Free DVD   Free DVD

Essential Test Tips Video from Trivium Test Prep

Dear Customer

Thank you for purchasing from Trivium Test Prep! Whether you're looking to join the military, get into college, or advance your career, we're honored to be a part of your journey.

To show our appreciation (and to help you relieve a little of that test-prep stress), we're offering a **FREE *ASWB BACHELORS Essential Test Tips* Video** by Trivium Test Prep. Our video includes 35 test preparation strategies that will help keep you calm and collected before and during your big exam. All we ask is that you email us your feedback and describe your experience with our product. Amazing, awful, or just so-so: we want to hear what you have to say!

To receive your **FREE *ASWB BACHELORS Essential Test Tips* Video**, please email us at 5star@triviumtestprep.com. Include "Free 5 Star" in the subject line and the following information in your email:

1. The title of the product you purchased.
2. Your rating from 1 – 5 (with 5 being the best).
3. Your feedback about the product, including how our materials helped you meet your goals and ways in which we can improve our products.
4. Your full name and shipping address so we can send your **FREE *ASWB BACHELORS Essential Test Tips* Video**.

If you have any questions or concerns please feel free to contact us directly at 5star@triviumtestprep.com.

Thank you, and good luck with your studies!

Social Work Licensing Bachelors Exam Guide

3 Practice Tests and ASWB Study Prep

B. Hettinger

Copyright ©2024 Trivium Test Prep

ISBN-13: 9781637986622

ALL RIGHTS RESERVED. By purchase of this book, you have been licensed on copy for personal use only. No part of this work may be reproduced, redistributed, or used in any form or by any means without prior written permission of the publisher and copyright owner. Trivium Test Prep; Accepted, Inc.; Cirrus Test Prep; and Ascencia Test Prep are all imprints of Trivium Test Prep, LLC.

The Association of Social Work Boards (ASWB) was not involved in the creation or production of this product, is not in any way affiliated with Trivium Test Prep, and does not sponsor or endorse this product.

Image(s) used under license from Shutterstock.com

Table of Contents

Introduction i
What Is the ASWB? i
What's on the ASWB–Bachelors? i
How Is the ASWB Scored? ii
How Is the ASWB Administered? ii
About Trivium Test Prep iii

1. Human Growth and Development 1
Elements of Developmental Psychology 1
Cognitive and Language Development 6
Life Span Developmental Theory 9
Personality 15
Motivation and Stress 17
Answer Key 21

2. Human Behavior in the Social Environment 23
Systems Theory 23
Family Dynamics and Functioning 25
Psychological Defense Mechanisms 32
Addiction Theories and Concepts 33
The Dynamics of Interpersonal Relationships 41
Other Theories 49
Answer Key 52

3. Diversity, Social Justice, and Oppression 53
Systemic Discrimination 53
Gender and Sexuality 55
Disability 57
Culture, Race, and Ethnicity 58
Social, Economic, and Criminal Justice 59
Environment 60
Answer Key 62

4. Biopsychosocial History and Collateral Data 63
Assessing the Client 63

Intake and Initial Observations 69
Overview of Medical Terminology and Medications 74
Common Medications and Side Effects 75
Answer Key 82

5. Assessment Methods and Techniques 83
Problem Formulation 83
Principles for Building Helping Relationships 84
Assessment Instruments 91
Diagnosis 105
Answer Key 110

6. Concepts of Abuse and Neglect 112
Indicators of Abuse and Neglect 112
Types and Effects of Abuse 115
Characteristics of Perpetrators 118
Answer Key 120

7. Indicators and Effects of Crisis and Change 121
Indicators of Traumatic Stress and Violence 121
Effects of Displacement 129
Trauma-Informed Care 132
Crisis Intervention Theories 136
Answer Key 139

8. Intervention Processes 140
Planning Treatment Strategies 140
Interviewing the Client 146
Establishing Goals 150
Client Considerations 153
Working with the Client 157
Treatment Termination 160
Answer Key 166

9. Intervention Techniques 168
Goals and Objectives of Case Management 168
The Role of Case Managers in Different Settings 169
Evidence-Based Interventions 170

Other Techniques 174
Answer Key 176

10. Use of Collaborative Relationships 177
Community-Based Intervention 177
Consultation Approaches 183
Roles and Responsibilities of the Social Worker 188
Accommodations 189
Answer Key 192

11. Professional Values, Ethical Issues, and Documentation 193
Defining Professional Ethics, Values, and Principles 193
Principles of Documentation and Record Management 198
Answer Key 202

12. Confidentiality 203
Confidentiality 203
Referrals and Confidentiality 206
Answer Key 208

13. Professional Development and Use of Self 209
Social Worker and Client/Client System Relationship 209
Advocacy 218
Answer Key 220

Practice Test 1 221
Answer Explanations 1 253
Practice Test 2 268
Answer Explanations 2 300

Online Resources

Trivium includes online resources with the purchase of this study guide to help you fully prepare for the exam.

Practice Tests

In addition to the practice tests included in this book, we also offer an online exam. Since many exams today are computer based, practicing your test-taking skills on the computer is a great way to prepare.

From Stress to Success

Watch "From Stress to Success," a brief but insightful YouTube video that offers the tips, tricks, and secrets experts use to score higher on the exam.

Reviews

Leave a review, send us helpful feedback, or sign up for Cirrus promotions—including free books!

Access these materials at: triviumtestprep.com/aswb-bachelors-online-resources

Introduction

Congratulations on choosing to take the Association of Social Work Boards (ASWB) licensing exam! By purchasing this book, you've taken the first step toward becoming a social worker.

This guide will provide you with a detailed overview of the ASWB, so you will know exactly what to expect on test day. We'll take you through all of the concepts covered on the exam and give you the opportunity to test your knowledge with practice questions. Even if it's been a while since you last took a major exam, don't worry; we'll make sure you're more than ready!

What Is the ASWB?

The **Association of Social Work Boards (ASWB)** develops exams as part of licensure for social workers throughout the United States and Canada. ASWB tests are part of licensure nationwide, but some states may require additional tests. Check with the board of social work in your state or province for complete information.

Licensing helps ensure that new and experienced social workers practice safely and ethically. ASWB exams measure the skills necessary to safely practice as a social worker. There are five categories of practice for which the ASWB licenses social workers:

- Associate
- Bachelors
- Masters
- Advanced Generalist
- Clinical

This book will prepare you for the ASWB–Bachelors licensing exam. Candidates for the ASWB–Bachelors exam must have a bachelor's degree in social work.

What's on the ASWB–Bachelors?

The ASWB consists of **170 questions**. Only 150 of these questions are scored; the remaining twenty are unscored, or *pretest* questions. Pretest questions are included to evaluate their suitability for inclusion in future tests. You'll have no way of knowing which questions are unscored, so treat every question like it counts.

The questions on the ASWB are multiple-choice with four answer options. The ASWB has **no guess penalty**. In other words, if you answer a question incorrectly, no points are deducted from your score; you simply do not get credit for that question. You should therefore always guess if you do not know the answer to a question. You will have **four hours** to complete the test.

What's on the ASWB?		
Subject	Approximate Number of Questions per Subject	Percentage of Exam
Human Development, Diversity, and Behavior in the Environment	42	25%
Assessment	50	29%
Interventions with Clients/Client Systems	44	26%
Professional Relationships, Values, and Ethics	34	20%
Total	**170 multiple-choice questions (150 scored)**	**4 hours**

How Is the ASWB Scored?

The ASWB is a pass/fail test. Of the 170 questions on the test, 150 are scored. Your score is determined by how many of the 150 scored questions you answer correctly.

If you pass the test, your official scores will be reported to ASWB and to your state social work board or school within fourteen days. If you do not pass the test, you may retake the test after a three-month waiting period.

The number of correct answers needed to pass the exam will vary slightly depending on the questions included in your version of the test. That is, if you take a version of the test with harder questions, the passing score will be lower. For security reasons, different versions of the test are administered every testing window.

How Is the ASWB Administered?

To take the ASWB, you must first apply to the social work board in your state for your license. Once you have applied for your license and paid the fee, you will receive approval to take the ASWB exam. You can then register with the ASWB for the exam and receive an authorization to test. At that point, you can schedule your testing appointment with Pearson VUE.

The ASWB is administered at Pearson VUE testing centers around the nation. Plan to arrive at least **thirty minutes before the exam** to complete biometric screening. Bring at least one form of **government-issued photo ID** and be prepared to be photographed and have your palms scanned. You may also be scanned with a metal detector wand before entering the test room. Your primary ID must be government-issued, include a recent photograph and signature, and match the name under which you registered to take the test. If you do not have a proper ID, you will not be allowed to take the test.

You will not be allowed to bring any personal items into the testing room, such as calculators or phones. You may not bring pens, pencils, or scratch paper. Other prohibited items include hats, scarves, and coats. You may, however, wear religious garments. Pearson VUE provides lockers for valuables. You can keep your ID and locker key with you.

About Trivium Test Prep

Trivium Test Prep uses industry professionals with decades' worth of knowledge in their fields—proven with degrees and honors in law, medicine, business, education, the military, and more—to produce high-quality study guides for students.

Our study guides are specifically designed to increase any student's score. Our books are also shorter and more concise than typical study guides, so you can increase your score while significantly decreasing your study time

1. Human Growth and Development

An understanding of human growth and development is essential for any social worker. This chapter reviews theories of human growth and development.

Elements of Developmental Psychology

Life Span Development and Behaviorism

Development begins at conception and continues throughout a person's lifetime. **Developmental psychology** studies how people change over time. Because most developmental changes occur during childhood, this is the emphasis of this field:

- **Cephalocaudal development** refers to the concept that human development and growth start at the head and move down. The head is the first to grow, and then the body grows to fit the size of the head.

- **Heredity** is the passing on of genetic traits from parents to their offspring through genes, chromosomes, and DNA.

- **Hereditability** refers to the possibility that a trait or condition can be passed from parents to offspring and to the portion of a trait that can be explained via genetic factors.

There are several significant debates in developmental psychology, one of which concerns whether biology or the environment have a greater impact on human development. Psychologists have determined that both play a significant role.

Every person has certain biological traits that shape their personality traits. For example, research has found that some people have neurons that are sensitive to overstimulation. These people tend to be introverts (in fact, as a general rule, introverts have these neurons).

However, some of these people are raised in ways that help them overcome this sensitivity to an extent—perhaps their parents required them to engage frequently in lengthy conversations with other adults—leading them to become extroverts.

The concept of **power of the environment** centers around the fact that humans do not live in a vacuum. Rather, they are influenced by people, places, ideas, and conditions in the world around them.

Empiricism is the theory that all data comes from the senses or through measurable observations or quantifiable data. Empiricism is a forerunner of behaviorism, which theorizes that developmental changes are quantitative and experience creates knowledge.

Behaviorism is the psychological theory that all human behavior is learned through the various forms of conditioning that people encounter from experience. It can be measured and changed by modifying behaviors. The psychologist **B. F. Skinner** was often referred to as the "father" of behaviorism. He believed that all behavior is learned and therefore all behavior can be shaped through operant conditioning.

Applied behavior analysis (ABA) is a method of behavioral therapy. Most often used with children with autism spectrum disorders, ABA can also be applied to a variety of issues that require a purely behavioral intervention. The therapy uses the principles of conditioning to gradually change behaviors.

> **Did You Know?**
>
> John B. Watson coined the term *behaviorism* in 1913.

Organismic theorists look at human development and personality as a total experience where developmental changes are qualitative and require a holistic perspective.

Practice Question

1. A 16-year-old male client has symptoms of schizophrenia. During the intake, the social worker learns that his grandfather and paternal uncle had similar symptoms, though they were never officially diagnosed. This indicates that schizophrenia is what?
    A) heritable
    B) cephalocaudal
    C) empirical
    D) organismic

Motor Sensory Development

The greatest changes in sensory, motor, and perceptual development happen in the first two years of life. When babies are born, most of their senses operate in a similar way to those of adults. For example, babies are able to hear before they are born; studies show that babies turn toward the sound of their mother's voice just minutes after being born, indicating they recognize the mother's voice from their time in the womb.

The exception to this rule is vision. A baby's vision changes significantly in the first year of life. Initially, an infant has a range of vision of only eight to twelve inches and no depth perception. As a result, infants rely primarily on hearing; vision does not become the dominant sense until around the age of twelve months. Babies also prefer faces to other objects. This preference, along with their limited vision range, means that their sight is initially focused on their caregivers.

While babies' senses might be similar to those of adults, their ability to interpret sensory inputs is very different. They must learn to **perceive**, or interpret, the sensory information they receive. This occurs as they interact with their environment, their caregivers, and as they age.

Eleanor Gibson conducted an experiment in which she created a "visual cliff" by extending a plexiglass ledge off a wooden table. All babies looked to their mothers for guidance when they approached the cliff; older babies refused to cross it regardless of their mothers' expressions. Gibson posited that while all

babies could see the cliff, the older babies had a more complex perception of it because of their more advanced development and their experiences with crawling (and falling).

In early psychology, babies were not believed to have any innate motor skills; the brain was considered to be **tabula rasa**, or a blank slate. However, later research revealed that all humans are actually born with certain reflexes which then later disappear. These include:

- **rooting**—turning the head and opening the mouth in search of food when the cheek is touched
- **sucking**—moving the mouth to draw milk from a nipple
- **grasping**—the tight clenching of anything placed on a baby's palm
- the **Moro reflex**—a startle reflex in which a baby throws the arms out and pulls them back in
- the **Babinski reflex**—when a baby extends the big toe when the bottom of the foot is touched.

These reflexes fade through the process of **maturation**, the biological process of aging. Maturation is also a key component of other motor developments—a baby cannot perform certain skills until the body has properly matured. For example, no matter what a parent tries to do, a six-month-old baby cannot run or jump.

Practice Question

2. Which of the following senses is most different at birth as compared to adulthood?
    A) sight
    B) smell
    C) hearing
    D) taste

Attachment Theory

In 1953, psychologist **John Bowlby** posited his attachment theory to explain the nature of the relationship between caregivers and children. Bowlby argued that in infancy, babies form an **attachment**—an enduring emotional bond to a particular figure, usually the primary caregiver.

Whereas psychologists previously attributed attachment to the association between being fed and the caregiver, Bowlby noticed that babies often maintained a strong attachment to their mothers, even when they were not the ones doing the feeding. So, he theorized that attachment is actually evolutionary in nature, developed for an infant's survival.

Having someone who will provide that care allows babies to then use them as a base to explore their world, returning to them when they feel threatened. Attachment is not about food, but about care and responsiveness to needs. Thus, attachment is essential to development as a prototype for future relationships; disruption of attachment leads to difficulties in adulthood. Bowlby identified the ages between birth and five years as critical periods for the development of attachment.

In the early 1970s, **Mary Ainsworth** empirically proved Bowlby's attachment theory through her experiment "the strange situation." Ainsworth conducted an experiment where she first had the mother and the baby in a room and then introduced a stranger. The mother then left the baby alone with the stranger for a few minutes. After this, the mother returned and the stranger left. Next, the mother left the baby alone in the room, after which the stranger returned, followed shortly thereafter by the mother, and then the stranger left again. Ainsworth concluded that babies exhibited three types of attachment related to the care provided by the attachment figure:

>**1. Secure Attachment:** In this case, the baby is very secure in its relationship with the attachment figure. The baby uses this figure as a base for exploration and is soothed easily by her when upset. The baby is unhappy to see her go but calms quickly when she returns. Ainsworth found that secure attachment resulted from a caring and attuned caregiver.
>
>**2. Ambivalent Attachment:** In this case, the baby exhibited extreme fussiness and clinginess. The baby was unhappy when left alone with the stranger but was not easily soothed by the caregiver. This resulted from an inconsistent level of responsiveness from the caregiver.
>
>**3. Avoidant Attachment:** In this case, the baby was completely detached from the caregiver. The baby explored the room without any orientation toward the attachment figure and responded equally to the caregiver and the stranger.

Practice Question

3. A baby who cries when approached by a stranger, but who calms quickly when held by her primary giver, is exhibiting which of the following?
    A) conditioned response
    B) ambivalent attachment
    C) avoidant attachment
    D) secure attachment

Baumrind's Parenting Styles

Diana Baumrind developed the theory of parenting styles based on her interactions with children and their parents. Underlying Baumrind's theory is the idea that children need both structure and warmth. Baumrind theorized three main parenting styles, which are described in Table 1.1.

Table 1.1. Baumrind's Parenting Styles	
Style	**Definition**
Authoritarian	<ul><li>focused on structure</li><li>parents often described as strict</li><li>limited freedom, warmth, or love toward children</li><li>no explanations provided to help children make choices</li></ul>
Permissive	<ul><li>little structure</li><li>allows children to do what they want</li><li>offers children more warmth and love</li><li>few boundaries</li><li>indulges children</li></ul>
Authoritative	<ul><li>balanced version of the authoritarian and permissive styles</li><li>considered the ideal mode of parenting</li><li>boundaries, limits, and structure balanced with warmth and love</li><li>rules and the consequences for breaking them understood by children</li><li>children's knowledge that they are loved even when making bad choices</li></ul>

Practice Question

4. Michelle is fifteen and in therapy for anxiety. When asked to describe her parents, she calls them "drill sergeants." Which parenting style does this indicate?
   A) authoritative
   B) authoritarian
   C) permissive
   D) involved

Harlow's Maternal Deprivation Theory

Harry Harlow is most known for his experiments with **rhesus monkeys**, which explored the effects of maternal deprivation and attachment. His theory was that the bonding process between mother and infant requires not only attachment but also **contact comfort**, or the tactile sensation of comfort. In the

1. Human Growth and Development

experiment, he separated baby monkeys from their mothers at birth and put them in cages with two different artificial "mothers":

- One of the fake mothers was made of wire and provided the baby monkeys with food.
- The other mother was wrapped in soft cloth but did not offer food.
- Harlow found that the baby monkeys spent most of their time with the soft mother.

In a variation of this experiment, Harlow introduced a frightening stimulus. Again, the babies sought comfort from the soft mother. Finally, when the monkeys developed into adults, those with artificial mothers had more social problems with other monkeys compared to the ones who grew up with their real mothers.

Practice Question

5. What did Harry Harlow's experiments with monkeys reveal about mother-infant attachments?
   A) Baby monkeys need food to grow strong.
   B) Baby monkeys need contact comfort for healthy development.
   C) Having a mother makes no difference to development.
   D) Contact comfort is not necessary for monkeys.

Cognitive and Language Development

The study of cognitive development looks at the ways in which people—mostly children—think about and evaluate the world and how this perception changes over time. The most significant figure in cognitive development is **Jean Piaget**.

Piaget theorized that children view the world through **schemata**—cognitive rules for interpreting the world which are developed based on their experiences. When they encounter new information or have a new experience, they either incorporate it into their existing schemata, called **assimilation**, or—if the new information is contradictory or does not fit—they adjust their schemata based on the new information; this is called **accommodation**. The balance between assimilation and accommodation is called **equilibration**.

For example, all the men in a girl's life may have short hair. She then believes that all men have short hair. If she encounters a young boy with short hair, she will assimilate the information into the existing schema: all males have short hair. If, however, she encounters a man with long hair, her first reaction might be surprise, confusion, or even amusement. She will then accommodate the information by adjusting her schema: most men have short hair, but some have long hair.

Piaget's Stages of Cognitive Development

Piaget identified four stages of cognitive development:

Sensorimotor Stage (birth – age 2): In this stage, a baby's behavior is governed by its senses, and its schemata are based on its reflexes. Most significantly, during this time, babies develop **object permanence**—the understanding that, even if an object is outside of their perceptual range, it still exists. If a four-month-old baby is fussing for his father's keys, the father needs only to put the keys away, and the baby will forget they exist.

Preoperational Stage (ages 2 – 7): The most important development during this stage is **language**. Children learn to use symbolic schema—through speech, drawing, letters, and numbers—to represent real-world objects. Their memories are developing, and they are able to use their imaginations; however, they still cannot understand more complex ideas like cause and effect, time, and comparison (e.g., when a three-year-old pours her milk over her dinner plate in an attempt to understand cause and effect). During this stage, children are also completely **egocentric**; they cannot think beyond their own worldview. Children in this stage demonstrate **centration**, focusing on a singular aspect of a situation or object without noticing other elements of it.

Concrete Operations (ages 8 – 12): During this stage, children begin to develop logical thinking. They understand the passage of time and can comprehend that an action causes a certain reaction. Piaget identified **conservation** as the biggest developmental leap during this stage. Children in this stage can understand that the properties of an object stay the same even when its shape changes. For example, they understand that a rope is still a rope whether it is stretched out long or wrapped into an intricate knot. Another important step is developing the **concept of reversibility**, the idea that an action can be undone.

Formal Operations (ages 12 – adulthood): In this final stage, humans develop abstract reasoning and consider ideas and objects in their minds without physically seeing them. For example, they can formulate a hypothesis about what will happen in an experiment before ever running the experiment. People are also able to engage in **metacognition**—thinking about *how* they think. While this is the final stage, Piaget argued that not everyone reaches this stage; some remain at the concrete operations stage.

In recent years, critiques of Piaget's theory have emerged. For one, Piaget's primary research subjects were his own children; he lacked a diverse group of research subjects, and his judgment may have been clouded. Furthermore, psychologists believe that many children go through Piaget's stages more quickly than he posited.

Other psychologists question the validity of stages in general. These psychologists support the **information processing model**, which follows the same development path as Piaget but in a continuous manner, rather than in stages.

> **Helpful Hint**
>
> The terms *conservation*, *concept of reversibility*, and *concrete operations* all start with the letter C.

Practice Question

6. A group of students are discussing the best ways to study for an upcoming exam. This is an example of which of Piaget's stages of development?
    A) concrete operations stage
    B) formal operations stage
    C) preoperational stage
    D) sensorimotor stage

Vygotsky's Cultural-Historical Theory

An alternative theory, the **cultural-historical theory** of cognitive development was posited by **Lev Vygotsky**. Vygotsky believed that society and culture were critical in a child's cognitive development. Vygotsky's work is based on the assumption that children learn about their culture—and how it interprets and responds to the world—through their formal and informal interactions with adults.

For example, a child is reading a book with her mother about animals that live in the forest. The mother points out the squirrels in the trees and the deer munching grass. In this way, the child learns how her culture classifies and talks about animals.

Vygotsky also assumes that for cognitive growth to take place, children need both challenging tasks and room to play. Challenging tasks force children to stretch cognitively, making new connections and furthering their understanding; however, for this process to be most effective, they need an adult—or anyone with more knowledge and experience than them—to **scaffold** (i.e., demonstrate) their learning by helping them through the process of acquiring new skills.

Returning to the mother and child, the child is now trying to complete an animal puzzle. The mother scaffolds this process by encouraging her work, asking guiding questions, and helping her place a few pieces until she can do it on her own. Vygotsky called this learning area—the area between what a child can do without help and what she can do with help—the **zone of proximal development (ZPD)**.

Practice Question

7. The term *scaffolding* came from which of the following theories?
    A) Lev Vygotsky's zone of proximal development
    B) Howard Gardner's multiple intelligences theory
    C) Albert Bandura's social learning theory
    D) Erik Erikson's psychosocial development theory

Language Development

Adults—and even children—cannot remember a time when language and thinking were separate. Once language is acquired, the two processes are completely intertwined.

But how does language develop? Researchers have found that, regardless of the language a baby is learning, all babies go through the same stages of acquisition. Around four months, babies begin to babble, practicing the sounds of the language (or languages) that they hear regularly. Around their first birthdays, the babbling turns into single words, like "book." By eighteen months, babies begin to bring together their single words into two-word phrases with clear meaning but no syntax. So "Book!" becomes "Mommy book!"

Syntax begins to develop as the child advances into forming three- and four-word phrases. At first, young children often misapply or overuse grammatical rules, a process called **overgeneralization**.

For example, knowing that one uses the suffix *–ed* to create the past tense, a child in the **telegraphic** phase might say, "Daddy throwed the ball," not understanding that it does not apply to every word. This is corrected through modeling—when adults or older children use correct grammar so that the younger children can model their mode of speaking.

There is debate over the actual process of language acquisition. Psychologists who study behavior have argued that language is acquired through a process called conditioning. Essentially, this means that when children use language properly, they receive praise and positive feedback (which may even be just receiving an item they request) from their parents or caregivers. This then encourages them to use the language in the same way again.

Cognitive psychologists argue, however, that people deprived of this kind of parental conditioning are still able to develop language. **Noam Chomsky** put forward the **nativist theory of language**, which states that each person is born with a language acquisition device inside. This device allows for language acquisition unless it is interrupted or damaged during a critical period. Current researchers have concluded that language is acquired both through behavior modification and natural development during that critical period.

Practice Question

8. Which of the following is an example of overgeneralization in language development?
   A) "Mommy, I eated all of my vegetables!"
   B) "Mommy, monkey."
   C) "Baby cracker eat."
   D) "Book!"

Life Span Developmental Theory

Piaget, Vygotsky, Bowlby, and Ainsworth focused primarily on infancy and early childhood in their theories because this is where the majority of developmental change happens. Other psychologists, however, developed theories that examine development across the entire life span of a human.

Erikson's Psychosocial Development Theory

The most well-known life span developmental theory is **Erik Erikson's psychosocial development theory**. Erikson was trained in the psychoanalytic school of psychology, so his theory is based on that rather than on evidence-based research. However, it has still heavily impacted psychology as a whole, particularly the treatment and schooling of children.

Erikson theorized that development occurs in eight stages, with each stage centered on a specific social conflict. The way the conflict is resolved impacts who the person ultimately becomes.

Stage 1 (birth – age 1): Trust versus Mistrust

Babies determine if they can trust their caregivers. If they can, as adults they will appreciate the value of relationships and interdependence. If they cannot, they will remain untrusting and disconnected.

Stage 2 (ages 1 – 3): Autonomy versus Shame and Doubt

Toddlers attempt to exert their will over their own bodies. This manifests itself through activities like potty-training and learning to dress themselves. If toddlers are able to develop a level of independence, as adults they will have a strong sense of autonomy. If not, they will experience feelings of shame and self-doubt.

Stage 3 (ages 3 – 5): Initiative versus Guilt

This is also known as the "why?" stage. Children develop curiosity and a desire to exert control over their environment as well (because they feel they have some control over themselves and trust in the adults around them). If this initiative is encouraged, they will have a strong sense of curiosity and purpose going forward. If not, they will feel guilt and avoid future curiosity.

Stage 4 (ages 6 – 11): Industry versus Inferiority

This is the beginning of children's formal education. If they feel that they are as good academically and socially as their peers, they will develop confidence. If not, they will develop an **inferiority complex**, a generalized feeling of incompetence and performance anxiety.

Stage 5 (ages 12 – 18): Identity versus Role Confusion

During adolescence, the primary social task is to discover one's most comfortable social identity. All teenagers will try on different roles. If they find their identity, they will have a stable sense of self. If not, they will encounter an **identity crisis**, a period of profound identity confusion.

Stage 6 (ages 19 – 40): Intimacy versus Isolation

Young adults must develop loving relationships with others while balancing their work needs. Success leads to strong, lasting relationships; failure leads to isolation and loneliness.

Stage 7 (ages 40 – 65): Generativity versus Stagnation

Individuals in middle adulthood strive to create something that will outlast them—through raising children or engaging in meaningful work. Those who succeed feel fulfilled and accomplished. Those who do not succeed endure a **midlife crisis**, becoming disengaged from the world or trying to change the direction of their lives. They may change their identities or attempt to exert more control over those around them. The fear of death is greatest in this period.

Stage 8 (ages 65 – death): Integrity versus Despair

As individuals near the end of life, they will reflect to determine whether they are satisfied with their life choices. If they are, they will develop wisdom. If not, they will experience despair.

Practice Question

9. According to Erikson, toddlers who develop a sense of control over their own bodies will experience which of the following as adults?
    A) trust
    B) industry
    C) autonomy
    D) identity

Table 1.2. Kohlberg's Three Levels of Moral Development

Stage	Age Range	Description
Pre-Conventional Level		
1. Obedience/Punishment	preschool	The focus is on avoiding punishment: Heinz should not steal the drug because he might get caught and put in jail.
2. Self-Interest/Reward	elementary school	The focus is on rewards instead of punishment; the goal is to maximize benefits to oneself: Heinz should steal the drug because having his wife live would make him happy.
Conventional Level		
3. Interpersonal Accord	middle school	The focus is on being perceived as a "good" person and being liked:

Table 1.2. Kohlberg's Three Levels of Moral Development		
Stage	Age Range	Description
Pre-Conventional Level		
		Heinz should steal the drug because he will be seen as a hero.
4. Law and Order	high school	There is reliance on the perceived fixed rules of conduct (e.g., learned from parents, peers): Heinz should not steal the drug because stealing is wrong.
Post-Conventional Level		
5. Social Contract	high School/young adulthood	There is an understanding that legally right and morally right are not always the same; laws are for the majority's benefit and may conflict with the best interest of the individual: Heinz should steal the drug because, while theft is illegal, the protection of life is more important than the protection of property.
6. Universal Principles (only achieved by some)	adulthood	There are self-defined and protected ethical principles: Heinz should steal the drug because life must be preserved at all costs.

Theories of Moral Development: Kohlberg and Gilligan

Another perspective in examining human development can be seen in **Kohlberg's theory of moral development**. Lawrence Kohlberg became interested in the question, "How does the ability to reason in ethical situations change?"

To answer this question, he posed several dilemmas to people of varying ages. The most well-known is the **Heinz dilemma:** A man must decide if he should steal a drug that he cannot afford to save his wife's life. Based on the responses he collected, Kohlberg articulated three levels of moral development, each composed of two stages.

There are many critiques of Kohlberg's research. The primary criticisms are that the situations were fictional and unfamiliar for many of the participants. The participants ranged in age from ten to sixteen, so they had no frame of reference for making a decision about saving a dying wife.

Carol Gilligan critiqued Kohlberg for his bias. All the participants in the original study were male, and when girls were tested later, they demonstrated slower moral development. However, Gilligan argued that there is a difference in moral development based on gender, and Kohlberg's stages only articulate the development of male morality.

In her 1982 book ***A Different Voice***, Gilligan posits that male morality is based on absolute abstract ideas, with justice being the fundamental moral principle. Female morality is based on specific, individual situations, with caring for others being the fundamental moral principle. Later researchers have questioned Gilligan's gender distinctions, and this debate continues.

Practice Question

10. Which of the following is NOT a critique of Kohlberg's theory of moral development?
    A) He chose to examine a cross-section of participants rather than complete a longitudinal study.
    B) The study articulated a gender difference in moral reasoning that does not exist.
    C) His ethical dilemmas were artificial.
    D) Ethical decision-making can differ significantly in real-world versus hypothetical situations.

Daniel Levinson's Four Major Eras Theory

Daniel Levinson posited theories of adult development and divided them into four eras, or stages. He wrote about his ideas in two well-known books:

- *The Seasons of a Man's Life* focuses on the life span that men experience.
- *The Seasons of a Woman's Life* chronicles the life span unique to women's experiences.

Both books expanded on the four major eras theory:

- Preadulthood (childhood and adolescence) is a stage of development characterized by dependence on adults.
- Early adulthood occurs after the age of twenty-two, but the transition period takes place between the ages of seventeen and twenty-two.
    - This stage is characterized by solidifying one's identity; understanding how one fits into the world; and changing family relationships, culminating in pursuing a career and family.
- Middle adulthood occurs after the age of forty, but the transition period takes place between the ages of forty and forty-five, which is when most people experience the midlife crisis.
    - The **midlife crisis** is a period when people question the trajectory of their lives.
    - Levinson considered it a positive event that inspires change if it is needed; without it, a person can feel stagnation toward the end of life.
    - The midlife crisis occurs regardless of class.
- Later adulthood occurs after the age of sixty-five, with the transition period between the ages of sixty and sixty-five. This is the stage of life when people transition out of their careers into retirement and often look back at their lives.

Practice Question

11. Tamara is forty-two and has anxiety and depression. Her children are grown, and she does not know what to do with herself. She spent most of her time as a stay-at-home mom homeschooling her children, and now she has nothing to do, no purpose, and she feels lost. What might Tamara be experiencing?
    A) midlife crisis
    B) major depressive episode
    C) separation anxiety
    D) stress

William Perry's Four-Stage Theory of Intellectual and Ethical Development in Adults

William Perry developed a four-stage theory of intellectual and ethical development in adults. Perry's theory focuses on the cognitive and moral development of college students as they engage in higher learning and become more independent. He believed that students need to go through each stage (described in Table 1.3.) to become effective at critical-thinking skills.

Table 1.3. Perry's Four-Stage Theory of Intellectual and Ethical Development in Adults

Stage	Definition
Dualism	There is one right answer; a student just needs to find it.
Multiplicity	There is no right answer, but someone in authority must figure out the answer.
Relativism	One can prove any answer with enough evidence.
Commitment	One is open to independently learning and exploring for answers.

Practice Question

12. A college student who defers to the experts on a subject might be in which stage?
    A) dualism
    B) multiplicity
    C) relativism
    D) commitment

James W. Fowler's Theory of Faith and Spiritual Development

James W. Fowler was a theologian, minister, and human development professor who established the stages of faith development throughout the life span:

- **Stage 0: undifferentiated (primal) faith (birth – age 4, infancy):** A baby does not feel faith, per se, but experiences feelings of trust and assurance that can grow into faith or neglect, the latter of which will lead to lack of faith.

- **Stage 1: intuitive-projective faith (ages 2 – 7, early childhood):** A child develops the sense of right and wrong and learns faith stories without true understanding.

- **Stage 2: mythic-literal faith (childhood):** A child develops the sense of fairness associated with religious beliefs. The schema is simple: doing good deeds results in good things, and doing bad deeds results in bad things.

- **Stage 3: synthetic-conventional faith (adolescence):** An adolescent begins to identify with a belief system and form a sense of faith.

- **Stage 4: individuative-reflective faith (young adulthood):** Young adults explore faith further, often encountering conflict in their beliefs or developing a greater appreciation for them.

- **Stage 5: conjunctive faith (mid-thirties):** An adult comes to understand that faith is beyond basic religious beliefs.

- **Stage 6: universalizing faith (midlife):** Adults live out the tenets of their faith and are not bothered by differences in religious traditions.

Practice Question

13. Which stage of faith is associated with fairness and justice in its simplest forms?
    A) stage 0: undifferentiated
    B) stage 1: intuitive-projective faith
    C) stage 2: mythic-literal faith
    D) stage 3: synthetic-conventional faith

Robert Kegan's Six Stages of Life Span Development

Robert Kegan expanded on the work of Jean Piaget and theorized six stages of development based on how people create meaning, which grows throughout the life span. **Meaning-making** is the process of evaluating life events for their existential value. In particular, it means processing an event to find the good that comes from it that may not be readily apparent.

Table 1.4. Kegan's Six Stages of Life Span Development

Stage	Age Range	Definition
Incorporative	infancy – age 2	A child is completely dependent on the mother or primary caregiver.
Impulsive	ages 2 – 6	A child is guided by pursuing what she wants and giving in to impulses. Behavior is guided by rules and consequences.
Imperial	age 6 – adolescence	A child is more influenced by his relationships and whether others approve of him or not. Empathy develops, but much of how a child thinks of himself comes from the opinions of others.
Interpersonal	adulthood	Adults create mutual, interdependent relationships.
Institutional	adulthood	Adults exhibit autonomy and self-expression.
Interindividual	adulthood	Adults focus on intimacy and genuine relationships that contribute to identity.

The **holding environment** refers to the space that a social worker creates for a client and includes safety and nonjudgment. It is an attitude and approach that allow clients to express what they need to. Thus, the social worker "holds" the space for clients, so they feel safe in the relationship.

Practice Question

14. Robert Kegan's life span development stages focus on which aspect of human development?
    A) physical growth
    B) spiritual development
    C) relationships
    D) meaning-making

Personality

The study of personality is essentially the study of what makes people who they are. This is a complicated question, but one that is fundamental to psychology. There are four general approaches to answering this question: psychoanalytic, trait, social-cognitive, and humanistic.

Freud's Psychoanalytic Theories and Criticism

The most well-known **psychoanalytic** psychologist is **Sigmund Freud**. Freud believed that personality was set in early childhood. According to Freud, the stages of development were the following:

1. oral

2. anal

3. phallic (Oedipal/Electra complex)

4. latency

5. genital

If a child progressed through the stages of development without a problem, he would be well-adjusted. If, instead, the child experienced an unresolved conflict at a certain stage, he would develop a **fixation** or become stuck at that stage; this conflict would affect his adult personality. For example, if an individual experiences a conflict in the first stage—the oral stage—he may develop an oral fixation and need to constantly have something in his mouth. In addition to his developmental theories, Freud theorized that the personality was composed of three parts:

- **Id:** This is the unconscious or unknown mind that operates on instinct. Emotions reside here, as these are instinctive and not actively created by the individual.

- **Ego:** Existing partly in the unconscious mind and partly in the conscious mind, the ego follows the **reality principle**, and it negotiates between the id and the limitations of the environment.

- **Superego:** The superego is a person's conscience, which distinguishes right from wrong. It can influence the ego to account for moral considerations.

While extremely popular, Freud's theories face significant criticism. They are not based upon empirical evidence, and the nature of many of his structures (for example, the id) make them unprovable. His theories also have no predictive power. While they can be used to explain why someone acted a certain way, they cannot predict how someone will act in the future. Freud is also criticized for overemphasizing early childhood and sex and for being offensive to women (for example, he claimed that all women have penis envy).

On the opposite side of Freud is Alfred Adler's **individual psychology**. Diverging from Freud's pessimistic view of humanity, Adler had an inherently optimistic view, arguing that people are all ultimately striving for success or superiority. If a person enjoys success—meaning that she contributes to the community's benefit while maintaining her personal identity—her personality is unified. If not, or if the person strives for superiority (personal gain without real regard for others), she will be ultimately unfulfilled.

Practice Question

15. When accidentally rear-ended by another car, Mark becomes enraged and attacks the other driver. How would Freud explain Mark's actions?
    A) Mark's id was determining his actions.
    B) Mark's superego was determining his actions.
    C) Mark's ego was determining his actions.
    D) Mark's actions were the result of negotiations between his ego, his id, and his superego.

Trait, Social-Cognitive, and Humanistic Theories

Trait theories describe personalities by identifying main traits or characteristics. Characteristics of an individual's personality are considered stable and motivate his behavior. **Nomothetic theorists** argue that the same set of traits can be used to describe all personalities. For example, Hans Eysenck posited that a transection of an introversion-extraversion scale (essentially how shy or outgoing one is), originally created by **Carl Jung**, and a neuroticism scale (how anxious or fearful one is), could classify all personalities.

Idiographic theorists, on the other hand, argue that one set of traits cannot be used to describe everybody. Instead, people should be defined by the few traits that best define them, which can vary from person to person.

The primary criticism of trait theory is that it assumes that personalities are stable, when in fact people might behave very differently depending on the situation. For example, someone might be extremely talkative and social among her family, but shy and reserved in public.

According to social-cognitive theories, personality is the result of a combination of environment and patterns of thought. **Albert Bandura**'s theory of **reciprocal determinism** posits that personality results from the interaction between a person's traits, the environment, and the person's behavior. For example, a person might be naturally optimistic, but become less so after a series of disappointments and failures.

Julian Rotter's **locus of control theory** suggests that personality is determined by whether one feels in control of what happens to him. Those who have an internal locus of control—they feel in control of their lives—tend to be healthier and more engaged, while those with an external locus of control—they feel that luck or destiny controls their lives—tend to be less successful.

Humanistic theorists challenge the **determinism**—the idea that personality is determined by past events—that is innate in other personality theories. Instead, they argue that people are able to exercise free will to determine their own destinies.

According to humanistic theory, an individual's personality is determined by her overall feelings about herself (called **self-concept**) and the level of confidence she has in her own abilities (called **self-esteem**):

- **Abraham Maslow** argued that people strive to reach **self-actualization**, the maximizing of their own potential. (See below for more on Maslow.)
- **Carl Rogers** posited that people need blanket acceptance, which he called **unconditional positive regard**, from other people in order to self-actualize.

Humanistic theory is criticized for being overly optimistic and vague. For example, it is difficult to measure if a person has reached her full potential.

Practice Question

16. Bandura's theory of reciprocal determinism—that personality is the result of the interaction between the individual, his behavior, and his environment—is part of which school of personality theory?
    A) humanistic
    B) psychoanalytical
    C) social-cognitive
    D) trait

Motivation and Stress

The reason for an individual's behavior is called **motivation**. Motivations can be either conscious and obvious, or unconscious and subtle. Most of motivation theory is based on research in learning and personality.

Maslow's Hierarchy of Needs

Abraham Maslow theorized that motivation was based on needs, but needs are not all equal. He identifies five levels of needs, from basic biological needs for safety and survival to the need to fulfill life goals and self-actualization.

According to Maslow, each level of needs must be fulfilled before the next one can be addressed; however, there are examples that contradict this model. For example, Buddhist monks who practiced self-immolation (lighting themselves on fire) during the Vietnam War prioritized the need of self-actualization over the need for survival.

Self-Actualization
morality, creativity, spontaneity, acceptance

Self-Esteem
confidence, achievement, respect of others

Love and Belonging
family, friendship, intimacy, sense of connection

Safety and Security
health, employment, property, family and social stability

Physiological Needs
breathing, food, water, shelter, clothing, sleep

Practice Question

17. Which of the following is true of Maslow's hierarchy of needs?
    A) All needs ultimately relate to survival and safety.
    B) All needs must be met simultaneously.
    C) A level of need cannot be addressed until the previous level is met.
    D) Personal relationships are the ultimate need.

Sources of Motivation

Motivation comes from a variety of sources: internal, external, and environmental. The individual attitudes and goals of the people in an individual's life, as well as broader societal attitudes and goals, may serve as motivation for that individual. An example of this **social motivation** would be a student who works hard in school to gain admission to college because of the value society places on a college education.

If, however, that same student sought admission to college to master high-level skills and to better understand the world, that student would be propelled by **achievement motivation**. People who are motivated by achievement continually seek greater challenges.

All motivators can be classified as either **extrinsic motivators** (coming from outside of one's self) or **intrinsic motivators** (coming from within). For example, a person who wants to gain admission to college to get a good job or to be held in high esteem by others is extrinsically motivated. A student who seeks admission to college to feel a sense of accomplishment or achieve mastery in a particular discipline is intrinsically motivated.

Both types of motivation are effective in encouraging desired behaviors; however, once extrinsic motivators end, so does the behavior. Once the student looking for peer approval gains admission to college, he is more likely to perform worse than his intrinsically motivated counterparts. Therefore, extrinsic motivators are suitable for short-term behavior goals, while intrinsic motivators are better at encouraging long-term positive behaviors.

Practice Question

18. When Amy fails her math test, she decides it is because the questions were too confusing. This is an example of which of the following types of attribution?
    A) person-stable attribution
    B) person-unstable attribution
    C) situation-stable attribution
    D) situation-unstable attribution

Stress

Any situation that burdens one's coping abilities by threatening—or seeming to threaten—a person's well-being is considered **stress**. Common stressors include life changes, external and internal pressures, environmental factors, frustration, and conflict.

Acute stressors are relatively short in duration and have a clear end point, whereas chronic stressors are relatively long in duration and have no apparent time limit. Acute stressors have little negative impact and can even be beneficial at times. For example, short-term frustration—the thwarting of the pursuit of a goal—can act as a motivator for further achievement. **Chronic stressors**, on the other hand, have significant physiological and psychological consequences. Hans Selye detailed the body's stress response in his **General Adaptation Syndrome (GAS)** as it applies to all animals:

- **Alarm reaction:** The heart rate increases; blood is diverted away from other body functions to prepare the animal for action. This is also known as the **fight-or-flight response**, as the animal is prepared to either attack or flee.

- **Resistance:** Hormones are released to maintain the state of readiness. In chronic stress, this state is maintained for too long, depleting the body's resources.

- **Exhaustion:** The body returns to a normal state. If the resistance state lasted too long, the body will be more vulnerable to disease and sustain long-term damage. This is why chronic stress is associated with health problems like arthritis, ulcers, asthma, migraine headaches, heart disease, and depression.

Maintaining a resistance state resulted from some kind of stressful event—either acute or long-term (for example, war, sexual assault, watching someone die, or almost dying themselves)—can also lead to **post-traumatic stress disorder (PTSD)**. People with PTSD experience disturbed behavior—including nightmares, jumpiness, and temper flares.

Chronic stress also disrupts attention and inhibits memory. Chronic, or **toxic stress**, related to poverty can even change the chemical makeup of a child's brain, disrupting and weakening its circuits.

The best way to deal with stress is to use **constructive coping mechanisms**, such as confronting a problem directly, breaking it down into manageable pieces, maintaining flexibility, and remaining aware of one's coping and stress resources. Studies have also shown that maintaining **perceived control**, or the feeling that one is in control of a stressor, reduces the overall stress level. For example, the client who is given control of his own pain control medication reports a lower overall pain level than the client who is prescribed doses, even when the amount of medicine received is the same.

Practice Question

19. Hans Selye developed his general adaptation syndrome to describe which of the following?
    A) personality traits
    B) reactions to stress
    C) memory processes
    D) problem-solving processes

Answer Key

1. A: The client's symptoms and history indicate that the disorder was passed on through his family's generations.

2. A: At birth, babies can only see eight to twelve inches in front of their face. They do not gain full sight until they are one year old.

3. D: The baby's actions demonstrate a strong attachment to the caregiver.

4. B: Parents who are considered authoritarian impose rules and structure with very little explanation or warmth, similar to how a drill sergeant might enforce order.

5. B: The baby monkeys preferred the soft fake mothers even when they did not offer food, revealing that baby monkeys need contact comfort for healthy development.

6. B: The formal operations stage is the final stage of Piaget's stages of cognitive development wherein individuals develop the ability to engage in metacognition—thinking about how they think.

7. A: Vygotsky's zone of proximal development (ZPD) describes tasks students can perform with help and gradually learn to do on their own.

8. A: Overgeneralization describes the tendency of young children to misapply grammatical rules by assuming that the rules apply universally.

9. C: According to Erikson, autonomy emerges when a toddler develops a sense of independence. This occurs in the second stage.

10. B: Carol Gilligan critiqued Kohlberg for having a strong male bias in his theory, pointing to the fact that all the original participants were male and his own male perspective on moral reasoning impacted how he evaluated various types of reasoning. Gilligan herself articulated different types of moral reasoning based on gender, which has since been called into question.

11. A: A midlife crisis occurs when people question their life's purpose.

12. B: The multiplicity stage puts the burden of answers on authority figures.

13. C: Children at the mythic-literal faith stage associate good deeds with good outcomes and vice versa.

14. D: Kegan's developmental stages consider how people in each stage develop their social understanding, identities, and create meaning in their lives.

15. A: The id governs all emotions and impulsive behavior. When attacking the other driver, Mark was being driven solely by his emotions.

16. C: Social-cognitive theory looks at the ways individual thought and overall environment impact personality. Bandura was a prominent social-cognitive theorist.

17. C: According to Maslow, the ability to fulfill a need is dependent on the fulfillment of needs lower in the hierarchy.

18. D: Amy attributes her failure to the situation of the particular test, making it an unstable attribution and a situational one.

19. B: The general adaptation syndrome describes the physiological reaction all animals have to stress.

2. Human Behavior in the Social Environment

Systems Theory

Ecological systems theory, developed by Urie Bronfenbrenner, is one of the cornerstones of social work theory. **Systems theory** holds that people exist in systems, and these systems all interact with each other at varying levels that have different effects on each other:

- The **individual** is the smallest system, including
    - internal thought processes
    - experiences
    - personality.
- The **microsystem** includes places and people most influential in the individual's upbringing and daily life, such as:
    - parents/siblings
    - work
    - the school environment.
- The **mesosystem** describes how microsystems influence each other—how parents, teachers, peers, and coworkers interact with each other and how those interactions influence the individual.
- The **exosystem** consists of systems that do not have a direct impact on someone's upbringing but will have indirect effects on the individual, such as:
    - extended family
    - neighborhoods
    - mass media
    - parents'/guardians' workplaces.
- Finally, the **macrosystem** comprises the cultural elements of the individual's society, such as:
    - laws
    - social conditions

- culture
- history
- economic systems.

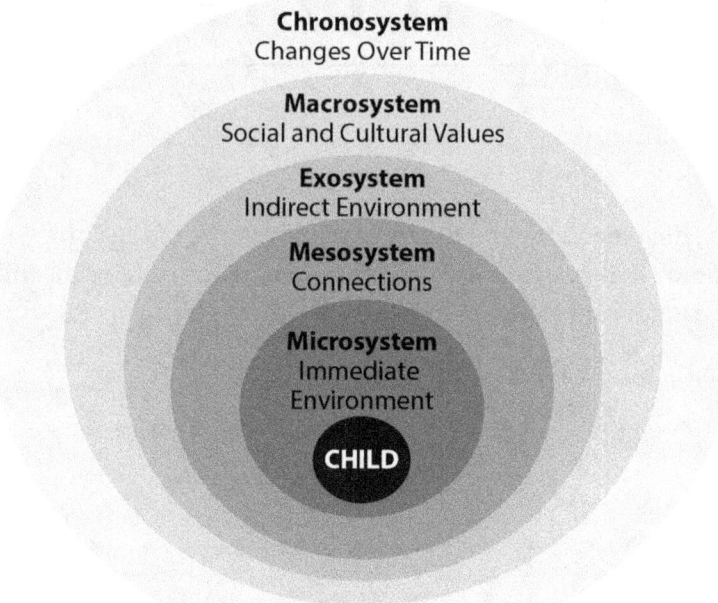

The impact of life events and stressors can be examined through a systems theory lens. The microsystem and mesosystem interact with each other, while the exosystem and macrosystem impact how an individual experiences life events and stressors.

Consider a situation where a child is being abused at home. She is experiencing life stressors from part of her microsystem (family). How other individuals in her microsystem and mesosystem respond will impact how the experience affects her. If a teacher in her microsystem notices the bruises, she might get help and intervention; if no one notices, she will continue to suffer, which will impact her personal experiences throughout life. If the teacher reports the bruises to child protection, then the child will enter the social services system—another macrosystem. She will be placed in a foster family and enter a new microsystem at home and a new mesosystem at school. How each of these systems reacts and responds to the situation will have a direct impact on the child's life and ability to succeed.

In the same way, large-scale political events can have impacts on smaller systems as well. Events such as natural disasters or political unrest play out on the national stage, with significant impacts on exosystems, mesosystems, microsystems, and individuals. For instance, political unrest or natural disasters could shut down schools, cause damage to infrastructure, displace families, or result in harm to loved ones.

Practice Question

1. A social worker is seeing a family who has recently been displaced by a hurricane. The social worker is attempting to get the family emergency housing through the Federal Emergency Management Agency (FEMA). Which part of Bronfenbrenner's systems theory does FEMA best fit into?
   A) microsystem
   B) mesosystem
   C) exosystem
   D) macrosystem

Family Dynamics and Functioning

Families

Families are an intrinsic part of our cultural fabric. The traditional nuclear family consists of a mother, father, and children; however, our understanding of family has shifted quite a bit over time. Today, single parenthood is common and accepted, as are families in which two parents are the same gender. In other families, grandparents or other relatives may serve as the primary caregivers of children.

Historically, a **couple** was defined as a man and a woman in a romantic relationship. Today, a couple is considered to be two people in a romantic relationship, regardless of gender identity. Some couples may open their relationships to other people, such as in **polyamorous** relationships.

Marriage is a union between a couple that grants them certain privileges and responsibilities. The main legal advantages include tax benefits and the right to make end-of-life decisions should a partner become incapacitated.

In the United States, the Defense of Marriage Act was ruled unconstitutional in 2013, paving the way for the Supreme Court's ruling in 2015 that same-sex marriage is legal and must be recognized by all states. Since then, anyone of any gender can marry whomever they please under the law.

Family composition can take many forms:

- Some families consist of single parents.
- Grandparents sometimes take the role of parents.
- Other relatives may be primary or secondary caregivers.
- Cousins may be raised in the same household.
- Families can also include stepparents and step- and half-siblings.

Cultural background may significantly influence the family composition. For example, many Asian families live with grandparents in the household; they serve as patriarchs and may also provide an important role in caregiving and teaching cultural traditions. Social workers should assume an attitude of cultural humility and learn from clients how their unique family systems function at their best in order to support them within their own cultural values.

Not every family is based entirely on biological kinship. A person's **family of origin** might be the family he lives with. People who were adopted, who live with foster parents, or who move out to be on their own may consider other significant people to be their family. Regardless of where people live, their family of origin can have a significant influence on their outlook on life, their values, and how they interact with the world.

Family member interactions vary widely from family to family. Exploring these themes can be enlightening, especially for adult clients who may be struggling in areas such as intimacy and healthy romantic relationships. The following questions can help clients better understand their own behaviors:

- What did their parents' relationship look like?
- Was it loving and communicative, or abusive?
- What were the parent-child dynamics like?
- How were children viewed in the family?
- What about gender roles?
- Were there healthy boundaries in the family or minimal boundaries?

Practice Question

2. How might culture influence family composition?
   A) by determining who lives in the household and who is in a position of authority
   B) by setting regulating behaviors of family members
   C) by making sure family members adhere to cultural rituals
   D) Culture rarely influences family composition.

Children and Parenting

Parenting can be a difficult process, especially when the parents have different ideas about how to raise kids. For example, one parent may take a more relaxed approach, while the other may have a more active style.

Inconsistency in the home environment can create childhood stressors and leave kids feeling confused and out of control. Whenever there is confusion or ambivalence, parents need to discuss the issues with each other and let the kids know what the expectations are for the family.

Co-parenting (joint parenting with an former partner) can present its own unique set of challenges. Since the children are staying with each parent separately, co-parents may not be aligned in parenting style or rules. Short of legitimate concerns of abuse or neglect, co-parents need to trust each other with their children's care and work to let go of less significant issues, such as one parent allowing a later bedtime or more sweets. Social workers can support their clients by helping them:

- recognize the importance of their children having strong and healthy relationships with both parents
- try to establish consistent rules between households
- learn to let go of control over how the child is parented when at the other parent's house.

Many parents seek help with children's **behavioral problems**. This can include behaviors like fighting in school, defiance at home, refusal to do homework, or elevated sibling rivalries.

Sometimes, a child's behavior may be unpleasant but is ultimately age appropriate and not a significant cause for concern, such as when a four-year-old experiments with "naughty" words. Consistency is a big part of working with children with behavioral issues, and social workers may need to work extensively with parents to improve consistent and measured responses to behavioral issues. Parents must not become emotionally reactive when their child is misbehaving; instead, they should be a source of calm and measured expectations.

A common reason parents may bring their child into therapy is because the child is experiencing **bullying**. In the past, bullying was seen as a normal part of childhood, but it is now recognized as a phenomenon that can have a lasting negative effect on a child's well-being and self-worth. Children who are bullied are often targeted because they appear vulnerable—they may have few friends and already experience low self-esteem. Social workers can work with children on how to improve confidence and self-esteem, which can make attacks less threatening, as well as how to seek out positive peer friendships in the classroom or other settings.

Some children—especially those who are very young—may go through periods of **separation anxiety** when apart from their families:

- In very young children (under age three), this is a normal developmental stage.
- If the anxiety is overwhelming even at school age, intervention may be necessary.

Separation anxiety may be triggered by

- a stressful life event
- stress or separation anxiety on the part of the parent.

Children who experience distress when separating from their parents often imagine that something bad will happen to them or their parents when they are not together, leaving them alone in the world. In some children, the anxiety can be so severe that they are distressed at the idea of going to school or playing alone with other kids. Social workers can help children by

- practicing cognitive behavioral therapy (CBT) techniques to manage emotions
- involving the parents in helping to support the children with their anxiety.

Child development issues, such as autism spectrum disorder, attention-deficit hyperactivity disorder (ADHD), and learning disabilities, can be very stressful for parents. Getting a diagnosis, learning about treatment, and advocating for a child is an involved process that can wear parents thin. Social workers can support clients by

- helping them manage their own stress by using techniques like CBT and developing positive coping strategies
- connecting parents with services and providers in schools and communities which can ease the burden of care.

A wide support system of friends, family, and neighbors can also help decrease the stress associated with raising children who have developmental delays.

Practice Question

3. Deborah is a single mom to Chloe (age nine). Deborah was recently in a car accident and had to stay in the hospital overnight. Ever since the accident, Chloe has been clinging to Deborah's side. She cries easily and refuses to stay with her grandparents alone, even though she used to love going to their house on weekends. How can the social worker help Chloe?

    A) Chloe and Deborah can engage in family therapy to learn coping skills for separation anxiety.
    B) Chloe should be referred to a child specialist for PTSD.
    C) The social worker should inquire if there is possible abuse going on with the grandparents.
    D) The social worker should observe if Deborah has been neglecting Chloe since the accident.

Blended Families and Adoption

Adoption is the process of parents raising a nonbiological child as if that child were their own biological child. Adoption can occur within families (such as kinship adoptions from grandparents or aunts and uncles), or it can take place with someone who is not a relative:

- Some adoptions are informal (never legally recognized). This may happen within extended families.

- In other adoptions, the caregivers go through a legal process to become the legal parents of the adoptee.

Despite the many benefits of adoption, it can be a fraught process for adoptees. There are seven core issues that are common among adoptees:

1. **Loss:** the loss of one's birth parents, relatives, and perhaps even culture/language

2. **Rejection:** feelings of abandonment that trigger feelings of rejection by the birth family

3. **Guilt and shame:** internalizing that the adoption was their fault, that they were given up because they were "too difficult" or not good enough

4. **Grief:** the grief of losing one's birth family, which is closely tied to loss

5. **Identity:** cultural, medical, and biological identities that come into play; integrating the past identity of an adoptee with his present identity

6. **Intimacy:** the emotional issues surrounding adoption that may cause a child to withdraw in an effort to self-protect

7. **Mastery/control:** a feeling of helplessness and lack of control that makes the adoptee feel that her life is out of her hands

Parents and caregivers can support their adopted children through these challenges with open communication and understanding. Caregivers should allow and encourage the children to feel all of their feelings and ask many questions, even uncomfortable ones such as "Why did my mom give me up?" Social workers who work with families may focus on supporting parents on how to best provide high levels of emotional support.

> **Helpful Hint**
>
> It is important to provide an open and nonjudgmental space for adopted children to process their feelings.

Blended families form when parents bring children from previous relationships into a new marriage or partnership. Some common challenges in blended families include:

- sibling rivalries
- adjusting to new people who may take up the parents' attention
- conflict with ex-partners
- parenting style differences.

Any conflict between adults must stay between the adults; the children should not be brought into disagreements. This can cause unnecessary pressure to "take sides" and may even cause the child to turn against a birth parent.

Sibling rivalries and the need for attention are often closely linked. Finding ways to create special time with each child, including stepchildren, in addition to group family activities can help ease the transition when bringing two families together.

Practice Question

4. Anna is a nine-year-old girl who was adopted by her current family when she was three. Recently, she has begun having outbursts around bedtime, refusing to listen to her parents and frequently shouting, "You're not my real mom!" The parents are distraught and do not know how to approach the issue. What should the social worker do?
   A) recommend that Anna reconnect with her birth mother
   B) advise Anna's parents about setting firmer boundaries with bedtime
   C) teach Anna's parents ways to empathically reflect Anna's feelings about her adoption
   D) recommend that Anna's father take over bedtime for a few weeks

The Family Life Cycle

The **family life cycle** is typically divided into six stages, each with its own **stage-critical tasks:**

1. **Leaving home:** developing self-identity, differentiating from family

2. **Marriage:** adjustment to and development of a satisfying married life, adjusting to a new kin network, navigating family planning

3. **Families with young children:** adjusting to the high needs of infants and toddlers, creating a satisfying family life for all members

4. **Families with adolescents:** encouraging academic success and planning for their future, balancing freedom with responsibility

5. **Launching children:** supporting young adults as they navigate careers, college, and relationships

6. **Families in later life:** coping with loss, living alone, adjusting to retirement

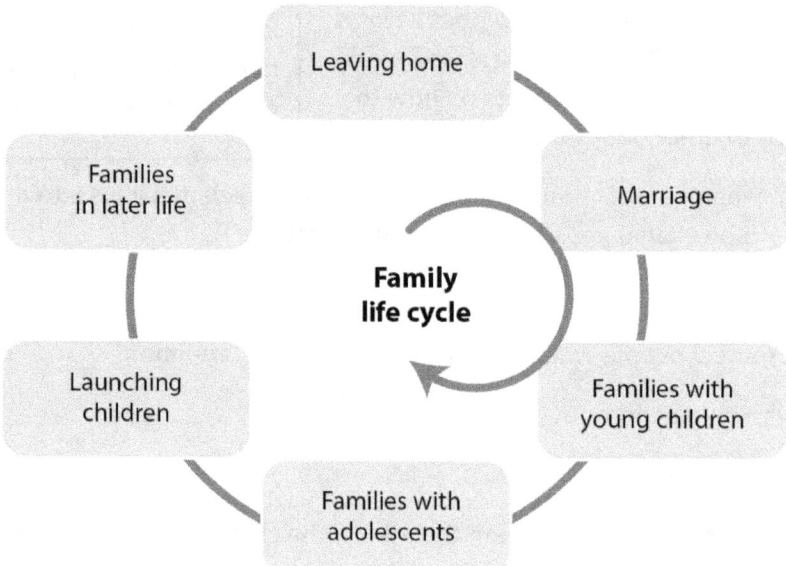

A social worker should know which stage in the family life cycle the client is in; that way, the social worker can determine which key areas the client is likely to be struggling with and which areas he needs to succeed in to feel accomplished and ready for the next stage.

Extended families can offer a wealth of resources and joy; but they can also contribute to family friction. When couples or young people diverge from the rest of the family's values, it can disrupt family norms and cause tension. Clients who are struggling with extended family relations may benefit from identifying boundaries to keep within their families and more comfortable ways in which to honor them.

Practice Question

5. Marta (twenty-six) and her fiancé, John (twenty-eight), have been having some difficulties with their family relations. Marta's family is religious and wants their wedding to be held in the Catholic church. While John is an atheist and does not wish to be wed in a church, Marta is ambivalent about a church wedding. How can the social worker help them?
   A) help the couple identify the pros and cons of either acquiescing to the family or doing what they prefer
   B) explain to John the importance of integrating with his new family
   C) encourage the couple to compromise
   D) work with Marta on setting better boundaries with her family

Physical and Mental Illness in the Family

Any time something is added or subtracted from a family system, the system will adjust. That adjustment can result in positive or negative consequences. Physical and mental illness can disrupt the family system and family dynamics in several ways.

Some physical and mental illnesses can create a **crisis situation**. For example, a family member has a heart attack or a psychotic episode. When a crisis occurs, all family energy centers around the crisis until the crisis passes. Once the crisis passes, residual issues commonly occur while the family tries to reestablish homeostasis. This recovery can also change relationships between family members or cause issues with changes in levels of attention.

An **acute physical or mental illness** creates a situation where the illness comes on fast and unexpected. It may or may not be a crisis, but it resolves through healing or recovery. For example, a new mother might experience postpartum depression, but through therapy and social support, she recovers completely. This episode can impact family dynamics and relationships, sometimes bringing them closer, sometimes not. It may also cause the family to rethink roles, rules, priorities, and other aspects of daily living.

Chronic physical or mental illness is one that occurs over a long time and may even be a lifelong condition. For example, a cancer diagnosis or the onset of schizophrenia can change family dynamics significantly. The family's financial situation may change, the focus of daily life may switch to the person with the condition, and the family's social participation may be affected.

Whether a **disability** is something a person is born with or acquired due to an accident, injury, illness, or other means, it can alter how the family operates. For example, parents who find out that their baby is deaf must adjust to a new lifestyle and method of communication not only with their child but between family members as well. This may also require special schools or other accommodations. Other situations may cause parents to change their employment status to take care of a child who is disabled or sick.

Any time a change occurs in the family system, the individuals within that system adjust. These adjustments can create tension or conflict. Even if individual family members seem to adjust to the changes, there will be emotional stress involved that mirrors the stages of grief that people go through when someone dies.

With each family member experiencing anger, denial, depression, bargaining, and acceptance, they may also be experiencing these feelings at different times, which can create challenges in family dynamics. Social workers can help families with changes due to physical or mental illness in several ways:

- Normalize and validate the family's experiences and feelings.
- Educate and guide the family through the stages of grief, mourning, and trauma that often accompany these changes.
- Connect the family to supportive resources, including social support, financial support, and support navigating health care and mental health systems.
- Help the family process how changes in the family system affect their relationships.
- Help the family recognize the negative consequences of the change and develop healthier coping and communication skills to restabilize relationships.

Practice Question

6. The Smith family's eighteen-year-old son recently experienced an acute psychotic episode that required an emergency room visit. Since that incident, the family says they have not been able to get back to "normal." The mother wants to pretend nothing happened, the father is angry at the mother for ignoring what happened, the son has completely withdrawn from the family and his friends, and the fourteen-year-old daughter recently started defying the rules and having emotional outbursts in school. What can the social worker say to the family members to explain what is happening to the family?
   A) "It sounds like your family needs some crisis intervention services."
   B) "What happened to your son was a crisis situation. Any time something like that happens, it is going to cause changes in the family system. Let's talk through some of that."
   C) "Which problem would you like to work on first?"
   D) "I can refer each of you to good therapists."

Psychological Defense Mechanisms

Defense mechanisms are another source of conflict within a therapeutic relationship. These are techniques clients use to protect themselves from feelings of anxiety or hurt. There are several defense mechanisms that people use. Some of the more common ones appear in Table 2.1.

Table 2.1. Defense Mechanisms

Mechanism	Definition	Example
Denial	ignoring reality	A parent denies that his child is misusing substances despite obvious signs.
Repression	deciding to avoid thinking about something distressing	A client pushes away memories of an ex-partner who treated her badly.
Regression	engaging in childlike behavior or emotions	A man speaks in baby talk when someone gets angry with him.
Intellectualizing	focusing on rationalizing an issue rather than on emotions	A client's loved one dies; she only talks about the person's illness, the course of treatment, and the inevitability of death without acknowledging the sad emotions.
Compartmentalizing	keeping a part of one's life separate from the others to reduce distress	A client works a very dangerous job but keeps it completely separate from her home life.

Practice Question

7. Samantha is a freshman in college, and despite attempts to make friends, she has made no meaningful social connections in the first semester. Her program of choice is engineering, and she is one of four women in the program, but those women do not seem interested in social relationships. She tells the social worker that her purpose in college is to earn good grades, pursue activities that will help her be the best engineer, and that she does not have much time for social stuff anyway because her program is hard and requires a lot of studying. Which defense mechanism is Samantha using?
- A) compartmentalizing
- B) regression
- C) intellectualizing
- D) repression

Addiction Theories and Concepts

Substance Use Disorders and Common Terminology

Substance use disorders are characterized by the excessive use of mind-altering substances to a degree that the user's life, relationships, and/or work are negatively impacted. People with substance use disorders, also known as addictions, cannot control their substance intake, even when they try to limit it or quit entirely.

People may be exposed to substances through recreational use. In other cases, habit-forming medications that have been prescribed by a doctor are misused. Some substances are easier to become addicted to than others. Common symptoms of substance use disorder include:

- needing more of the substance to reach a euphoric state ("get high")
- withdrawal symptoms when trying to quit
- an inability to quit despite trying to do so
- having urges to use the drug or substance that cannot be ignored
- continuing to use despite negative consequences
- spending more money than desired or can be afforded on the substance
- neglecting work or family obligations due to substance use
- engaging in risky behaviors while on the substance or in an attempt to obtain the substance (e.g., stealing or driving under the influence)

> **Helpful Hint**
>
> Illicit drugs present the greatest risk for people seeking opioids; they may be laced with other substances and not accurately measured, which can lead to emergent reactions and overdoses.

It is important to know the definition of some of the terms commonly used in addiction treatment; these are listed in Table 2.2.

Table 2.2. Addiction Treatment: Commonly Used Terms

Term	Definition/Description
Drug	<ul><li>a substance that has a physiological effect on the body when ingested</li><li>may or may not be addictive or produce a state of euphoria</li></ul>
Medicine	<ul><li>a drug prescribed to a client to treat a medical condition</li><li>may have the potential for abuse and have its use monitored</li></ul>
Misuse	<ul><li>using a drug in a manner or for a reason that differs from how it was prescribed</li><li>an unintentional type of use</li></ul>
Abuse	<ul><li>using a drug in a manner other than prescribed with the intention of getting high (e.g.,, taking too much)</li></ul>
Dependence	<ul><li>a state that occurs when drug or alcohol abuse persists for a prolonged time</li><li>can be both psychological and physical</li></ul>
Psychological dependence	<ul><li>a strong mental urge to use a drug to experience effects considered pleasant</li><li>drug or alcohol use to reach a euphoric state of mind</li></ul>
Physical dependence	<ul><li>when a person's body is accustomed to taking a drug</li><li>may include withdrawal symptoms when the drug is no longer present in the person's system</li></ul>
Cross dependence	<ul><li>when another drug is used to lessen the withdrawal symptoms of the drug of choice and/or replace the drug of choice</li></ul>
Tolerance	<ul><li>when the body adjusts to a drug over a prolonged time, altering its effects</li><li>often leads to taking larger amounts of the substance to try to achieve the same effects</li></ul>
Reverse tolerance	<ul><li>can cause a person to become more sensitive (rather than less sensitive) to a drug over a period of time</li><li>causes the substance to have a higher level of impact on the person</li></ul>
Dose	<ul><li>the amount of the substance taken at one time or over the course of twenty-four hours</li></ul>
Half-life	<ul><li>the amount of time a drug stays present in the body</li></ul>

Table 2.2. Addiction Treatment: Commonly Used Terms	
Term	**Definition/Description**
	▪ can be affected by metabolism and other factors, which differ from the specific half-life of the drug
Lethal dose	▪ a dose of a drug that is too potent and results in death
Therapeutic dose	▪ the amount of a drug needed to be effective
Drug interactions	▪ the way in which drugs interact with one another ▪ includes interactions among street drugs, prescription drugs, and alcohol

Practice Question

8. The amount of drug needed by a person in order for it to be effective is called what?
   A) the lethal dose
   B) the half-life dose
   C) the therapeutic dose
   D) the maximum dose

Progression and Severity of Substance Use Disorders

People with substance use disorders (SUDs) usually go through several stages with various levels of severity. It is therefore critical to understand the distinction between the terms *dependence*, *use*, *disorder*, and *addiction*:

- **Substance dependence** is a deep physical and/or psychological need to use a controlled substance to achieve a feeling of euphoria and/or calm.

- **Substance use** is the non-medically warranted consumption of medications or substances, such as tobacco, alcohol, or illicit drugs.

- **Substance use disorder** is the continued use of a medication without medical reason, or the excessive and intentional use of a controlled substance (e.g., alcohol, opioids).

- **Addiction** is the dependence on a substance or practice that is physically or psychologically habit-forming to the extent that it results in critical pain and damage.

People who misuse drugs and alcohol tend to exhibit common behavior changes that indicate that their use is becoming problematic; however, the misuse of drugs and alcohol does not necessarily signify an addiction or that a substance use disorder will develop.

Did You Know?

Some people may exhibit substance dependence without the behavioral characteristics of addiction.

Binge drinking is an example of alcohol misuse that can occur without the presence of a substance use concern. Other behavior changes observed when someone misuses substances can include:

- experiencing hangovers or tiredness after heavy use
- going to work hungover or sick;
- not being able to remember events because of alcohol or drug use.

Overall, there is minor impact on the day-to-day lives of people who misuse substances—they are often able to manage their responsibilities with no major noticeable changes to their behaviors. When people move from misusing substances to developing a substance use disorder, their use has a larger impact on their day-to-day lives. Indications of this include:

- a negative impact on their work performance
- an inability to manage day-to-day responsibilities
- interpersonal relationship struggles with family and friends
- denial of the consequences and severity of their use habits
- missing important events or withdrawing from usual hobbies
- new financial concerns
- new legal concerns (such as a DWI or possession charge)
- experiencing withdrawal symptoms
- being defensive about their use behaviors
- being irritable or angry more often
- signs of dishonesty or manipulation
- changes in their physical appearances (e.g., weight loss, changes in personal hygiene)
- changes in friends and problems at work or school
- appearing impaired more often than not (e.g., slurred speech, changes in pupils).

There is no cookie-cutter presentation for substance use disorders. With that being said, some or all of the above concerns may be noticed in clients. Additionally, the time it takes to develop an addiction will vary from person to person. Individuals who struggle with substance use disorders vary in age from adolescence to older adults.

There are a variety of tools that mental health professionals can use to assess the **severity** of a client's psychoactive substance use. Common assessments are discussed in depth in Chapter 5.

Practice Question

9. What is it called when a person uses another drug form to lessen the withdrawal he is experiencing from his drug of choice?
    A) dependence
    B) abuse
    C) cross-dependence
    D) reverse dependence

Models of Addiction Treatment

There are several **models** used to understand addiction and treatment. The model chosen by a social worker generally depends on the social worker's work experience and education and will have a direct impact on the theoretical approaches and interventions used with clients. An effective addiction model blends multidimensional aspects of addiction with various cultural and regional aspects, interpersonal preferences, and family concepts.

The **medical model** of addiction is well established among most rehabilitation centers. It is a descriptive model that does not lead to only one method of intervention. The medical model divides the process of addiction into stages, which can each be viewed as a target for intervention. This model helps social workers and medical professionals better judge the likelihood and severity of addiction in specific cases. Concepts integral to the medical model include those described in Table 2.3.

Table 2.3. Concepts Integral to the Medical Model of Addiction	
Concept	**Description**
Genetic predisposition	<ul><li>The client is genetically predisposed to addiction and has one or more family members who are also living with a substance use disorder.</li><li>This may explain why similar behavior leads to addiction in certain people.</li></ul>
Response to addictive chemicals	<ul><li>The person has a specialized response to substances.</li><li>This explains why taking a drug is unpleasant or not a compulsion for some people.</li></ul>
Risk factors	<ul><li>These include contexts.</li><li>Some contexts are social environment, preexisting mood disorders, drug availability, and life problems.</li></ul>
Practice	<ul><li>The individual has undergone a trial-and-error process, experimenting or "learning" how to use the drug.</li></ul>

Table 2.3. Concepts Integral to the Medical Model of Addiction

Concept	Description
	- The person has become addicted in the trial-and-error process.
Change from use to addiction	- This is when behavior changes from occasional use to full-blown addiction. - It involves hyposensitization and hedonic dysregulation (the inability to feel good without the drug).

According to the **cultural belief model**, a client's cultural beliefs must be addressed when providing client care:

> **Helpful Hint**
>
> The medical model does not apply to addictions that do not involve chemical substances.

- Certain behaviors may be attributed to the culture of the client, and it would be unethical to disrupt any behaviors that are related to culture.

- Different cultural aspects must be considered when first assessing the client's drug addiction and then taken into consideration again when creating an effective treatment method for the client.

Historically, addiction has been seen as a moral failing in many societies. Today, some people still treat addiction as a character flaw, considering it a moral failing, although this taboo is changing. The **moral model** has fallen out of favor because the medical community identifies addiction as a real disease process with a true genetic component.

Often confused with the moral approach, the **temperance model** focuses on the substance itself rather than the client. The temperance model developed during the Prohibition movement in the United States during the early twentieth century. It condemns the addictive substance and its potential to harm people and social institutions.

The **cognitive model** of addiction focuses on cognition, the mental process that relates to judgment, perception, and reasoning. Social workers work to discover the core beliefs that allow the person with addiction to engage in drug-using behavior, both conscious and unconscious.

The **biopsychosocial (BPS) model** of addiction attempts to explain how addiction starts, continues, and persists:

- The biological factors of the BPS model involve genetics and chemical changes that occur from drug use and are viewed as the primary causes of the addiction.

- The BPS model expands to include emotional (psychological) and social aspects of addiction, such as:
    - family matters
    - poverty
    - crime

- opportunity
- history of trauma
- mental disorders
- the influence of friends/peers.

- Critics of the BPS model feel that it is too broad and does not really identify a target to attack and treat.
- Practical addiction treatment blends the BPS model with the medical model. Along with medications, treatment is often more successful.

According to the **psychological model** (also known as the characterological model), addiction is caused by a psychological abnormality—the "addictive personality." Treatment under the psychological model includes psychotherapy and social support.

Addictive personality is not recognized as a personality disorder in the *Diagnostic and Statistical Manual of Mental Disorders* (*DSM*); however, the psychological model has been historically used in the treatment of SUD, and this model recognizes the concept of the addictive personality.

According to the **social education model**, addiction is a learned behavior. Based on principles of classical and operant conditioning, this integrative approach views addiction as the result of social influence or the client's imitating behavior, followed by ongoing cognitive processes.

Treatment includes training in impulse control and other social skills, cognitive exercises and reconditioning, suitable and realistic goal setting, and appropriate behavioral modeling overseen by cognitive and behavioral social workers.

The **biological model** of addiction is based upon genetic factors that influence addiction. Genetics, biochemistry, and metabolism all play a role in biological addiction factors:

- Some people may be unable to tolerate alcohol and other drugs, even when consumed in small amounts.
- The bodies of some people will act adversely to the substance, and behavioral issues will occur.
- Women tend to have a lower alcohol tolerance than men.
- People whose parents or siblings struggle with substance use are at a higher risk of developing an addiction; however, not all individuals with this circumstance will develop an addiction.
- There may be lower concentrations of certain enzymes in the brains of those who are susceptible to alcohol use due to their genetic disposition.

Genetics theory, or addictive inheritance theory, identifies the genetic factors of addiction separately from environmental factors:

- While there are many environmental components of addiction, studies have shown that the children of parents with alcohol use disorder (AUD) who are later adopted into families without this disorder have a greater risk of developing it than the general population.

- Certain populations are at a higher risk for addictive inheritance.
    - Due to a genetic predisposition to a deficiency in acetaldehyde production—the enzyme that degrades alcohol—they are hypersensitive to its effects.
- Sons are more likely to inherit alcohol use disorder than daughters.

Exposure theory assumes that addiction will eventually occur after the regular use of a substance:

- Due to drug use, the body undergoes metabolic changes.
    - The drug is mimicking the body's natural painkillers (endorphins).
    - The substance reduces the body's ability to produce endorphins naturally, causing chemical dependency and, ultimately, addiction.
- To avoid withdrawal, the body demands higher and more frequent amounts of a drug.

> **Did You Know?**
>
> The term *alcohol use disorder (AUD)* is now preferred by behavioral experts over the term *alcoholic* to describe the progressive nature of addiction as concerns the misuse or abuse of alcohol.

Similarly, **conditioning theory** posits that addiction is reinforced by drug use itself. Given the rewarding effect of the drug, the substance controls the user's behavior—the user becomes conditioned (addicted) to use the substance due to its rewarding effect.

According to **adaptation theory**, environmental, social, and psychological factors influence addiction and contribute to its potential. These include beliefs about the drug, subjective emotional experiences, and other internal and external dynamics. Adaptation theorists have investigated the psychodynamics of drug reliance; they also believe that some causes of addiction are problems in childhood, low self-esteem, and other psychological challenges.

People with SUD continue to seek out and use drugs and alcohol despite negative life consequences. They may wish to stop using and even try to stop but be unable to do so. The **disease concept of addiction** identifies addiction as a brain disease. This model recognizes that a person's brain changes in the way it functions, which leads to an abnormal reaction to a substance to which most people would react differently. For example, someone without an alcohol use disorder could have one or two alcoholic beverages and easily stop drinking. On the other hand, someone with an alcohol use disorder would feel compelled to continue drinking in a way the person without the disorder could never experience. It is thought that this compulsion is related to abnormalities concerning dopamine release and feedback in the brains of people who are addicted. Thus, people with an addiction may use more than one substance or seek out another substance if their drugs of choice are not available.

Practice Question

10. What is the term for using a drug in a manner or for a reason that differs from how it was prescribed, which is often unintentional?
    A) misuse
    B) abuse
    C) dependence
    D) tolerance

The Dynamics of Interpersonal Relationships

Social Interactions and Support Systems

Social support systems are an integral part of a healthy functioning life and are comprised of the people a person can turn to with emotional, physical, or spiritual needs. Social support systems may include:

- friends
- family members
- practitioners
- religious congregations
- clergy
- mentors
- teachers
- neighbors, and/or
- other community members.

Family of origin and close friends make up the majority of most people's support networks. Church congregations, clergy, mentors, teachers, neighbors, and other community leaders may make up part of the wider network of a person's support system.

Strong support systems are ideally rich in depth and breadth, with a variety of people who can offer different levels of support. People with a robust social support network can more easily deal with life challenges, such as financial difficulties, health issues, or relationship problems.

Social workers can help clients understand their current social systems and how they function by examining their systemic patterns of interaction. One way social workers do this is through the use of a genogram.

A **genogram** is a tool used by social workers and mental health professionals to help clients make sense of their family relationships so they can better understand where patterns of healthy and unhealthy behaviors are arising. Genograms have many different forms, but most have several elements in common, such as:

- squares represent men
- circles represent women
- lines between shapes represent relationships.

Some genograms can be simple, like the one in the figure below, while others can be more complex, with different types of lines representing different elements of a relationship. For example, zigzag lines might represent a hostile relationship, while dotted lines might represent estrangement.

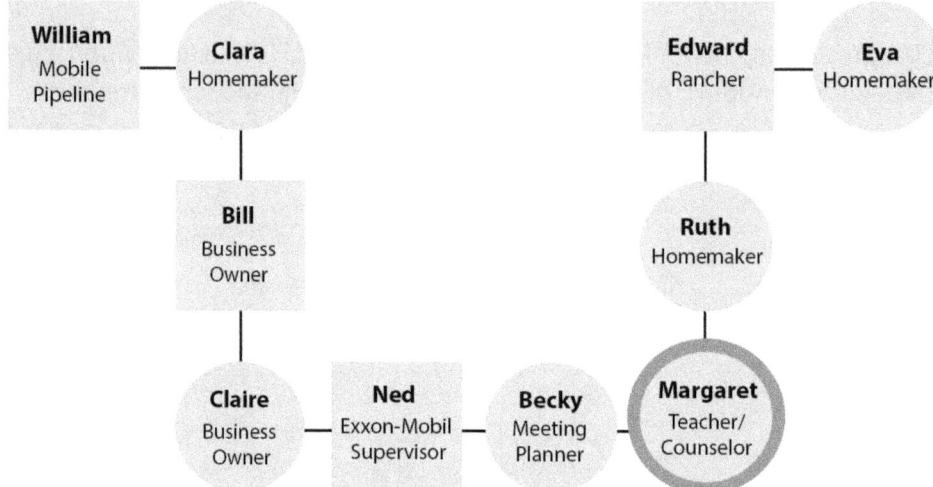

Another tool for describing relationships is an ecomap. Instead of focusing on individual relationships like genograms do, **ecomaps** explore broader systems in a person's life. Small systems like the immediate family, sibling relationships, and extended family might be included on an ecomap. But ecomaps also focus on other systems, such as:

- academic obligations/school environment
- community or professional organizations
- work/career relationships
- religious communities
- legal obligations.

An ecomap reveals the influence the external systems have on a client. For example, a client who is attending university and struggling in her classes might attribute her stress to the university system. This may influence other systems, such as family relationships. As with a genogram, different types of lines and shapes can be used to customize the ecomap to each individual's experience.

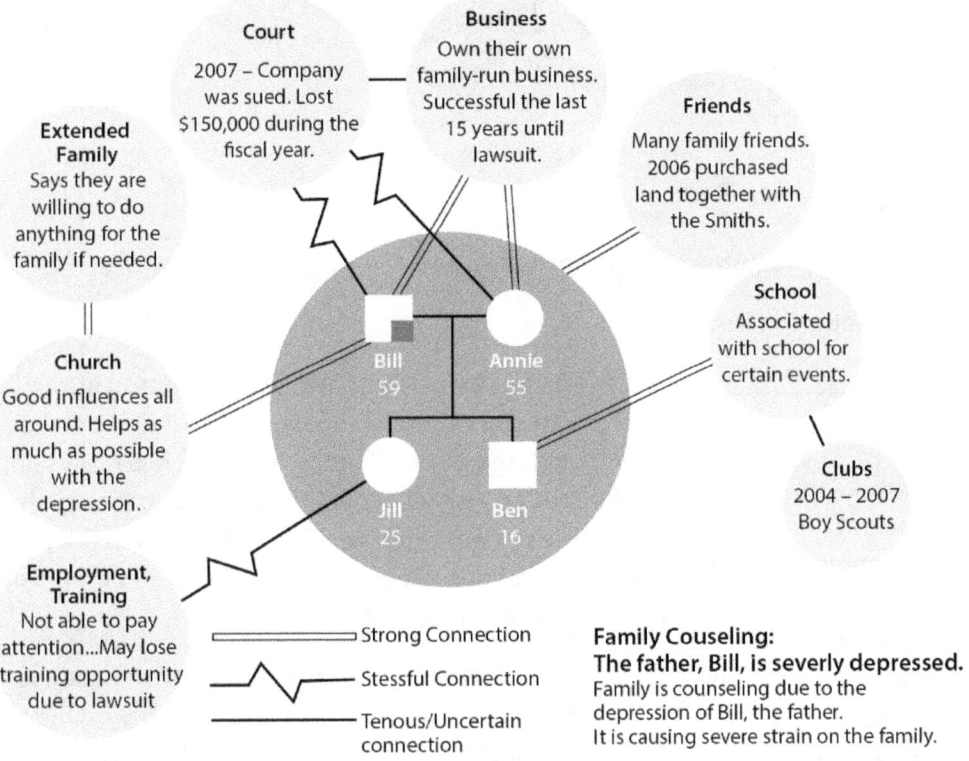

Figure 2.4. Ecomap

Some clients have very poorly developed support systems. This is especially common among adults who experienced abuse as children, since their family ties may be tenuous. Individuals with weak support systems are at a higher risk for feelings of loneliness and depression. **Loneliness** and depression can lead a person to retreat even further from society despite craving social interaction. Social workers should encourage clients struggling with loneliness to work on the following:

- strengthening existing support systems
- expanding new support systems
    - taking on new hobbies
    - joining communities with like-minded individuals

The social worker may discover unhealthy **interactional patterns** that stem from the client. For example, a client who habitually breaks up with his girlfriend after two to three months might be avoiding intimacy and vulnerability. Some approaches to use with this client may include:

- learning to identify intimacy fears
- developing coping strategies to self-soothe when faced with anxiety over intimacy.

Some relationships may take on a specific pattern known as codependency. **Codependency** is a type of relationship dynamic in which a partner enables the other partner's destructive habits, such as addiction, immaturity, or irresponsibility. The enabling partner may take on a role of self-sacrifice and feelings of responsibility for others' actions and behaviors, and thus may experience boundary issues and enmeshment. People who are codependent tend to have

- high rates of anxiety or depression
- compulsions
- hypervigilance
- experiences of recurrent physical or sexual abuse
- possible addiction issues.

Helpful Hint

In their relationships, individuals who are codependent may help their partners maintain unhealthy behaviors by enabling them, despite insisting that they want the behavior to end. Typically, this is motivated by a desire to be needed by their partners.

Codependency patterns are typically rooted in childhood issues, often among children who were parentified or whose feelings were ignored or punished. When the child grows up, he might ignore his own feelings and deny himself, feeling that he does not deserve to be treated well. People who are codependent may even have been expected to care for their parents due to addiction or mental health issues.

Social workers working with clients who are codependent may start by exploring childhood patterns and working to identify how those impact the client's current life. From there, issues such as developing healthy boundaries, sharing one's feelings, and building self-esteem can be introduced to allow the client to work toward better relationships.

Practice Question

11. Tammy and Fred have been married for over twenty-five years and are seeking therapy for Fred's alcohol abuse. They describe their relationship as very close and say they could not live without each other. Despite that, Tammy expresses exhaustion and disappointment with Fred's frequent drinking and subsequent poor behavior. On further questioning, the social worker learns that Tammy is the only one who does the grocery shopping and purchases all the alcohol for Fred, despite insisting that it is all his doing. What is the BEST response?
    A) recommend that Fred immediately enter a detox and rehab program to get his drinking under control
    B) pull Tammy aside and screen for domestic violence to see if Fred is forcing her to purchase the alcohol
    C) recommend that Fred begin doing the shopping with Tammy to make sure she does not purchase more alcohol
    D) broach the possibility that Tammy might be maintaining Fred's behavior by purchasing the alcohol for him

Dating and Marriage

For many people, **dating and marriage** are important parts of a fulfilling life. At the same time, they pose challenges. Some common disagreements that can arise in dating and marriage concern:

- finances/the use of money
- sex
- the division of household labor
- emotional expression
- levels of trust

Ultimately, the root of most relationship issues can be traced back to communication problems. Unspoken expectations, unkind language, and difficulty discussing feelings can all make healthy communication about difficult topics nearly impossible. Social workers should work with clients on identifying their communication styles and practicing building healthier communication habits.

Despite a desire to remain in one committed relationship, many people do end up remarrying or entering into more than one long-term relationship during their lives. **Remarriage** can come with its own unique set of challenges, including:

- a larger network of people involved in the relationship (e.g., children, ex-partners, co-parents)
- a renegotiation of family boundaries
- getting used to sharing a space again

As with all relationships, social workers should work with remarried couples and families to practice healthy communication, respect of boundaries, and ways to increase love and acceptance within the family unit.

Practice Question

12. George (fifty-eight) and Mary (fifty-four) are widows who recently remarried. They both have adult children who visit often. Tensions have started arising among the children: George's children complain that Mary takes up too much of George's time, and Mary's children do not like how George's children treat her. How can the social worker help?
    A) ask the children to work it out among themselves as adults
    B) encourage Mary's children to continue standing up for their mother
    C) advise the couple to separate themselves from the children for a while to strengthen their bond as newlyweds
    D) work with the family on identifying the main sources of conflict and practicing healthy communication and boundaries

Relationship Conflict

Communication problems are often the root of many sources of discord in relationships. Learning effective communication techniques to demonstrate care and respect for a partner in times of disagreement can smooth over many stressful interactions. Some of the most common unhealthy communication patterns are described in Table 2.4.

Table 2.4. Unhealthy Communication Patterns

Pattern	Description	Examples	Impact
"You" statements and directives	<ul><li>Directives tell the other person what to do.</li><li>"You" statements focus on the partner instead of the speaker.</li></ul>	<ul><li>"You are so rude to me."</li><li>"You need to be a better listener."</li><li>"You are lazy/sloppy/irresponsible."</li><li>"You have to meet my needs."</li></ul>	Nobody likes being told what to do. Using "you" language conveys negativity and criticism toward the receiving partner and does not actually communicate how the behavior is making the speaker feel or what the speaker would like done differently.
Universal statements	Universal statements often include the words *always* or *never*, *everyone*, *usually*, or *again*.	<ul><li>"You always interrupt me."</li><li>"You never put your clothes in the laundry."</li><li>"Everyone says you are lazy."</li><li>"You forgot to pick up the mail AGAIN."</li></ul>	These types of statements tell a partner that there is no room for any other kind of behavior from her, which can be hurtful and shut down communication. Such critical statements focus on *who* the listener is as a person, not *what* behaviors the speaker would like addressed.
Personalization	This technique focuses on *who* the person is instead of what the person is doing that is problematic.	<ul><li>"You are such a jerk."</li><li>"You are really stupid."</li></ul>	In the first example, it could be that the speaker is feeling hurt by something the listener said. By choosing to personalize the statement, the speaker loses focus on the undesired behavior (the listener's unkind words). Such statements perpetuate hurt and prevent intimacy and vulnerability.
Invalidation	This occurs when one partner expresses a hurt,	<ul><li>"Why are you so upset about this?"</li></ul>	Having a vulnerable thought or feeling ignored, dismissed, or

Table 2.4. Unhealthy Communication Patterns

Pattern	Description	Examples	Impact
	desire, want, or need, and the other partner dismisses or undermines these feelings.	• "I don't see what the big deal is." • "This happened to me before; I didn't cry about it."	belittled drives a wedge between partners and communicates to the hurt person that his feelings do not matter to his partner.

Social workers can work with their clients to identify which unhealthy communication patterns they are engaging in and help them replace these with more effective communication patterns. Healthier communication patterns include:

- focusing on "I" statements
- focusing on communicating feelings
- demonstrating love and respect throughout the conversation (e.g., through words or even small actions, like holding hands)

> **Did You Know?**
>
> Invalidation is an extremely harmful communication pattern in a relationship because it typically occurs after a moment of vulnerability on the other partner's part.

Intimate partner violence (IPV) occurs when one or both partners in a relationship engage in physical violence, sexual violence, stalking, or psychological aggression against the other:

- Globally, about one in three women will experience IPV in her life.
- Men can also experience IPV, though less is known about the statistical frequency.

The violence rarely decreases, making IPV a very dangerous situation. In fact, the violence typically increases over time and can lead to the death of the person experiencing the violence.

> **Helpful Hint**
>
> Universal statements are typically used with "you" statements.

Abuse tends to follow a very predictable cycle of tension, outburst, honeymoon period, and calm. As tensions arise and emotions get heated, incidents with various levels of verbal and physical abuse, sexual coercion, and psychological abuse arise.

After the incident, the attacker will often be contrite and may apologize, promise to make it up to the other person, or even agree to go to therapy or other treatments. Then, there is a period of calm when there are no incidents, leading the person experiencing the abuse to fall into a lull of false security.

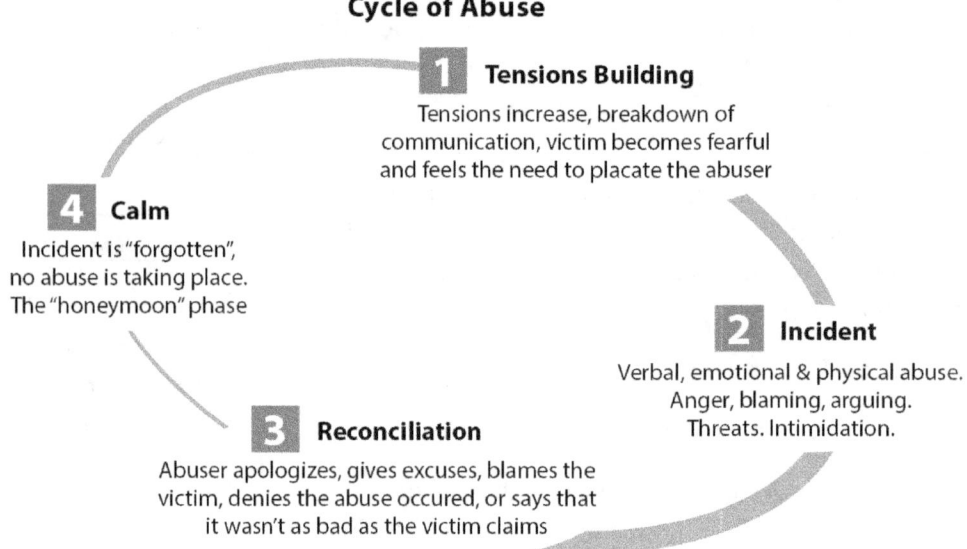

Cycle of Abuse

Social workers working with people experiencing IPV must keep an open door of communication and encourage their clients to develop a safety plan. A client's **safety plans** could include:

- moving money to a separate account
- seeking employment or skill development
- having a safe person with whom the client can move in if a decision to leave is made.

People who experience abuse may take years to leave their partners—if they ever do. Certain factors that prompt someone to stay in an abusive relationship include:

- financial dependence
- shared children
- a hope that the relationship will improve.

Divorce is the legal dissolution of a marriage. It is a high-stress time in a client's life, typically involving the ending of a years- or even decades-long relationship in which all of one's financial assets are tied up with another person. The emotional, financial, and logistical stresses of divorce can be overwhelming.

Social workers can work with clients to build up their support systems to help cushion the pain of a divorce, develop coping skills outside of the relationship, and learn how to live alone after many years of sharing a life.

Practice Question

13. Denise and her husband, Tony, have come to therapy to seek help with their relationship. They report fighting constantly and having difficulties resolving issues. During intake, Tony remarks, "This won't help anyway; Denise never listens to anyone." Which negative communication pattern is Tony engaging in?
    A) "you" statements
    B) universalization
    C) personalization
    D) invalidation

Other Theories

Role Theories

Role theory centers on the behaviors people engage in based on social expectations. It suggests that an individual may have many roles to play. For example, a woman may have roles such as mother, wife, sister, daughter, and caretaker, and others have expectations about who she is and what she does based on those roles. Those roles also include various rules that are imposed by social expectations. For example, a mother's role is to take care of her children, and when she engages in behavior that does not conform to society's expectation of that role, she may be stigmatized.

Problems arise due to tensions or conflict of roles either within an individual, between individuals, or between individuals and society. There can be tension or conflict within an individual between the different roles she has. For example, there are women who experience role conflict when they hold the role of mother as well as employee, especially when work has expectations of her that take her away from her role as a mother. Other sources can include the differences between an individual's perception of his role and societal expectations of his role. For example, men who stay at home and raise their children do not conform to societal expectations of a husband and father as the primary breadwinner in a family. This is an example of role strain—when a person experiences distress because he cannot meet the expectations of the role. Those expectations might be self-imposed or imposed upon the individual by others.

In families, there are additional dimensions to roles in that a role is associated with an individual's place in the family hierarchy, what the person's function is within the family, and the social expectations associated with it. For example, a traditional role for an oldest child is that of role model and caretaker for younger siblings. When that child does not conform to the family's expectation to fulfill that role, it can cause significant problems within the family system. Social workers apply role theory in therapeutic settings in multiple ways:

- Identify current roles.
- In each role, identify self-expectations and the expectations of others.
- Identity sources of role strain and role conflict.
- Determine if roles are consistent with the client's values and priorities.
- Make changes to expectations or roles to minimize strain and conflict.

Practice Question

14. Jessica says her mother is never happy with anything she does. As the oldest child of four, Jessica is expected by her mother to be home right after school to take care of her younger sisters until their mother gets home from work. What is Jessica experiencing?
    A) role theory
    B) role strain
    C) not fulfilling a role
    D) role dissolution

Group Development and Functioning

When people form groups, there are several defined **stages in the group process:**

- forming
- storming
- norming
- performing
- mourning

The **forming** stage of the group process is the start of the group when members join, introduce themselves, and determine their positions in the group. This part of the group process involves establishing the group rules, getting used to the format, and gaining an understanding of what the group will accomplish.

The **storming** stage involves conflict among group members. This can include testing boundaries, ascertaining whether other members really belong in the group, challenging the authority of the social worker, or resisting the way the group has decided to operate. Not every group goes through this stage, but the group's success depends on a healthy resolution; otherwise, members will be stuck in this stage and not get to the group's actual work.

The **norming** stage involves healing and repairing following the storming stage. If there is no conflict within the group, it occurs immediately after the forming stage. This is the stage when group members become comfortable with each other, understand what is expected of them, and settle into the routine of the work.

The **performing** stage describes the phase of real group work being done. The leader's function is reduced because members take on the roles of encouraging interaction with each other. It is in this stage that much of the therapeutic work is accomplished.

The **mourning** stage occurs at the end of the group and begins the process of group termination. During group therapy, members can become close, and the end of the group can be a sad event. Therefore, to ensure a successful termination of the group, the leader might facilitate an event or ritual to commemorate the successes of the members and to celebrate their accomplishments. Honoring this stage of the group process helps members transition out of the group.

Social workers need to be aware of which stage the group is in to make sure members are ready for a particular intervention. If a proposed intervention is not appropriate for the stage, then it will not be

effective. For example, a role-play intervention to teach assertiveness might not be effective during the storming stage because of the level of group conflict; however, adjusting that intervention to teach healthy conflict resolution skills would be appropriate. A social worker should therefore always think about whether members are ready for a particular intervention and if it will help them move toward the stated goals.

Practice Question

15. At the end of a group session, the social worker highlights the way three members achieved deep insight into their issues and thanked the other four members for helping with validation, feedback, and encouragement of those three members. Which developmental stage is this group likely in?
    A) forming
    B) norming
    C) storming
    D) performing

Answer Key

1. D: The Federal Emergency Management Agency (FEMA) is a national organization and best fits into the macrosystem because it is run by laws and government. The neighborhood or area affected would be part of the exosystem. The family's place of work and school make up the mesosystem, whereas the family itself makes up the microsystem.

2. A: Cultural values that include honoring elders may result in grandparents or other aging family members living in the household and holding a position of authority over family decisions.

3. A: Family therapy to learn about separation anxiety and develop coping skills can help treat the symptoms of separation anxiety.

4. C: Anna is likely experiencing identity issues and feelings of loss surrounding her adoption. Reflecting Anna's feelings and putting them into emotion-based language can help Anna better process her emotions and feel safe opening up to her adoptive parents.

5. A: Marta and John are beginning their married relationship and would benefit most from practicing making decisions together based on their own values and dynamics. This may be a time to set a boundary with the family, or it may be a time to be flexible—it is not clear based on the information.

6. B: The goal is to explain to the family how the son's episode impacted the family system. Each family member seems to be reacting to it differently, but the family does not relate those changes to the crisis.

7. C: Samantha gives intellectual and rational reasons for focusing on school and remains detached from her emotions related to social rejection.

8. C: The therapeutic dose is the amount of drug needed by a person in order for it to be effective.

9. C: With cross-dependence, a person may use another drug form to lessen the withdrawal he is experiencing from his drug of choice. Abuse is using a drug in a manner other than that prescribed, with the intention of getting high, such as taking too much of one drug within a short period of time.

10. A: Misuse is using a drug in a manner or for a reason that differs from how it was prescribed. Misuse is unintentional.

11. D: Tammy and Fred's relationship is highly codependent. Bringing awareness to the dynamic can help both partners recognize patterns and begin to make changes in their relationship.

12. D: Helping the family work on their communication and set expectations and boundaries early in the marriage will benefit the entire family unit in the long run.

13. B: Words like *always* or *never* indicate universalization, which can pigeonhole someone and prevent positive growth in the relationship.

14. B: Jessica is not fulfilling her mother's expectations of Jessica's role as the oldest child.

15. D: Performing is the stage of group therapy when real work gets accomplished. The session described includes positive group interactions that contributed to positive outcomes for multiple group members, so the group is likely in the performing stage.

3. Diversity, Social Justice, and Oppression

Systemic Discrimination

Discrimination is the act of treating or considering people differently based on specific classes or characteristics, such as race, class, gender, or sexual orientation:

- Discrimination can be experienced at the individual level; for example, a gay man being harassed on the street for holding hands with his partner.
- Discrimination can also be experienced at the systemic level; for example, laws barring women from acquiring divorces without their husbands' permission.

Systemic discrimination is when discrimination is formally instituted and upheld through laws, institutions, and standardized practices. Systemic discrimination can occur across many categories, including race, class, gender, age, or sexual orientation.

The concept of **race** is the pseudoscientific delineation of people based on skin color and geographic ancestry. Black, Asian, and White are some examples of race groups. Though these terms are commonly used and understood, they are not accepted by scientists or biologists as legitimate groupings of humans, as all humans make up the same species.

Despite the rejection of the scientific theory of race, many people still operate on the idea of the legitimacy of race. This can lead to **racism**—the hatred and mistreatment of people of different races based on the belief that one's own race is superior to other races.

Systemic racism is the intersection of prejudice (individual racism) towards people for their racial background and systemic power to uphold that prejudice. Systemic racism is only possible when systems and institutions uphold laws and practices that discriminate against people based on their race. Examples of systemic racism include:

- segregation laws
- redlining
- police brutality

Sexism is discrimination based on someone's sex or gender. Sexism can affect anyone, but historically, girls and women have been the primary targets of sexism. At the individual level, this can look like sexual harassment and sexual violence, domestic violence, gender-based stereotyping, and more.

Systemic sexism involves the use of institutional power to discriminate based on sex. In the US, for example, women were not legally allowed to vote until 1919. Laws barring property ownership, financial independence, and limiting parental rights were other areas of systemic sexism that women have historically faced in the United States.

Homophobia is the fear or hatred of individuals who are gay or lesbians. At the individual level, this may look like harassing or targeting people who are gay on the street or in the workforce, subjecting them to physical violence, and more.

To this day, being gay is a crime in at least 69 countries around the world. In some cases, being found out to be gay can land one in prison or even lead one to face the death penalty. Same-sex sexual activity was not legalized in the US until 2003, and gay marriage was not legalized until 2013 with the overturning of the Defense of Marriage Act.

Ageism is discrimination and prejudice against individuals based on their age. It can occur for any individual; however, older adults are the most vulnerable to ageism. Ageism can take place in the form of elder abuse (physical, emotional, and/or verbal), neglect, and financial abuse. Older adults are particularly vulnerable to financial abuse because they have often accumulated some wealth over their lifetimes but may not have the necessary faculties to manage their finances independently. Elder abuse can be perpetrated by family members, hired caregivers, or strangers.

Other forms of ageism can include discrimination in the workforce through denied jobs or promotions. Although institutional ageism in the form of laws or policies is less common, older adults are a vulnerable population who need additional legal protection against abuse and mistreatment and increased access to care and services.

Discrimination can have wide-reaching **effects** on individuals and communities. Besides the obvious effects of barring the free movement and rights of individuals based on immutable characteristics, discrimination can have significant internal effects on the recipient.

People who have experienced individual or systemic discrimination often report feeling demoralized and humiliated by the experience. They may feel lower self-esteem, have greater rates of anxiety and depression, and suffer other emotional effects.

Long-term discrimination can shape one's identity if that individual begins to believe the negative ideas propagated about them by society. As they move through society, these individuals may experience that most people also see or treat them in a similar way, which may further internalize the negative belief structures.

Some groups of people may become empowered to fight back against discrimination and seek political and socioeconomic power by banding together as a group. This can have a positive impact on the community at large, as it can lead to increased feelings of competence, self-worth, and agency.

Practice Question

1. A client who is Black is applying for a loan for his first house. Despite having good credit, a stable job, and good rental history, he was denied a loan by the first two lenders he approached. What should the social worker do NEXT?
    A) Report the banks that denied the client a loan.
    B) Counsel the client to try at a credit union.
    C) Assess the client's financial situation together to make sure everything is in order.
    D) Recommend the client to wait one more year to save more for his house.

Gender and Sexuality

Feminism is the political movement dedicated to the upholding of women's rights around the world. **Feminist theory** is the philosophical and theoretical discourse surrounding feminism. Feminist theory seeks to understand gender inequality. Some basic concepts commonly explored include:

- discrimination
- objectification
- oppression
- patriarchy
- stereotyping.

Feminist theory is used in social work as a lens when working with clients. Even though women are afforded more protection and standing in society today than they have in the past, issues such as the wage gap, gender-based violence, and sexual assault still plague our society.

Feminist theory overlaps significantly with broad social work theories, such as systems theory (discussed below). The social worker recognizes these issues:

- Female clients operate in a system that privileges men and masculinity.
- Female clients face systems that are skewed against them and uphold gender-based oppression.

Sexual orientation describes a person's attraction and desire for intimate relationships. People can be attracted to those of the opposite sex, those of the same sex, or both sexes. Sexual orientation involves romantic attraction and sexual attraction.

Relationships that are not heterosexual have historically been taboo in American public life. Gay and lesbian people have faced discrimination and even imprisonment for their sexuality. Some have lived in secret, even marrying into traditional marriages to avoid raising suspicion.

Still, clandestine relationships and communities embracing nontraditional sexuality have existed throughout US history and earlier. On the heels of the civil rights movement, gay and lesbian people began fighting for increased rights and recognition. Over time, this group has coalesced into the **lesbian, gay, bisexual, transgender, and queer (LGBTQ)** movement to fight for better treatment, rights, and protection from discrimination in the workforce and throughout everyday life.

> **Did You Know?**
>
> In recent years, terms like *heteroromantic*, *biromantic*, and *pansexual* have been developed to better describe various orientations and acknowledge the fluidity of gender and its relationship to sexual attraction.

People in the LGBTQ community still face discrimination today. Some LGBTQ people report a feeling of solidarity in their identity and may prefer to socialize with other members of the LGBTQ community for feelings of safety, understanding, and a greater sense of camaraderie and closeness.

Gender identity is a person's self-perceived identification and alignment with their presenting gender. A person may identify as male, female, a combination of both, or neither.

Some people identify as the opposite gender. In other words, a person born with a penis may identify as female, while a person born with a vagina may identify as male. When an individual's genitalia and gender identity do not match, they are known as **transgender**. Furthermore, some people identify as **nonbinary**, which means that they feel their gender identity does not fit well into the categories of male or female.

People who are transgender may experience **gender dysphoria**—a feeling of unease and dissatisfaction with their physical body because it does not align with how they perceive themselves internally. This is typically treated through **transitioning:** living one's life as the gender that they identify with internally.

Transitioning can range from smaller interventions, like changing one's name or clothing, to medical interventions with hormone blockers and hormone replacement therapy. Some people undergo gender-affirming surgery to add or remove breast tissue or alter their genitalia. Not all transgender people choose surgery or hormones; the degree to which one chooses to physically transition may have to do with several factors, including the level of gender dysphoria, their physical health, affordability of treatment, and more.

Transitioning can be an emotionally fraught process for individuals who are transgender. They may face pushback or lack of understanding from friends and family, and they may have difficulty accessing adequate care and face discrimination in school or workplace settings.

When people transition, frequently their feelings of dysphoria lessen. Still, other challenges can arise. They may face issues in schools or workplace settings with regards to which bathrooms they are permitted to use, for example. Laws protecting transgender rights are limited at this point and are primarily found on a state-by-state basis as opposed to federal law.

Because of the stigma associated with a transgender identity, people who are transgender may experience challenges in their relationships with family and friends. They may also have trouble finding relationships due to the stigma associated with transitioning. Like gay and lesbian people, some people who are transgender may find solace in socializing more exclusively with members of the LGBTQ community, where they are likely to find greater camaraderie and understanding through shared experiences.

LGBTQ Pride emerges from the historic gay rights movement which focused on eliminating shame and being proud of one's sexual or gender identity. Commemorations of the Stonewall Uprising of June 1969 evolved into Pride month. Pride remains central to the LGBTQ community today and is celebrated across the country. Pride festivals and Pride parades occur globally during June.

Practice Question

2. A client comes to a clinic seeking help with identity questions. She states that she often feels dissatisfied with her appearance when she looks in the mirror and does not like being perceived as a girl. In particular, she reports a lot of distress with her breasts and says she wants to cut her hair short to appear more boyish. Which of the following BEST describes the client's state of being?
   A) gender dysphoria
   B) agoraphobia
   C) dissociative identity disorder
   D) borderline personality disorder

Disability

A **disability** is a condition that limits or prevents a person from typical achievement in a certain area. A disability may be permanent (such as being born without limbs) or temporary (such as experiencing PTSD). Disabilities can be physical or developmental. Severe mental illness can also qualify as a disability.

Physical or developmental disabilities can be **congenital**, meaning that the person is born with the condition. Common examples include Down syndrome or cerebral palsy. Other times, disabilities can occur later in life through trauma, such as losing a leg in war or suffering brain damage after a car accident.

Severe psychological problems that rise to the level of disability tend to manifest in adolescence or early adulthood (e.g., bipolar disorder, schizophrenia). Some psychological disabilities may be temporary; others may become lifelong conditions.

Living with a disability can have significant effects on a person's well-being. Securing and keeping jobs, navigating transportation, and engaging in social aspects of life may be challenging.

The limitations on accessible locations or ease of navigation can lead to isolation and loneliness for individuals with disabilities. They may find themselves staying home more often to avoid having to plan and navigate going out into the world. They may not be able to find work or may be limited in their work options, which can lead to financial difficulties, including struggles with paying their medical bills to care for themselves.

Individuals with disabilities have varying levels of needs and abilities. With adequate support, people with disabilities can lead thriving and fulfilled lives, including maintaining their health, relationships, and mental wellbeing. Some individuals may need concrete physical support, such as braces, braille writing, or wheelchair ramps. Others may need more intangible support, such as job training, help finding socialization opportunities, or financial assistance.

Many people with disabilities find it emotionally fulfilling to meet with and socialize with other people with similar disabilities, either through support groups, online forums, or in other manners. The shared experiences and difficulties of living with their disabilities can create intimacy and friendship through their unique perspectives.

Practice Question

3. A social worker is assisting a client who uses a wheelchair due to diminished mobility. The client's current home is not wheelchair accessible, and he has to wait for relatives to come over to help him when he needs to run errands. The social worker has located a new apartment for him to move into, but the client does not want to move in because they do not allow pets. What is the BEST response from the social worker?
    A) The social worker should insist on transfer to the new location for safety reasons.
    B) The social worker should reassess the client's needs and values related to housing.
    C) The social worker should inform the client's son about the client's unwillingness to move.
    D) The social worker should educate the client on the dangers of remaining in his current home.

Culture, Race, and Ethnicity

Everybody exists in a culture, whether they are aware of it or not. Some people describe cultural norms as like water to a fish—it is the entire environment and is everywhere, although one may not even be aware of it. Some cultural norms in the US include things like dating practices (men should pay for the first date, online dating is acceptable, "hookup culture," and so on), family setup (nuclear family or variations of it are the norm as opposed to extended family living under the same roof), or expectations of dress (suits to the office, jeans on the weekend, swimsuits at the beach). Culture tends to develop through geographic proximity and shared values, norms, and expectations.

As discussed earlier, race is a pseudoscientific category based on outdated ideas of phenotype and genetics. While it is true that people of the same race share general common ancestry, researchers have found that there are more genetic differences between individuals of the same race than there are between individuals across racial groups. Some people in a racial group may have shared cultural norms within their subgroup, but cultural norms rarely are shared by all members of a racial group.

Ethnicity is a distinctive group that is identified by shared culture or historical lineage. Shared language, cuisine, religion, values, dress, and cultural norms may all be aspects of what makes an ethnicity distinct. Ethnicity and culture are similar ideas; however, **ethnicity** is more commonly tied to ancestral heritage, while **culture** can be ancestral or geographic. An example is a country like the US, where there is a common language and many broad shared values and norms, but ancestral heritage is diverse and comes from countries all over the world.

Cultural competence is a necessity for good social work practice. The National Association of Social Workers (NASW) states that social workers should have a knowledge of their clients' cultures, approach culture from a strengths perspective, and be able to provide culturally sensitive services regardless of background. The main areas that a social worker should focus on developing cultural competence are through communication, medical and mental health care treatment, and spirituality.

The primary concern with communication is language. Linguistically appropriate services are a bare minimum necessity for successful work with clients. If services are not being provided in a language the client is comfortable in, the competence of service is lacking and inadequate. Social workers should be aware of a client's comfort in the language the social worker delivers and check for comprehension if it is not the client's first language. Cultural differences in the use of nonverbal communication cues, such as eye contact and body language, should be noted and accommodated for as well.

When providing medical or mental health care across cultures, the social worker must be aware of the client's cultural relationship with mental disorders, which can be taboo in some cultures. Other conditions may be culturally specific, and the social worker should be sure to consult and review possible culturally bound diagnoses in the *Diagnostic and Statistical Manual of Mental Disorders* (*DSM-5*) should symptoms arise. Conversely, some symptoms may be perceived as psychological problems from a Western perspective, while in other cultures they may be seen as normal, such as seeing ghosts or spirits.

Spiritual beliefs can complement social work practice very well for the well-prepared social worker. Some clients may seek out counsel from spiritual leaders, such as guides, priests, or ministers, to assist them with their problems. Culturally competent social workers will become knowledgeable about a client's spiritual beliefs and incorporate them into the practice to the comfort level of the client.

Practice Question

4. A teenager who is Muslim is referred to a social worker for truancy. When speaking with the social worker, she reveals that she is not being allowed to pray when she attends school, so she prefers to stay at home. Which of the following BEST describes the client's experience?
   A) racial discrimination
   B) cultural autonomy
   C) religious discrimination
   D) systemic oppression

Social, Economic, and Criminal Justice

At its core, **social justice** is about fairness for all people, including fair treatment under the law, respect for all individuals—with special concern for those who are marginalized—and the equal distribution of resources for community members. The core of social work is focused on social justice work—efforts to ameliorate the inequalities in the world for people who are marginalized. Social justice work can occur at the individual level, such as helping a client advocate for herself in the face of workplace discrimination. But the most effective social justice work is done at the macro level in policy work, institutional change, advocacy, lobbying, and more.

Economic justice is specifically focused on the economic aspects of social justice and tools used to further those goals, such as welfare, housing assistance, fair minimum wages, and other economic efforts to create more economic equality.

The **criminal justice system** encompasses several connected organizations that serve different but related roles:

- police
- courts
- corrections system
- parole system

Most people first interact with the criminal justice system when they encounter the police. **Police** are responsible for enforcing laws. They issue warnings and fines, arrest suspects, and bring charges against individuals who break laws.

The next stage of the criminal justice system involves the courts. In the **courts**, an individual accused of a crime will stand before a judge and can defend himself against the charges with a trial or accept the charges and take a plea. If a person is found guilty of a serious crime, he will be sentenced by a judge and placed in a corrections institution, which is its own system.

The **corrections system** has multiple levels of prisons depending on the severity and level of violence of the crime. When a person has completed his sentence, he is then placed into the **parole system**, where he will have several requirements he must fulfill and will have to meet with a parole officer regularly to ensure that he is following the terms of his parole. There are other parts of the justice system as well, such as the juvenile justice system (which has its own courts), rehabilitation centers, and regulations.

Environment

In social work, the environment is an essential element of analysis and planning for treatment. **Person-in-environment (PIE) theory** is a social work perspective that highlights the importance of understanding an individual's behavior based on the environment that she is in. PIE theory comes out of a long history of social work theory, such as Bronfenbrenner's systems theory, and understandings about the systems that people exist in and move through.

An individual's environment is made up of many elements: his family of origin, his social circles, and the community he lives in are all part of his environment. But so are the cultural norms he shares: his society at large, political activity, economic movement, and more. His exposure to these elements has innumerable influences on him in big and small ways. City planning is an easy example to think of how environment changes one's behavior. When communities are spread out, roads are wide, and necessities are far from people's homes, people are more likely to drive to their destinations; however, when roads are narrower, have bike lanes, and stores and markets are on the same streets as residential areas, people are more likely to walk or bike to their destinations. Of course, cultural norms play a big role in this as well—what is considered too far to walk for a midwestern suburbanite might be very different from how far a New Yorker, for example, would walk.

Environment can impact behavior on a larger scale as well. Laws make up the fabric of the society, and they significantly impact behavior in positive and negative ways. Pro-segregation laws in the past upheld and protected racist behavior against Americans of African descent. It also led to protests, marches, and political movements and sparked massive social change.

Laws affect how large institutions (e.g., the medical or pharmaceutical industry) impact individuals, families, and communities on a daily basis. Such laws influence access to medication and health care, the costs of those goods and services, and even the legality of goods and services, such as access to abortion or family planning care.

Just as laws can impact the environment, the political environment itself can impact policymaking. This is true in both positive and negative ways. Often, laws are enacted after significant social and political pressure. A good example is the repeal of the Defense of Marriage Act (DOMA). When DOMA was repealed, many states had already made same-sex marriage legal through referendums or through the legislature, making the repeal of DOMA a very popular move among constituents and politicians.

In the same way, the current Supreme Court is a more conservative political environment, which has influenced their ruling on several key issues, most notably their recent overruling of Roe v. Wade, which made abortion rights no longer protected or guaranteed in the US and were instead left to the states to decide. Political environment changes frequently over time based on public opinion and who is in office. Responsible social workers recognize the role of the political environment and policymaking in the day-to-day work whether it is with individuals, groups, or institutions.

Poverty

Poverty is the state of having insufficient funds or material goods to satisfy one's basic needs. According to Abraham Maslow, basic needs include physiological and safety needs. Survival requires food, water, a safe place to rest, shelter from bad weather, and safety from physical harm. Poverty makes it difficult or impossible to meet one or more of these needs. (See Chapter 1 for more on Maslow's hierarchy of needs.)

The effects of poverty can be debilitating. At its most extreme, people in poverty lack the resources necessary to feed themselves, keep themselves adequately clothed, keep their homes warm, or may lack housing altogether. Living on a daily basis with the basic needs not being met can have deep psychological impacts on individuals, leading one to experience high rates of stress and anxiety, difficulty focusing on work or school due to greater worries, difficulty forming meaningful relationships, and more. People who live in poverty may also be likely to be exposed to higher rates of interpersonal violence, property theft, and witness violent crimes. It can lead to significant stress on family units, even causing families to have to be separated due to an inability to care for all family members. Children in families with extreme poverty are likely to be exposed to higher rates of parental fighting due to the stress of lacking the funds to care for basic needs and are more likely to accumulate adverse childhood experiences (ACE) than peers from middle- or upper-class homes.

When an entire community is in poverty, the effects can become even more widespread. Schools in impoverished communities will receive less funding, leading to overcrowding, insufficient resources, and outdated materials. Building infrastructure in impoverished communities may languish and decay over time with no funding to repair or rebuild old structures. Impoverished communities may be exposed to more environmental stressors, such as living near highway systems, experiencing high rates of noise and physical pollution, or having insufficient access to clean drinking water. Communities in poverty may experience more violent crime and gang activity as well.

Answer Key

1. C: To better understand the client's financial situation, the social worker should assess the client's finances to make sure everything is in order. Only after understanding the client's finances can the social worker determine whether reporting the banks for discrimination, recommending a local credit union, or saving for one more year is the best course of action.

2. A: Gender dysphoria best describes the client's stated symptoms. Agoraphobia is an anxiety or fear about being in certain environments and can lead to fear of leaving one's home. Dissociative identity disorder is when an individual has two or more distinct and unique identities or personality states. Borderline personality disorder is a personality disorder characterized by unstable interpersonal relationships, a distorted sense of self, and strong emotional reactions.

3. B: Reassessing the client's needs and values respects the client's autonomy and is the best response in this situation. Insisting on transferring does not respect the client's right to autonomy, and telling the client's son is a Health Insurance Portability and Accountability Act (HIPAA) violation. Educating the client on the dangers of remaining in his current home is an acceptable response but not the best response in this situation.

4. C: The client is experiencing religious discrimination by not being allowed to practice her faith in school. Racial discrimination is discrimination based on one's racial background. Cultural autonomy is what the client would like to be experiencing (the freedom to practice her cultural faith). Systemic oppression refers to widespread and policy-level discriminatory practices. These may be at work here, but it is not clear from the example.

4. Biopsychosocial History and Collateral Data

Assessing the Client

General Types of Assessments

A **psychological assessment** is used to determine and treat psychological, psychiatric, and personality disorders as well as developmental delays. Psychological testing can be further categorized into four main types: clinical interview, assessment of intellectual functioning (IQ), personality assessment, and neuropsychological assessment.

The **clinical interview** is a basic but integral component of any psychological testing. Also known as an "intake" or "admission interview," it is generally a comprehensive assessment to collect information about an individual's background and family relationships. Only a licensed clinician may perform a clinical interview.

Intellectual functioning refers to intelligence, and intelligence quotient **(IQ)** tests are used to measure typical intelligence. These tests are divided into subsections that evaluate verbal comprehension, perceptual reasoning, working memory, and processing speed.

The **personality assessment** was developed to help health care professionals gain better insight into an individual's personality. Two different types of objective tests used to evaluate personality are the Minnesota Multiphasic Personality Inventory-2 (MMPI-2) and the Sixteen Personality Factors Questionnaire (16PF).

A **neuropsychological assessment** is used to measure capacity regarding memory, reasoning, concentration, motor skills, and other cognitive elements.

> **Helpful Hint**
>
> The intellectual functioning and personality assessments require special training; an entry-level social worker cannot administer these without that training.

Practice Question

1. Which of the following assessments is the FIRST one a social worker should conduct with a new client?
    A) IQ test
    B) personality assessment
    C) clinical interview
    D) neuropsychological assessment

Biopsychosocial Assessment

There are multiple domains to a **biopsychosocial assessment**. The **biological** assessment focuses on a person's physical health and wellness:

- What is the client's birth story? (Was there trauma, premature birth, poor maternal health, low birth weight, and so on?)
- Did the client meet physical developmental milestones?
- Has the client experienced any illnesses—acute or chronic—throughout his life?
- Has the client experienced any surgeries or hospitalizations while young?
- Has the client experienced any physical trauma or injuries related to accidents?
- How does the client sleep?
- What is the client's diet like?
- Does the client engage in physical exercise?
- Is the client taking any medication prescribed by a doctor?
- Has the client experienced adverse side effects from medication?
- Does the client use alcohol or illicit substances?
- What is the client's gender and genetic predisposition for health or mental health issues?
- Does the client have any disabilities?

The **psychological** domain of the assessment evaluates the client's mental and emotional health:

- What are the client's personality, temperament, and character traits?
- How are the client's emotional health and coping skills?
- What are the client's values, beliefs, and attitudes?
- How does the client's family relationships and environment affect her thoughts and emotions?
- What is the status of the client's ability to learn, pay attention, and concentrate?
- How does the client cope with thoughts and emotions?
- How well does the client practice self-awareness?
- Can the client self-regulate thoughts and emotions?

Finally, the **social** domain of the assessment evaluates how the client interacts with others:

- What is the client's family history, including culture, composition, and the dynamics between generations?
- Is there any intergenerational trauma?

- How does the client do in school or work?
- How does the client interact with the community and community organizations he is part of?
- What is the client's socioeconomic status?
- What are the client's peer relationships like?
- What cultural issues are important to the client?
- What is the client's relationship with religion/spirituality and a religious community?

These questions are a sample of what a social worker can ask a client in each domain. The goal is to gather as much information as possible about the client's current status in the various systems and then look for sources of conflict or tension between them. Additionally, the social worker needs to assess for strengths and resources in each area that can be considered protective factors and potential areas of support during the therapy process.

The exploration of all these areas is important because they are all interrelated. There are **biopsychosocial responses to illness and disability**, such as physical illness contributing to mental health issues like anxiety and depression. It works the other way, too, because mental health issues like anxiety, depression, and PTSD can contribute to physical illness. In addition, understanding trauma is integral to understanding the link between mental health and physical health. Body and mind are connected, so what happens to one will affect the other. Trauma can occur in any domain and at any age. For example, there is evidence to suggest that infants and toddlers who undergo surgery suffer the consequences of that traumatic experience solely based on the biological response to trauma. This is important to consider when working with children who have emotional or behavioral issues, which could be a response to a traumatic event they do not remember.

The **biopsychosocial perspective on mental health** suggests that biological, psychological, and social factors converge and contribute to a client's level of mental health. The goal of the social worker is to gather as much information as possible from the client and then determine which areas are risk factors and which are protective factors. Risk factors are those things that increase someone's risk for an issue and can be balanced by protective factors which reduce the risk. For example, a teenager with a family history of alcohol use disorder in her parent's and grandparent's generation may have that as a genetic risk factor. Another risk factor might be that her father died from alcohol poisoning when she was young and her mother never remarried; however, that teenager is involved in sports and a volunteer organization in the community, both of which act as protective factors.

Practice Question

2. How does the biopsychosocial perspective describe the relationship between physical health and mental health?
   A) They have nothing to do with each other.
   B) Mind and body are connected and influence each other.
   C) Mental health should always be the priority in therapy.
   D) A social worker should refer someone to a doctor to deal with physical health.

Reliability and Validity

It is important to understand if the data are reliable and valid. **Reliability** refers to the consistency of the measurement. Take, for example, an employee performance scoring system. To be reliable, the system must measure employees in the same manner. Though their scores may be different, *how* the employees are evaluated is consistent.

Validity refers to what is being measured and whether it is relevant. In the example of a performance review, if an employee's performance on a nonwork-related issue is being measured, that item is not valid. It may be a reliable measurement, but it is not accurate or relevant to the actual review.

> **Helpful Hint**
>
> The concept of reliability can be thought of in the same way as a person who is reliable. A reliable person behaves as expected every time. A reliable assessment instrument does this as well.

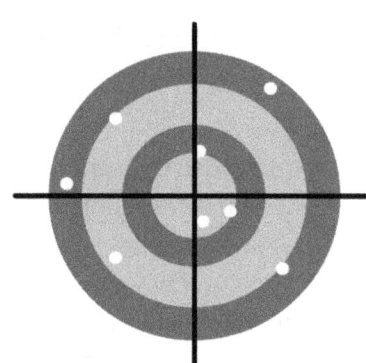
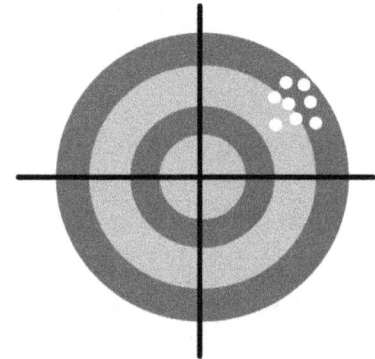

Valid and reliable
Data is meaningful and can be repeated.

Valid but not reliable
Data is meaningful but cannot be repeated.

Reliable but not valid
Data is not meaningful but can be replicated.

Figure 4.1. Reliability and Validity

Practice Question

3. Which of the following is an example of high validity?
   A) a math exam to determine how well students know the material
   B) an oven that can consistently change temperatures but does not display the correct temperature
   C) using GPA to determine athletic ability
   D) a scale that is five pounds off but always reads the same weight

Mental Status Exam

A **mental status exam (MSE)** is an informal assessment typically conducted during the initial clinical interview and periodically throughout the therapeutic relationship. It does not involve formal questions for the client or even a formal scoring method; instead, it is based on the social worker's observations and impressions of the client's behavior and how he presents himself, which provide indications of his mental health status.

Although the MSE is based on the clinician's personal observations, the social worker's goal is not to state her opinion of the client but rather to record her observations objectively and in a fact-based manner. She should not write, for example, "The client has a bad attitude." A more appropriate and objective observation would be, "The client sat in a slouched position during the appointment and gave one- or two-word responses to questions."

The information obtained in a mental status exam is an essential part of the social worker's initial assessment and working diagnosis. The social worker is gathering information about the client's level of interest in treatment, insight into how the client perceives his issues and the world, and potential clues that can lead to a formal diagnosis. **Appearance** is a common assessment in an MSE. The social worker should observe the following:

- How is the client dressed?
- How does the client hold herself? (E.g., Does she slouch and cross her arms or have a calm and relaxed posture?)
- Is she unkempt and unwashed or meticulously groomed?

Another domain includes **motor behavior**, which relates to a client's physical movements. Excessive fidgeting can be a sign of attention deficit hyperactivity disorder (ADHD) or anxiety disorders; very slow movement can be a sign of major depressive disorder. Involuntary limb movements or impaired gait may signify physical disorders like Huntington's disease or schizophrenia. Documenting physical movements that seem abnormal will be essential for diagnosing more complex disorders.

> **Did You Know?**
>
> Poor hygiene can be a symptom of several clinical diagnoses, including mood disorders and psychotic disorders.

Mood is based primarily on the client's self-report. It is the clinician's job to translate the client's self-report into clinically appropriate language:

- **euthymic:** normal or mildly positive mood
- **depressed/sad/dysphoric:** sad, "low" mood
- **anxious**
- **irritable**
- **euphoric/expansive/elevated:** abnormally positive mood

Clinical students often confuse mood with affect. While mood concerns how a client may describe her internal feelings, **affect** describes how the client presents externally. Affect is observed based on the client's facial expressions, posture, reactivity, and vocal quality. (Is it expressive and variable based on speech, more of a monotone, or something in-between?) The following terms are used to describe affect:

- **normal/congruent with mood:** affect matches described mood
- **labile:** affect swings wildly or is highly variable
- **constricted:** limited range of emotional display
- **blunted:** extremely limited range of emotional display
- **flat:** little or no display of emotional range

Orientation refers to the client's state of mind. Is he aware of where he is, the date, why he is in the social worker's office? Clients with poor orientation may be suffering from brain injury, hallucinations, or dementia. Orientation typically assesses the following:

- **orientation to time:** Does he know the day and year?
- **orientation to place:** Does he know where he is, or is he confused?
- **orientation to situation:** Does he know and understand why he is in the social worker's office?

Thought process and form refer to *how* the client thinks and are based on the clinician's observations of the quality of the client's thoughts: is the client logical with coherent, linear thoughts, or does she display disorganized or tangential thoughts?

- **linear:** coherent, goal-directed, clear
- **tangential:** racing thoughts, jumps from topic to topic, difficult to follow

Categories under thought process and form include the following:

- poverty of thought (having few thoughts)
- blocking (being unable to form thoughts)
- racing thoughts, flight of ideas (having rapid thoughts)
- loose associations (when a person's thoughts are disconnected)
- circumstantiality (when a person is able to get to the point but adds additional details along the way)
- tangentiality (when a person doesn't answer a question even though her thoughts are related to the question asked)

Thought content, on the other hand, refers to *what* the client thinks. Does the client exhibit any signs of hallucinations or delusions? Is she fixating on anything? Categories under thought content include the following:

- **suicidal/homicidal ideation:** suicidal or homicidal thoughts, plans, means, and intention to follow through
- **hallucinations:** auditory, visual, olfactory, gustatory, tactile, hypnagogic (having hallucinations upon waking or falling asleep)
- **delusions:** grandeur, jealousy, persecutory, somatic, love, religious
- **obsessions/compulsions:** religious, contamination, fear of losing control of one's actions, sex
- **phobias:** more intense than a fear, consistent and long-term, negatively impact the client's quality of life due to avoidance of everyday activities to prevent having to deal with the fear

Speech refers to the quality of the client's language production. Is it very fast or slow? Is it loud? Speech quality can provide important information about symptoms that relate to schizophrenia, autism spectrum disorder, personality disorders, and more:

- **quality/fluency:** Does the client speak easily or stumble over his words?
- **rate:** Does the client speak very quickly or noticeably slowly? Does the client speak in a monotone, clipped voice or have other unusual vocal inflections?
- **volume:** Is the client's speech noticeably louder or softer than normal?
- **quantity:** Does the client use appropriate and concise words? Does she only offer minimal or monosyllabic words, or does she provide extensive, elaborate details?

> **Helpful Hint**
>
> This list of elements for a mental status exam is not exhaustive. Each clinic will have its own forms or expected observations for MSEs. This list covers the topics that are typically found in the MSE; however, questions and terminology may vary.

Insight refers to how well the client can describe her own condition and circumstances. For example, a client who experiences hallucinations but is able to express to her social worker that she knows no one else can see them and doesn't believe them to be real would be described as having good insight.

Practice Question

4. Which of the following is an element of a mental status exam?
    A) client's level of insight
    B) case notes from prior social workers
    C) an IQ assessment
    D) client's past drug use

Intake and Initial Observations

Indicators of Mental and Emotional Illness

There are multiple indicators of mental and emotional illness throughout the lifespan. One indicator that is consistent throughout the lifespan is noticeable change. When an individual changes drastically in his thoughts, emotions, or behaviors, those around him are wise to inquire and investigate what caused the change.

Children do not have the capacity to think about themselves abstractly and often do not have accurate language to describe what they are feeling. Some older children can, but many children signal something is wrong through their behavior. Relevant indicators include the following:

- emotional outbursts that cannot be soothed in usual ways
- sudden defiance of parental instructions
- isolating themselves from the family
- regressive behavior (e.g., wetting the bed after being trained)
- thumb sucking

- changes in appetite
- changes in how they relate to siblings and peers
- refusing to go to school
- drastic changes in grades
- sudden onset of illnesses that have no medical cause, in particular gastrointestinal issues

While **adolescents** are more able to articulate their thoughts and feelings, they are also in a stage of development where peers are more influential in their lives than parents and family members. Therefore, the indicators of mental health issues may also be behavioral and can include the following:

- changes in friend groups
- drastic changes in dress or appearance without explanation
- grades dropping
- changes in activity engagement (e.g., dropping out of sports or school groups)
- significant changes in mood and behaviors:
    - sleep behaviors
    - appetite changes
    - weight changes
    - increased irritability and anger
    - increased incidents of interpersonal problems
- getting in trouble at school or with the law
- sudden physical illness:
    - gastrointestinal issues
    - headaches
    - muscle aches
    - extreme fatigue

Adults are the most capable of self-awareness, yet they may still struggle to articulate their thoughts and feelings. Also, adults may stay in a state of denial regarding their mental health, or they may put off dealing with mental health issues because they have other responsibilities. In adults, other indicators of mental health issues may include:

- changes in appetite, weight, and sleep behaviors
- an increased use of substances in order to function
- social isolation

- changes in interpersonal relationships or recreational activities
- increased mood lability
- irritability
- anger
- sudden onset of physical illnesses
- neglecting responsibilities to family or work.

There are several biopsychosocial factors related to mental health:

- biological: sleep changes, appetite and weight changes, gastrointestinal issues, headaches, muscle aches, heart palpitations, extreme fatigue
- psychological: attention, concentration and memory issues, mood lability, increased anger and irritability, increased emotionality (crying for no apparent reason), inability to self-regulate emotions, excessive rumination and worry
- social: isolating from others, instigating conflict with others, engagement in high-risk activities such as unsafe sex or criminal activity

When a person experiences illness and/or disability, there are several biopsychosocial responses that may occur:

- biological: sleep changes, appetite and weight changes, fatigue, and symptoms of additional physical illness
- psychological: grief, panic, mourning, depression, increased irritability and anger, emotional lability as well as changes in memory, attention, and concentration
- social: withdrawing from friends and family, stopping participation in community groups or recreational groups, changing or quitting a job

Somatization is a phenomenon where mental health manifests as a physical symptom and then the person seeks help from a physician. For instance, clients might experience anxiety as physical gastrointestinal issues or headaches. Somatization can happen to people who experience mental health issues over a long period of time, such as people with anxiety or panic disorders who develop cardiovascular issues.

There are multiple ways that people can **feign or fake illness**. Some people fake physical illness or disability, while others fake mental illness. **Malingering** is a way of faking, exaggerating, or prolonging an illness or mental illness in order to gain something, such as disability compensation, time off from work, or attention. Characteristics of a person who malingers include:

- being very willing to volunteer information about his symptoms
- seeking attention
- blaming other people for what the client experiences

- discussing symptoms in a way that sounds rehearsed but without exhibiting observable indications of those symptoms
- always claiming to have the symptoms

In **illness appropriation,** people read about symptoms of a mental illness and claim they have the illness. Illness appropriation is a trend among people who use social media a lot because there are places online that glamorize mental illness and give people a sense of belonging as a result. The more diagnoses a person has or the more serious the diagnosis, the more the person achieves a certain level of status online. Indications of illness appropriation include the following:

- multiple serious diagnoses that do not actually tend to occur concurrently
- evidence of social media use related to mental illness
- a person's ability to rattle off a list of symptoms as if she is reading them from the *Diagnostic and Statistical Manual of Mental Disorders* (*DSM*)
- an inability to describe her lived experience of those symptoms

Practice Question

5. Which of the following is an indicator of mental health issues that is consistent across the lifespan?
   A) physical illness
   B) self-report of mental health problems
   C) noticeable, drastic change in behavior or moods
   D) losing track of time

Crises and Emergencies

A **behavioral crisis** is a change in behavior during which the client does not act in an acceptable or normal manner (as defined by family, friends, and/or cultural norms). Examples of a behavioral crisis include a person sitting at a bus stop eating raw chicken while talking to himself or a person yelling at a tree.

A **psychiatric emergency** is an acute incident in which the client is in psychological distress:

- The client may be a danger to herself or others.
- An example would be a client who has suffered a recent loss and is having suicidal ideations.

Behavioral crises or psychiatric emergencies can be the result of

- psychiatric conditions (e.g., bipolar disorder)
- underlying medical conditions (e.g., stroke)
- psychosocial issues (e.g., depression after divorce).

Common medical conditions that cause altered behavior may include:

- hypo- or hyperglycemia
- hypo- or hyperthermia

- hypoxia
- stroke
- head injury
- exposure to toxins

Organic brain syndrome refers to behavioral or psychological issues caused by an identifiable injury or disease process (e.g., Alzheimer's disease, TBI, drug exposure).

Functional disorders are psychological or behavioral issues without an obvious physiological abnormality (e.g., depression).

Practice Question

6. If a person starts to yell and argue with someone whom no one else can see, what might that person be experiencing?
    A) a psychiatric emergency due to hallucinations
    B) a medical condition
    C) malingering
    D) anger issues

Readiness to Change

The **transtheoretical model (TTM) of behavior change**, developed by researchers James Prochaska and Carlo DiClemente, offers a useful perspective on the birth and growth of behavioral change. It defines a five-step process that is determined by an individual's readiness or willingness to change:

1. precontemplation stage (not ready to change)
2. contemplation stage (getting ready to change)
3. preparation stage (ready to change)
4. action stage (performing the action that will bring about change)
5. maintenance stage (integrating the action into one's lifestyle and making it habit)

A social worker must determine readiness and willingness to change in all clients. A client's willingness shows how successful she will be in self-managing her condition(s).

Practice Question

7. Gene is a 48-year-old male who wants to stop smoking. He has given it some thought, but he still enjoys his two-pack-a-day habit and will not listen when his daughter lectures him about quitting. In which stage of the transtheoretical model is Gene?
    A) contemplation
    B) precontemplation
    C) maintenance
    D) action

Overview of Medical Terminology and Medications

Basic Medical Terminology

Social workers should be familiar with basic medical terminology. The human body is made up of small units called cells. A **cell** is a microscopic, self-replicating, structural, and functional unit of the body that performs many different jobs.

Tissues compose the next-largest group of structures in the body. They are a collection of cells that all perform a similar function. The human body has four basic types of tissue:

> **Helpful Hint**
>
> **Serotonin syndrome** is a set of symptoms (including fever, fast heart rate, and agitation) caused by excess serotonin. It may occur with the use of any serotonergic drug but is more common when multiple serotonergic

1. Connective tissues—which include bones, ligaments, and cartilage—support, separate, or connect the body's various organs and tissues.

2. Epithelial tissues are thin layers of cells that line blood vessels, body cavities, and some organs.

3. Muscular tissues contain contractile units that pull on connective tissues to create movement.

4. Nervous tissues make up the peripheral nervous systems that transmit impulses throughout the body.

After tissues, **organs** are the next-largest structure in the biological hierarchy. Organs are a collection of tissues within the body that share a similar function. For example, the esophagus is an organ whose primary function is carrying food and liquids from the mouth to the stomach.

Organ systems, a group of organs that work together to perform a similar function, rank above organs as the next-largest structure on the biological hierarchy. The esophagus is part of the digestive organ system, which is the entire group of organs in the body that processes food from start to finish.

Finally, an **organism** is the collection of all the parts of the biological hierarchy working together to form a living being.

The **nervous system** processes external stimuli and sends signals throughout the body. **Nerve cells**, or **neurons**, communicate through electrical impulses and allow the body to process and respond to stimuli. **Neurotransmitters**, such as serotonin, dopamine, and histamines, are molecules that carry communication between nerves. Many medications (e.g., opioids) act by mimicking neurotransmitters or by altering their levels (e.g., selective serotonin reuptake inhibitors).

The **central nervous system (CNS)** consists of the brain and spinal cord. It is where information is processed and stored. The **peripheral nervous system (PNS)** transmits information throughout the body using electrical signals.

The **autonomic nervous system** controls involuntary actions that occur in the body, such as respiration, heartbeat, digestive processes, and more. The **somatic nervous system** is responsible for the body's ability to control skeletal muscles and voluntary movement as well as some involuntary reflexes.

The autonomic nervous system is further broken down into the **sympathetic nervous system** and **parasympathetic nervous system**. The sympathetic nervous system is responsible for the body's reaction

to stress. It induces a "fight-or-flight" response that increases heart rate and blood pressure. In contrast, the parasympathetic nervous system is stimulated by the body's need for rest or recovery.

Many common nervous system disorders are caused by chronic degeneration of nervous system tissue. Disruptions in hormone levels, electrical activity, or blood flow in the brain can also cause neurological symptoms that can signal the following conditions:

- **Mental health conditions** may be treated with medications and include anxiety, depression, bipolar disorder, schizophrenia, attention deficit hyperactivity disorder (ADHD), and post-traumatic stress disorder (PTSD).

- **Migraines** are intense headaches accompanied by nausea and light sensitivity.

- **Seizure** is caused by abnormal electrical discharges in the brain that disrupt brain function and may cause convulsions. **Epilepsy** is a condition characterized by recurrent seizures.

- **Alzheimer's disease** is characterized by the loss of memory and deteriorating cognitive function, usually later in life, due to the degeneration of neurons in the brain.

- Other degenerative nerve diseases include multiple sclerosis (MS), amyotrophic lateral sclerosis (ALS), and Parkinson's disease.

- **Stroke**, or **cerebrovascular accident (CVA)**, occurs when a blood vessel in the brain ruptures or is blocked. The resulting lack of oxygen to the brain can result in significant brain damage or death.

- **Peripheral neuropathy** is impairment of the peripheral nerves. It is often caused by diabetes (diabetic neuropathy).

Practice Question

8. What is responsible for the body's reaction to stress?
   A) sympathetic nervous system
   B) parasympathetic nervous system
   C) central nervous system
   D) autonomic nervous system

Common Medications and Side Effects

Social workers should be familiar with commonly prescribed medications and their common side effects and contraindications. Table 4.1. provides a list of the fifty most commonly prescribed drugs in the United States.

Table 4.1. Fifty Most Commonly Prescribed Medications in the United States

Generic Name (Brand Name)	Drug Class	Adverse Effects and Contraindications
atorvastatin (Lipitor) simvastatin (FloLipid, Zocor) rosuvastatin (Crestor) pravastatin (Pravachol)	HMG-CoA reductase inhibitors (statin)	ADR: muscle/joint pain Interactions: grapefruit/grapefruit juice, some antibiotics (e.g., cyclosporine, clarithromycin), some antifungals (e.g., itraconazole) Pregnancy: Category X
levothyroxine (Synthroid)	synthetic hormone	BBW: weight reduction ADR: dysrhythmias, trouble breathing, headache, nervousness, irritability, weight loss Interactions: iron supplement, calcium supplement, antacids Counseling: take with water 30 minutes before eating
lisinopril (Prinivil, Zestril)	ACE inhibitor	BBW: fetal toxicity ADR: cough, hypotension, dizziness Interactions: other medications that lower BP
metformin (Fortamet, Glucophage) glipizide (Glucotrol)	antidiabetic	ADR: hypoglycemia, diarrhea, nausea, headache Interactions: alcohol, miconazole (glimepiride) Counseling: take with food (metformin); take 30 minutes before food (glipizide)
amlodipine (Amvaz, Norvasc)	calcium channel blocker	ADR: headache, edema, tiredness, dizziness Interactions: other drugs that lower BP

4. Biopsychosocial History and Collateral Data

Table 4.1. Fifty Most Commonly Prescribed Medications in the United States

Generic Name (Brand Name)	Drug Class	Adverse Effects and Contraindications
metoprolol (Toprol-XL, Lopressor) carvedilol (Coreg) atenolol (Tenormin)	beta blocker	BBW: abrupt discontinuation ADR: dizziness, fatigue, weight gain Interactions: other drugs that lower BP
albuterol (Ventolin HFA, Proventil HFA, Combivent Respimat, DuoNeb, ProAir HFA)	bronchodilator	ADR: headache, fast heart rate, dizziness, sore throat, nasal congestion Interactions: beta blockers, digoxin, MAOI, tricyclic antidepressants
omeprazole (Prilosec) pantoprazole (Protonix)	proton pump inhibitor	ADR: headache, abdominal pain, nausea, diarrhea, vomiting Interactions: digoxin, clopidogrel, benzodiazepines, warfarin
losartan (Cozaar)	angiotensin II receptor blocker	BBW: fetal toxicity ADR: dizziness, headache, fatigue Interactions: potassium supplements, other drugs that lower BP Pregnancy: Category D
gabapentin (Gralise, Neurontin)	anticonvulsant (also indicated for neuropathy)	ADR: drowsiness, dizziness, edema, angioedema (pregabalin), suicidal thoughts, emotional changes Interactions: alcohol, other CNS depressants

Table 4.1. Fifty Most Commonly Prescribed Medications in the United States

Generic Name (Brand Name)	Drug Class	Adverse Effects and Contraindications
acetaminophen; hydrocodone (Norco, Vicodin, Lortab) tramadol (Ultram) oxycodone (OxyContin)	opioid	BBW: addiction, misuse, and abuse; respiratory depression; accidental ingestion; neonatal opioid withdrawal syndrome; risk from use with other CNS depressants ADR: constipation, light-headedness, dizziness, nausea, and vomiting Interactions: MAOI, serotonergic drugs, alcohol, other CNS depressants Counseling: may impair the ability to perform potentially hazardous activities
hydrochlorothiazide (Microzide) furosemide (Lasix)	diuretic	ADR: hypotension, weakness, dizziness, blurred vision Interactions: alcohol, other antihypertensive drugs, NSAIDs
sertraline (Zoloft) escitalopram (Lexapro) fluoxetine (Prozac) trazodone (Desyrel) citalopram (Celexa)	selective serotonin reuptake inhibitor (SSRI)	BBW: increased risk of suicidal thoughts/behaviors ADR: insomnia, headache, agitation, dizziness, drowsiness, dry mouth, nausea, vomiting Interactions: MAOIs
bupropion (Wellbutrin, Zyban)	dopamine/norepinephrine-reuptake inhibitor	
duloxetine (Cymbalta) venlafaxine (Effexor)	serotonin-norepinephrine reuptake inhibitor	

Table 4.1. Fifty Most Commonly Prescribed Medications in the United States

Generic Name (Brand Name)	Drug Class	Adverse Effects and Contraindications
montelukast (Singulair)	bronchodilator	BBW: neuropsychiatric symptoms ADR: respiratory infection, fever, headache, sore throat, cough
fluticasone (Flonase, Flovent)	corticosteroid (nasal, oral inhalant)	ADR (nasal/oral inhalation): headache, nasal/throat irritation, nose bleed, cough, worsening of infections
amoxicillin (Augmentin)	antibiotic (penicillin)	ADR: diarrhea, nausea
acetaminophen (Tylenol)	analgesic, antipyretic	BBW: hepatotoxicity ADR: nausea and vomiting Contraindications: hepatic impairment
prednisone (Sterapred)	corticosteroid (oral tablet)	ADR (oral tablet): fluid retention, hyper/hypoglycemia, hypertension, changes in behavior/mood, weight gain, worsening of infections Interactions (oral tablet): antidiabetics, anticoagulants, oral contraceptives, NSAIDs
amphetamine and dextroamphetamine (Adderall) methylphenidate (Ritalin)	ADHD treatment	BBW: potential for abuse/dependence ADR: insomnia, headache, fast heart rate, mood changes, decreased appetite, vomiting, dry mouth Interactions: MAOIs
insulin glargine (Lantus)	insulin	ADR: hypoglycemia, injection site reactions Interactions: other insulin products

4. Biopsychosocial History and Collateral Data

Table 4.1. Fifty Most Commonly Prescribed Medications in the United States

Generic Name (Brand Name)	Drug Class	Adverse Effects and Contraindications
ibuprofen (Advil, Motrin) meloxicam (Mobic)	NSAID	BBW: cardiovascular thrombotic events, GI bleeding ADR: abdominal pain, diarrhea, upset stomach Pregnancy: Category D (>30 weeks)
tamsulosin (Flomax)	alpha-1 blocker (indicated for BPH)	ADR: orthostatic hypotension, sexual disorder, dizziness, headache
alprazolam (Xanax) clonazepam (Klonopin)	benzodiazepine	BBW: risk of respiratory depression and death when used with opioids; risk of abuse/dependence ADR: drowsiness, sedation, fatigue, memory impairment Interactions: alcohol, other CNS depressants
potassium	supplement	ADR: nausea, vomiting, flatulence, abdominal pain/discomfort, and diarrhea Interactions: potassium-sparing diuretics
clopidogrel (Plavix) aspirin	anticoagulant	BBW: bleeding, abrupt discontinuation ADR: bleeding Interactions: omeprazole/esomeprazole (clopidogrel), NSAIDs
ranitidine (Zantac)	histamine H2 antagonist	ADR: headache, constipation, diarrhea, nausea, vomiting Interactions: warfarin

Table 4.1. Fifty Most Commonly Prescribed Medications in the United States

Generic Name (Brand Name)	Drug Class	Adverse Effects and Contraindications
cyclobenzaprine (Flexeril)	muscle relaxant	BBW: abrupt discontinuation (baclofen) ADR: drowsiness, dizziness, dry mouth, nausea, and vomiting Interactions: alcohol, other CNS depressants, MAOIs, serotonergic drugs Contraindications: use of MAOIs (cyclobenzaprine)
azithromycin (Zithromax)	antibiotic (macrolide)	ADR: diarrhea, nausea Interactions: anticoagulants, antidiabetics
allopurinol (Lopurin, Zyloprim, Aloprim)	antigout	ADR: rash, nausea, vomiting, drowsiness Interactions: anticoagulants Counseling: may impair the ability to perform potentially hazardous activities
BBW: black box warning ADR: adverse drug reactions		

Practice Question

9. Which drug class suffix refers to benzodiazepines?
    A) –artan
    B) –pam
    C) –ine
    D) –olol

Answer Key

1. C: A clinical interview, also known as an intake interview, is an informal assessment that makes up the first part of any clinical relationship.

2. B: People with physical health issues are more likely to develop mental health issues and vice versa.

3. A: Performance on a math test generally provides a fairly accurate assessment of how well students understand the material, which makes it a valid measure of student knowledge.

4. A: A client's level of insight, or how aware she is of the content of her thoughts, appearance, behavior, and condition, is a key part of a thorough mental status exam.

5. C: For all age ranges, these kinds of changes indicate that something is wrong either emotionally or mentally.

6. A: Hallucinations are visual or audio occurrences that a person experiences that no one else can see or hear; they can indicate a psychotic episode.

7. B: The precontemplation stage is when the individual is not thinking about behavioral change and is not ready to take steps to change.

8. A: The sympathetic nervous system is responsible for the body's reaction to stress. It induces a "fight-or-flight" response that increases heart rate and blood pressure.

9. B: The suffix *–pam* refers to benzodiazepines.

5. Assessment Methods and Techniques

Problem Formulation

Problem formulation is the part of the assessment process that includes identifying the client's issues and conceptualizing potential underlying risk and protective factors associated with the problem. Social work approaches problem formulation from the person-in-environment perspective, with the client's collaboration. The person-in-environment approach is supported by several theoretical frameworks that provide a basis for approaching client issues, and a social worker can use one or all of them.

An ecological or systems approach uses the systems theoretical framework that suggests that the individual exists within multiple layers of the environment. Problems are caused because of tension or conflict between the individual and those systemic layers or between the systemic layers. This requires the social worker to evaluate the client in terms of those layers that include the microsystem, mesosystem, and macrosystem.

> **Helpful Hint**
>
> See Chapter 3 for more on person-in-environment perspective.

For example, the social worker may explore relationships between the client and family or friends in the client's immediate environment, relationships between the client and school or work, relationships between the client's family and school or work, the relationships the client has within the community, and how the environment influences the client's thoughts, feelings, and behaviors.

A psychodynamic approach to problem formulation inspires the social worker to explore the client's upbringing, early personality formation, and some of the unconscious drives that might be contributing to the client's behavior. Using this framework, the social worker might ask about the client's earliest memories and what his life was like as a child.

Another approach to problem formulation involves inquiring about the client's cultural experiences and how those experiences influence the client. This may include race, ethnicity, sexual and gender identity, religion, and spirituality. Sometimes, a problem arises due to tension in these areas, whereas other times these cultural factors can be used as protective factors.

Regardless of the method used for problem formation, the client must be a collaborative partner. The information used to formulate the problem comes from the client, so establishing a trusting relationship with her at the beginning of the assessment process will increase the likelihood that she will tell the social worker the truth.

Second, the social worker must make sure that he is hearing and understanding the client by requesting feedback from her. If the social worker has not fully understood the client, these are the times to get more clarification.

Finally, as the social worker formulates the problem, checking in with the client about whether the problem formulation makes sense is essential to keeping the client engaged. For example, a client shares information about substance use and explains how his parents did drugs and how all his friends do as well. The social worker would formulate the problem of substance use within the ecological systems context of family and social influence: "It sounds like substance use is all around you, in your family, friends, and neighborhood. So, the problem is not just substance use, it is also a problem of how you make changes in your life without alienating the people you love. Does that make sense to you?" Using statements like this shows the client that the social worker understands that the problem is more complex and complicated but checks in with the client to get that assumption validated.

Even if the client disagrees with the social worker's problem formulation, it can prompt more conversation about how the client would define the problem. The point of achieving understanding about the problem is that it will drive the treatment plan.

Practice Question

1. Which approach to problem formulation includes a person's family, peers, and environment as part of determining the problem?
   A) psychodynamic
   B) behavioral
   C) systems
   D) medical model

Principles for Building Helping Relationships

Social Work Attributes

Many basic attributes form the foundation of the therapeutic relationship with a client and distinguish the professional social work relationship from other interpersonal relationships:

1. **Genuineness** is a social work attribute that refers to authenticity.
   - Social workers should say what they mean and mean what they say.
   - Social workers should be authentic in sessions with clients and not put on a false front.
   - For example, if a social worker smiles when greeting a client, the smile should be authentic and not forced.

2. **Congruence** is similar to genuineness. The psychologist Carl Rogers defined congruence as the genuineness necessary for a social worker to provide unconditional positive regard and empathy. Rogers believed that when social workers show congruence in their sessions, they appear more trustworthy, which strengthens the therapeutic alliance. Social workers should be fully attentive to both their clients and themselves while practicing transparency:
   - Social workers' insides should match their outsides.
   - Social workers should be completely honest with clients about what the social workers experience.
   - For example, if a social worker cringes in response to a client's remark, a congruent social worker will explain that reaction to the client.

3. **Nonjudgmental stance** requires social workers to remain open-minded to the clients' experiences and refrain from evaluating the clients, their issues, or their behaviors:
    - This attribute emphasizes the benefits of practicing self-awareness and self-reflection.
    - Judgment can be communicated both verbally and nonverbally, so social workers must learn to remain neutral in words and body language during sessions with clients.
    - A social worker can exhibit a nonjudgmental stance with a client by:
        o keeping facial expressions pleasant and neutral
        o staying in a relaxed body posture
        o maintaining eye contact regardless of what the client says

4. **Positive regard** expands on the nonjudgmental stance. A social worker practicing positive regard
    - projects an attitude of acceptance of the client as a person
    - adopts a worldview and philosophy of seeing all people as worthy of dignity and respect regardless of their thoughts, emotions, or behaviors, which are separate from people's inherent worth.

A social worker exhibits positive regard by

- verbally affirming that the client is worthy of dignity and respect no matter what
- treating the client with dignity and respect in sessions
- reinforcing the idea that clients are not defined by their thoughts, feelings, or behaviors
- clarifying that even if social workers disapprove of a client's behavior, they accept the client as a person.

Practice Question

2. A client discloses to the social worker that he uses illicit substances at night when his kids are in bed. The social worker believes this behavior is risky and could endanger the children. Which of the following statements would BEST reflect the implementation of social work attributes?
    A) "You need to stop using immediately, as it could put yourself and your children in danger. What if there is an emergency and you're unable to respond?"
    B) "The potential of something bad happening concerns me, and I don't agree with your choices, but I am here to help you if you would like to make better ones. I know you can do it."
    C) "If this continues, I will have to report you to child welfare for putting your children at risk. You could be facing serious charges."
    D) "What kind of parent does something like that? You should reconsider your choices and think about your kids from now on."

Communication and Active Listening

The basic elements of communication and active listening form the foundation of a social worker's rapport and relationship with the client. To build a strong rapport with a client, the social worker must

- be engaging

- be an active listener
- avoid interrupting the client.

Clients will trust that the social worker cares about their issues and advocates for their well-being. A social worker who actively listens will deliver on guarantees, establish and maintain boundaries, and build trust with clients. Building trust can take time, but doing so makes managing the client's condition easier for all involved. The theory of basic communication is made up of several components:

- **sender:** the individual or thing sending the message
- **channel:** the method by which the sender transmits the message
- **receiver:** the individual or thing translating the message
- **destination:** the individual or thing for whom the message is targeted
- **message:** the information transferred from the sender to the recipient

People use these elements in everyday conversations without even realizing it. The sender will transfer information through the channel to the receiver, who interprets or translates the message to the destination. In recent times, oral conversation has given way to texting, emailing, and using social media; sometimes, the intended tone of the message can be lost without aural cues.

Active listening means paying attention to the speaker, not just hearing his words. The listener makes eye contact with the speaker to indicate interest in what is being said. An active listener repeats important points the speaker has made to ensure understanding, asks follow-up questions, and does not interrupt. The goal is threefold: to convey to the speaker that the listener understands the message, to show the speaker that the listener cares about what the speaker is saying, and to let the speaker know that the listener empathizes with the speaker. The dos and don'ts of client communication are listed in Table 5.1.

Table 5.1. Dos and Don'ts of Client Communication	
Do...	Don't...
<ul><li>make eye contact with the client</li><li>introduce yourself and use the client's name</li><li>speak directly to the client when possible</li><li>ask open-ended questions</li><li>speak slowly and clearly</li><li>show empathy for the client</li><li>be silent when appropriate to allow the client time to think and process emotions</li><li>use person-first language</li><li>maintain pleasant facial expressions</li><li>use relaxed body language</li></ul>	<ul><li>use medical jargon</li><li>threaten or intimidate the client</li><li>lie or provide false hope</li><li>interrupt the client</li><li>show frustration or anger</li><li>make judgmental statements</li><li>make accusations</li><li>tell the client what to do</li><li>force clients to answer questions</li></ul>

In addition to active listening, a variety of techniques are used for therapeutic communication:

- Sharing observations may open up the conversation to how the client is feeling.

- Using touch, such as a gentle hand on the shoulder or arm, when appropriate or welcome, can offer comfort; however, this may not be appropriate in mixed-gender relationships, with those who have experienced trauma, or with clients with other relational differences.

- Silence allows the client a moment to absorb or process information and sit with emotions to experience them fully.

- Summarizing and paraphrasing information back to a client helps ensure or confirm understanding and convey empathy.

- Asking relevant questions that pertain to the situation helps the social worker gather information for decision making and can lead to insight for the client.

- Reframing is a technique that social workers use to offer the client another way to consider a situation. It offers an alternative perspective while demonstrating that the social worker understands the client.

Communication includes both verbal and nonverbal components:

- **Verbal communication** uses language to convey information. Characteristics of verbal communication include tone, volume, and word choice.

- Nonverbal communication includes behavior, gestures, posture, and other nonlanguage elements of communication that transmit information or meaning.

Finally, attending and reflecting are foundational skills for social workers:

- **Attending** is a basic skill whereby the social worker communicates to the client that she is present and listening.

    o   Attending is a vital skill for establishing rapport with clients because it lets them know that the social worker's attention is solely on the client.

    o   A social worker can practice attending verbally through greetings, showing interest in the client's life, and asking questions, when necessary, to clarify what the client said.

    o   A social worker can convey attending to a client nonverbally through eye contact, facial expressions, and gestures that encourage a client to keep talking.

- **Reflecting** is a skill that demonstrates attention, understanding, and empathy. Just as a mirror shows a reflection, reflecting in the therapeutic setting is a way of repeating what the client says.

    o   Reflecting shows that the social worker is listening, which increases the connection with the client.

    o   When clients feel that they are truly heard, they feel valued, which increases positive feelings toward the social worker.

- A social worker demonstrates reflecting by repeating what the client just said.
- For example, a client tells a story about a family conflict and says, "I just wanted to hit someone, but I didn't."
- The social worker might say, "You wanted to hit someone, but you didn't."
- This shows the client that the social worker heard what he said and invites him to say more without asking a direct question.

Practice Question

3. Which of the following scenarios demonstrates attending behaviors by the social worker?
    A) maintaining eye contact with the client and smiling to encourage the client to keep talking
    B) using a laptop to type notes while the client talks
    C) fidgeting and looking at the clock many times throughout the session
    D) sitting tensely and still with a neutral facial expression

Empathy

Empathy is the ability to understand and accurately perceive the feelings and experiences of clients from their perspective. Carl Rogers viewed empathy as a state of being that facilitates being nonjudgmental and accepting.

Empathy differs significantly from sympathy. Although both involve emotions, empathy does not involve the social worker's personal experience, nor does it involve judgment. Sympathy, on the other hand, is the process of pitying or feeling bad for someone without really understanding that person's perspective; this means it includes judgment.

Sympathy is a surface-level intellectual understanding based on personal experience. Empathy is a deeper understanding and sharing of emotions based on the other person's perspective. Empathy builds connection; sympathy does not:

- Empathetic **attunement** combines empathy with attending skills. When using empathetic attunement, the social worker is aware of the client's emotions as well as his own.
    - The social worker communicates verbally and nonverbally that he recognizes the client's emotions.
    - For example, if a client starts to cry in a session, the social worker can demonstrate empathetic attunement by staying silent and relaxed, being present with the client, and allowing her to experience that emotion without judgment or comment.
- **Empathetic** responding is a verbal response from the social worker that tells the client that she understands what the client is feeling and why he feels that way.
    - This skill shows the client that the social worker respects and understands his emotions and the reasons for them.
    - Using the example of the client who feels like hitting someone during a family conflict, the social worker might empathetically respond by saying, "You feel intense anger because you feel that person is not listening to you."

Practice Question

4. A client tells the social worker that her spouse just gave notice of divorce. The client is in shock and asks questions in rapid succession, wondering what she missed, what is wrong with her, and what she will do now. She is taking short, shallow breaths and talking fast. How can the social worker demonstrate empathetic attunement in this situation?
   A) try to answer the client's questions or help her answer her own questions
   B) tell the client to calm down and speak more slowly so the situation can be discussed productively
   C) help the client identify the cognitive distortions forming in her mind that contribute to her feelings
   D) allow the client to continue to express her frustration without judging her

Assessing Client Motivation to Change

Motivation is the driving force behind people's actions. Social workers should assess clients' sources of motivation in the context of managing their mental health to better educate, encourage, and advocate for them:

- **Intrinsic motivation** is the desire to achieve a goal, seek challenges, or complete a task that is driven by enjoyment and personal satisfaction (e.g., exercising because it is enjoyable). Motivation comes from within the client.
  - People who are intrinsically motivated to pursue change are more likely to follow through with therapy.
  - For example, a client who struggles with depression and irritability and who is intrinsically motivated may come to therapy because she wants to be a happier person.

- **Extrinsic motivation** is the desire to accomplish a goal that is driven by external rewards or punishment (e.g., exercising to prevent anxiety). Extrinsic motivation comes from forces outside the client.
  - People who are extrinsically motivated may follow through with therapy, but they are less likely to do so than those who are intrinsically motivated.
  - For example, an adolescent forced into therapy by his parents may only come to therapy to avoid punishment. This will impact the level at which he engages in the process.
  - Another example is a client referred to therapy by a drug court proceeding whereby her success in therapy will determine whether or not she goes to jail for a drug offense. In this case, extrinsic motivation may positively influence the client.

Social workers should also consider a client's motivation for change as it pertains to the stated problem. In other words, a client may have intrinsic motivation to feel better but may not be ready to make the behavioral changes necessary to do so.

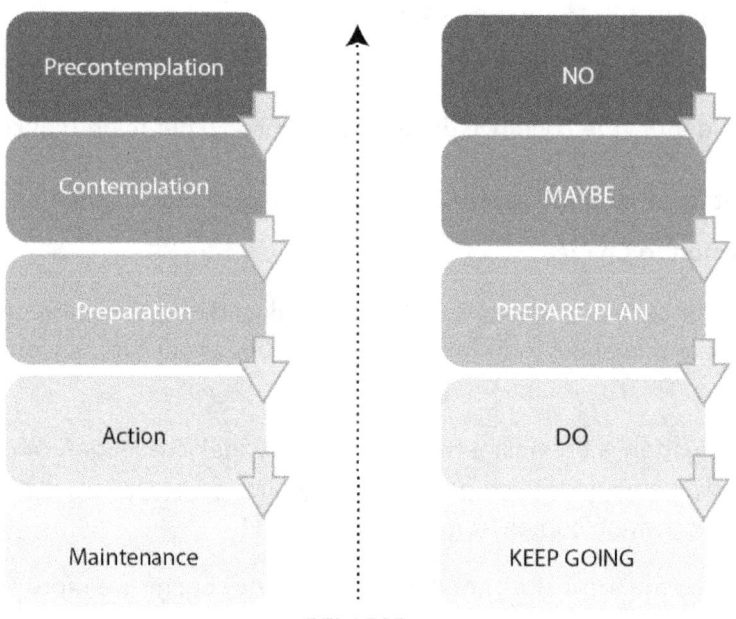

In these cases, the social worker should help clients discover and tap into their motivations to change. This will move them from the stages of change talk to change action. The **transtheoretical model (TTM) of behavior change(stages of change)** allows social workers to identify which stage of change clients are in and how to guide them to a stage of change where they are motivated to engage in change behavior:

- Clients with an **external locus of control** will attribute their successes or failures to outside forces. These clients tend to blame others for what they experience and feel there is little to nothing they can do to change these experiences. Some of these clients will feel helpless and hopeless that anything can change, while others recognize that even if those outside forces impact their success or failure, there are options to counter them.

- Clients with an **internal locus of control** will attribute their success or failure to themselves. Some of these clients will unrealistically take the blame and responsibility for everything that happens to them; others use their strengths to overcome adversity.

Practice Question

5. A college student comes to therapy seeking help for depression. The client says he is doing poorly in school and wants to quit. During the assessment, he says school is too hard, the professors are unfair graders, and his peers sabotage his work. What do the client's statements indicate?
    A) The client has an internal locus of control.
    B) The client is depressed.
    C) The client has an external locus of control.
    D) The client is motivated to change.

Assessment Instruments

An important part of being an effective social worker is understanding how to choose a good assessment. Considering whether the assessment has been tested and approved for a client's age, ethnicity, language, or presenting problem can help a social worker determine what is the best choice to make when assessing a client.

Statistical analysis of large groups of clients and how accurately an assessment measures their symptoms can help the social worker determine the assessment's efficacy. The following are several important statistical factors.

Assessing Trauma

Trauma is an emotional response or reaction to distressing events. Some common exposure events include natural disasters, war, witnessing or experiencing violence, witnessing or experiencing abuse, witnessing or experiencing rape or sexual assault, or being in an accident that leads to hospitalization. There are four main domains of trauma symptoms:

1. **Intrusion** includes intrusive memories, nightmares, flashbacks, or reactions to triggers.

2. **Avoidance** involves changing one's behavior to avoid certain thoughts, memories, or external reminders.

3. **Negative changes in mood and affect** include memory issues, low self-worth, thoughts that the event was their fault, consistent negative emotions, a sense of detachment, or difficulty feeling positive emotions.

4. **Increased reactivity** includes symptoms like irritability, hypervigilance, elevated startle response, attention issues, sleep issues, and self-destructive behavior.

For a client to be diagnosed with **post-traumatic stress disorder (PTSD)**, he must have been exposed to a traumatic experience, exhibited symptoms across all four domains, and experienced the symptoms for at least one month.

The **Clinician-Administered PTSD Scale for *DSM-5* (CAPS-5)** is one of the most commonly used assessments for PTSD. It is a structured diagnostic interview with thirty questions. It has high validity and reliability, making it a strong assessment for PTSD. The assessment takes about forty-five to sixty minutes to complete.

The **PTSD Symptom Scale Interview for *DSM-5* (PSSI-5)** is a twenty-four-question semi-structured interview used to assess for PTSD in adults. It is administered by a clinician and used to diagnose PTSD in adults.

> **Did You Know?**
>
> Assessments like the CAPS-5 require additional training for scoring and administration; an entry-level social worker cannot administer them without this training.

The **PTSD Checklist for *DSM-5* (PCL-5)** is a twenty-item self-administered checklist for PTSD symptoms. It can be used to make a provisional diagnosis of PTSD (contingent on further follow-up and assessment by a clinician). It can also be used as a way to monitor symptom severity over time.

The **Clinician-Administered PTSD Scale for *DSM-5*—Child/Adolescent Version (CAPS-CA-5)** is based on the **CAPS-5** assessment, with language and questions geared toward children. It is approved for use with children ages seven and up. Like the CAPS-5, it is a structured clinical interview that lists the symptoms that are key to a PTSD diagnosis; it has thirty questions.

The **UCLA Child/Adolescent PTSD Reaction Index for *DSM-5* (UCLA-RI)** is a semi-structured interview for children and adolescents. It covers a client's history of trauma experiences and screens for trauma symptoms based on the four domains found in the *DSM-5*.

Practice Question

6. Suzie was recently bitten by a dog and had to go to the hospital for treatment. Her mother is worried that she may have experienced trauma from the experience. Which of the following is a symptom of avoidance?
    A) Suzie reports frequent nightmares about dogs.
    B) Suzie's mom says that she has been yelling at her brother more often.
    C) Suzie's teacher reports that Suzie has not been paying attention in class.
    D) Suzie refuses to visit a neighbor who has a dog.

Assessing Substance Use

Substance use is the nonmedically warranted consumption of medications or substances such as tobacco, alcohol, or illicit drugs. **Substance dependence** is a deep physical and/or psychological need to use a controlled substance to achieve a feeling of euphoria and/or calmness. **Substance abuse** is the continued use of a medication without medical reason or the excessive and intentional use of a controlled substance (e.g., alcohol or narcotics). Finally, **addiction** is dependence on a substance or practice that is physically or psychologically habit-forming to the extent that critical pain and damage result.

The **Tobacco, Alcohol, Prescription medication, and other Substance use (TAPS) Tool** is a four-question screening tool for adults that determines if the client is using tobacco, alcohol, prescription medications, or other substances and how often he used them in the previous twelve months. It can be self-administered or administered by the clinician.

The **Drug Abuse Screening Test (DAST-10)** is a ten-question assessment to determine drug abuse. It has been approved for adults and young adults (ages sixteen and up). It can be administered by the social worker or the client.

The **National Institute on Drug Abuse (NIDA)-modified Alcohol, Smoking, and Substance Involvement Screening Test (NM-ASSIST)** is a clinician-administered online assessment that asks the client about lifetime prescription and illegal drug, alcohol, or tobacco use. If the client indicates any usage, the questions progress to frequency and the degree to which the use has negatively impacted the client's life.

The **CAGE questionnaire** consists of four questions that can be worked into an intake assessment or an individual session. CAGE is an acronym for "cut down, annoyed, guilt, and eye-opener."

The **Alcohol Use Disorders Identification Test (AUDIT)** is a ten-item tool that helps social workers recognize when a client's drinking behaviors have become dangerous for the client's health.

The **Michigan Alcohol Screening Test (MAST)** is a twenty-five-item assessment that helps social workers better understand the lifetime severity of a client's alcohol use. The MAST is often used to help guide treatment plans.

The **Clinical Opiate Withdrawal Scale (COWS)** is an eleven-item screening tool administered by clinicians. It measures objective symptoms of opiate withdrawal, such as heart rate, joint pain, stomach issues, goosebumps, sweating, and more. The assessment is used to help clinicians understand the level of opiate dependence and how severe a client's withdrawal symptoms are.

The **Car, Relax, Alone, Forget, Friends, Trouble (CRAFFT)** is a screening tool approved for youth ages twelve to twenty-one to determine substance use. It can be administered by a social worker or through self-assessment. It begins with three questions to determine any level of drug or alcohol use in the previous twelve months. If the client affirms any usage, screening moves on to query about six situations. The final portion is a brief intervention.

The **Drug Abuse Screening Test for Adolescents (DAST-A)** is a modified version of the DAST-10. It is a twenty-eight-question screening tool to determine adolescent abuse of prescription or illegal drugs, tobacco, or alcohol. It can be administered by the social worker or self-administered.

The **Screening, Brief Intervention, and Referral to Treatment (SBIRT)** is used by clinicians to determine alcohol use. It can be used with adolescents and adults. The client's reported alcohol consumption is placed into different danger levels depending on his weekly consumption, which is then discussed with him, and possible motivation for change is assessed. If the client is amenable, the final part of the SBIRT involves referral to treatment.

Practice Question

7. The social worker is seeing a 14-year-old client for the first time. She was referred for missing school and poor family relationships. Her mother suspects she has been using marijuana with friends. Which of the following would be the BEST tool to screen for drug usage?
    A) TAPS
    B) CRAFFT
    C) COWS
    D) SBIRT

Risk Assessment

Social workers are legally required to report any serious threats of suicide or homicide to the police for intervention. Self-injury with no suicidal intent and relationship violence are not reportable events, but responsible therapy involves ongoing monitoring and assessment of these aspects of a client's life to ensure safety.

> **Helpful Hint**
>
> Some people are afraid that asking about suicidal ideation (SI) can make a person suicidal. Research shows that this is not true and that assessing for SI can be lifesaving.

As part of ongoing assessment, social workers have a responsibility to screen for **suicidal** or **homicidal ideation (SI/HI)**—thoughts of harming oneself or others:

- Frequency and duration: How often does the client think about harming herself or others, and for how long?
- Intensity: Are the thoughts fleeting and easy to ignore, or are they pressing and disturbing?
- Plan: Does the client have a plan for how he would kill himself or others, or is it more of a vague wish to be dead?
- Means: If the client has a plan, does she have the means to carry it out? For example, if the client has contemplated shooting herself, does she have access to a gun?
- Intent: How seriously is the client considering enacting his plan? Does he have a specific time and date on which he is planning? Does he deny any intent? Is it something in between?

Nonsuicidal self-injury (NSSI) is any form of self-injury without intent to kill oneself. The most common forms of NSSI include cutting, burning, and head banging or hitting. Other forms include scratching, hitting oneself or other objects, ingesting harmful substances, and more.

It is important to refrain from judgment or reacting emotionally when assessing for NSSI. Although cutting is the most common form of NSSI, it is important to screen for other types of NSSI behaviors, as they can be easily missed by social workers.

The **SOARS model** is a brief assessment used in clinics to screen for NSSI:

- **S**uicidal ideation: Is the NSSI motivated by or paired with suicidal ideation?
- **O**nset, frequency, methods: When did the NSSI begin? When was the most recent time? How often does it happen? What methods were used?
- **A**ftercare: How are the wounds cared for? Has medical attention for the wounds ever been required?
- **R**easons: What prompts or motivates the client to harm herself (emotional release, anger, self-hatred, and so forth)?
- **S**tages of change: Does the client think about stopping? Does he want to stop?

Relationship violence, also known as "domestic violence" or "intimate partner violence," occurs when one or both partners are enacting physical, emotional, financial, or psychological abuse on the other partner. Intimate partner violence is dangerous and can be life-threatening. Despite that, it is not reportable, except in cases where children witness the abuse or if the abuse is aimed at an older adult.

Important areas of assessment for people who experience domestic violence include:

- frequency and duration of attacks (can be helpful to use a calendar)
- type of attack (whether a weapon was used, level of injury)

- partner stability (employment, drug/alcohol use, mental health concerns, suicide threats)
- controlling behavior (money, stalking, controlling whom the partner sees)
- attacks on others (children, pets, family members).

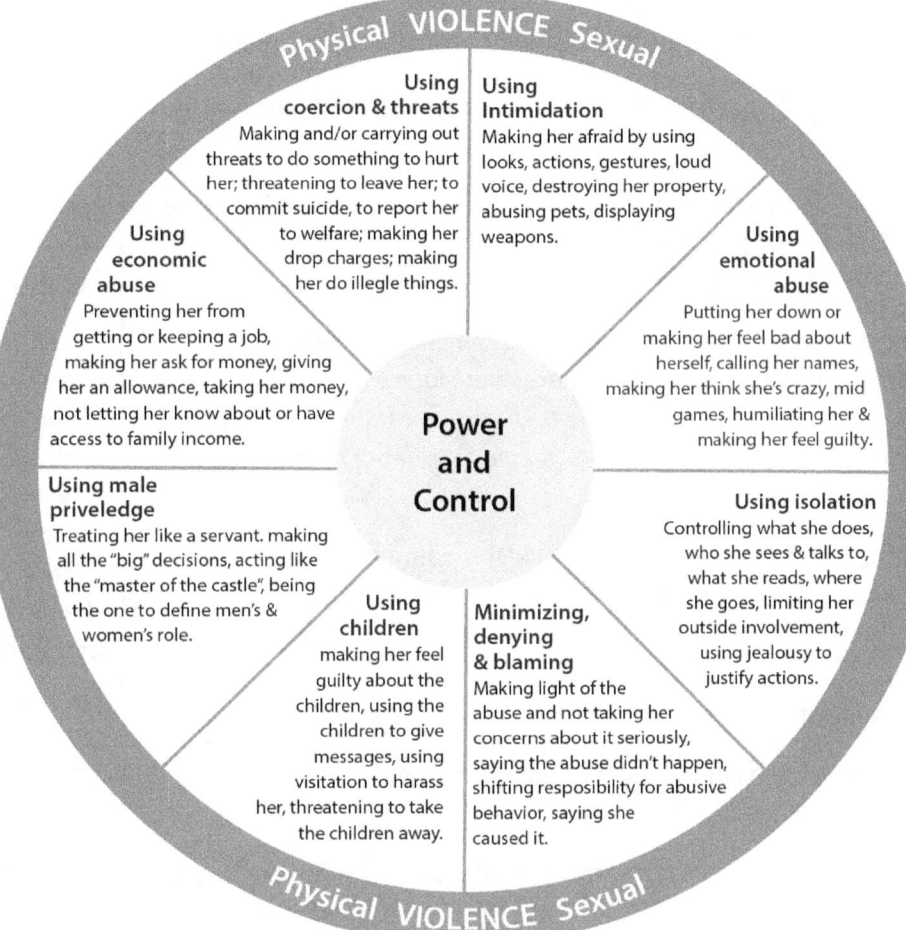

Safety planning is of paramount importance for clients who experience relationship violence. It often takes a long time for them to leave their abusers. Planning where to go, saving enough money, and childcare are all crucial elements of treatment planning for clients who experience relationship violence.

Practice Question

8. Which of the following is the FIRST thing to determine in assessing for suicidality?
   A) if the client has access to weapons
   B) if the client has any suicidal thoughts
   C) if the client has a specific plan for killing himself
   D) if the client has planned a time and place where she would kill herself

Assessing Depression and Anxiety

Several assessment tools are available to diagnose depression and anxiety, screen for these issues, or measure the severity of symptoms in clients.

The **Suicide Assessment Five-Step Evaluation and Triage (SAFE-T)** helps social workers identify suicide risks in clients. The social worker follows five steps:

1. Identify risk factors that can be changed to reduce the client's risk.

2. Identify protective factors that can be increased to reduce the client's risk.

3. Conduct a suicide assessment to understand the client's thoughts, plans, behaviors, and suicidal intent.

4. Determine the client's risk level and the appropriate response to ensure the client's safety; intervene as necessary.

5. Document the assessment of the client's risk level with the supporting evidence discussed, the interventions used, and follow-up steps.

The SAFE-T is available as a pocket card or app.

Many assessments exist to screen for depression or evaluate the level of depression in clients. The psychiatrist David Burns developed the **Burns depression test** to screen for depression. The test is meant to be completed by the client. It asks about thoughts and feelings, personal relationships, physical symptoms, and suicidality.

The **Hamilton Rating Scale for Depression (HAM-D)** is commonly used for individuals who already have a depressive disorder diagnosis:

- It measures suicide risk and physical and emotional symptoms.
- It can be used with both children and adults.
- There are two versions of the HAM-D: one includes seventeen items (HAM-D-17); the other has twenty-one (HAM-D-21).

> **Helpful Hint**
>
> Social workers should discuss their recommendations with clients and develop a plan collaboratively before documenting the assessment.

> **Did You Know?**
>
> The Hamilton Rating Scale for Depression can also be referred to as the Hamilton Depression Scale or the Hamilton Depression Rating Scale.

The **Montgomery-Åsberg Depression Rating Scale (MADRS)** is a ten-item tool. It helps the social worker get a better understanding of depressive symptoms in clients who have a mood disorder. Like the Hamilton scale, it is not used to diagnose; instead, it helps the social worker determine the severity of symptoms. The MADRS should be used with adult clients.

Like the MADRS, the **Zung Self-Rating Depression Scale** measures the severity of depression. It is a twenty-item assessment that rates four common symptoms of depression:

1. pervasive effect

2. psychological equivalents

3. psychomotor activities

4. other disturbances

Several assessments are available for diagnosing and screening for anxiety. Some of the more common follow.

The **State-Trait Anxiety Inventory (STAI)** is useful for diagnosing anxiety in adults. Twenty assessment items cover trait anxiety; another twenty questions cover state anxiety. Differentiating between the two types of anxiety helps reveal a client's levels of anxiety on a day-to-day basis (trait anxiety) as opposed to levels of anxiety in response to perceived stressors (state anxiety). The STAI can also help the social worker differentiate between depression and anxiety symptoms in a client.

The **Beck Anxiety Inventory (BAI)** is a relatively quick anxiety screening tool for adults. It can be done verbally during a session or self-reported before a session. In the BAI, the client rates the severity of several physical and emotional anxiety symptoms. This assessment is a good predictor of anxiety disorders, making it a helpful tool when trying to formulate a diagnosis. The BAI produces valid results. The BAI can also be used to help gauge the client's progress in therapy. Results before and after beginning therapy and/or medications can be compared.

Another anxiety screening tool is the **Generalized Anxiety Disorder 7-item (GAD-7)**, a quick seven-question assessment asking about the severity of anxiety. It is generally self-administered by the client and useful to track treatment progress.

The **Hamilton Anxiety Rating Scale (HARS or HAM-A)** was one of the original anxiety screening assessments. It is administered by a clinician and addresses fourteen categories of physical and psychological symptoms.

Research has found that reliability and validity of the HAM-A is improved when guidance for a structured interview is provided. As a result, the **Hamilton Anxiety Rating Scale Interview Guide (HARS-IG)** was developed. The HARS-IG is considered more reliable and valid.

Practice Question

9. Susan is a client who has been struggling with depressive symptoms since her husband unexpectedly passed away. Since the loss, Susan has been sleeping more than normal, has a depressed mood, and has lost a significant amount of weight. Because of Susan's symptoms, the social worker uses the SAFE-T assessment. What is the correct order of events for this assessment?
   A) document, identify risk factors, conduct suicide inquiry, identify protective factors, and determine risk level/intervention
   B) identify risk factors, identify protective factors, conduct suicide inquiry, determine risk level/intervention, and document
   C) conduct suicide inquiry, identify protective factors, identify risk factors, determine risk level/intervention, and document
   D) conduct suicide inquiry, identify risk factors, identify protective factors, determine risk level/intervention, document

Assessing Personality

Personality assessments are used to tell a social worker about a client's behavior patterns and interpersonal interactions. These can be used to help a social worker determine how to build rapport with a client and choose treatment plans and interventions. They have also been used to assess for career paths. These assessments are a somewhat controversial tool in the world of psychology and therapy because many of them have low reliability and validity, and because one's personality changes frequently throughout a lifetime. The results are usually not shared with the client and are instead used to inform treatment.

Projective tests are assessments in which the client must interpret some type of ambiguous stimuli. These tests require formal training before a clinician can administer and score them:

- The most well-known of these is the **Rorschach inkblot test**, which asks clients to describe what they see in an inkblot.

- Similarly, the **Holtzman inkblot technique** uses a client's interpretation of an inkblot to detect personality.

- The **Thematic Apperception Test (TAT)** is a projective test in which the client describes what is happening on different cards featuring people in ambiguous situations.

Overall, projective tests are seen as unreliable because they rely heavily on the social worker's interpretations and have low validity and reliability.

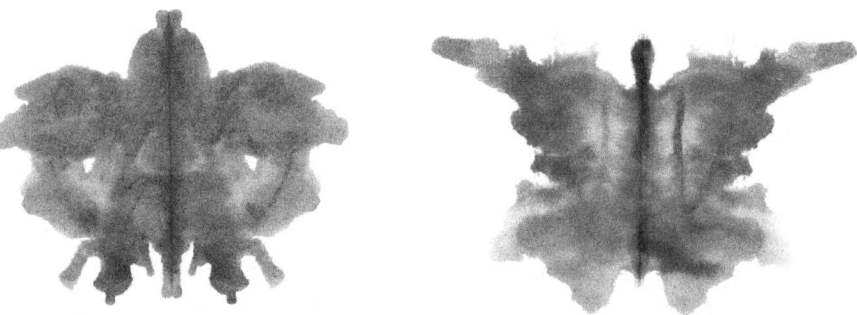

Self-report inventories are questionnaires in which people provide information about themselves in response to various prompts. The most common is the **Minnesota Multiphasic Personality Inventory-2 (MMPI-2)**, which assesses personality traits such as:

- paranoia
- social introversion
- psychopathology.

The MMPI-2 is not generally used to evaluate people with healthy personalities; rather, it measures dysfunction within an individual's personality. Like the CAPS-5 and projective tests, the MMPI-2 requires specific training to administer and score.

The **Sixteen Personality Factors Questionnaire (16PF)** focuses on sixteen fundamental personality characteristics and functions to assist in comprehending where someone's personality may register among

those characteristics. The behavioral assessment serves to provide greater understanding of an individual's behavior and causative factors or thought processes behind those behaviors.

The 16PF underwent a factor analysis that distilled the personality traits into five main traits and eventually developed into the **Big Five personality traits**, which measure the client's level of openness, conscientiousness, extraversion, agreeableness, and neuroticism.

The **Woodworth Personal Data Sheet** is regarded as the first personality test. It was developed to screen war veterans for shell shock (now known as PTSD). It is not typically used by clinicians today.

The **Myers-Briggs Type Indicator (MBTI)** is a self-administered questionnaire used to determine four personality factors with opposing domains. The domains include:

- introversion versus extraversion
- sensing versus intuition
- thinking versus feeling
- judging versus perceiving.

Though widely popular and easy to test online, the MBTI is not generally used by clinicians due to its low validity and reliability.

The **Edwards Personal Preference Schedule (EPPS)** is a series of forced-choice objective questions administered by a clinician. The assessment is designed to illuminate personality through motives and needs and to determine how one would react in certain situations. The assessment has limited validity and reliability and is not a standard personality assessment.

The **HEXACO Personality Inventory (HEXACO-PI)** addresses six characteristics:

1. humility
2. emotionality
3. extraversion
4. agreeableness
5. conscientiousness
6. openness to experience

Scoring for this assessment uses a scale, so the social worker can gauge the significance of the characteristics. However, some critics of the HEXACO Personality Inventory feel that it does not adequately reflect cultural influences.

Practice Question

10. Which of the following personality assessments would be the BEST choice to determine if a client has psychopathic tendencies?
    A) the Edwards Personal Preference Schedule
    B) the Big Five personality traits

C) the Minnesota Multiphasic Personality Inventory-2
D) the Rorschach test

Career Assessment

Career assessments are standardized inventories that allow people to explore their areas of interest and skills and the types of work environments they would thrive in. Social workers frequently use career assessments with high school and college students who are unsure of the career paths they want to take or for adults who want to revisit their current career choices. The following are some of the most common career assessment tools.

The **Strong Interest Inventory (SII)** is used for high school and college students as well as adults who are seeking guidance for a career path. It involves 291 questions across six domains in areas such as occupations and activities interests. It does not measure personality or aptitude. It is a reliable and valid assessment that social workers can use for clients who are unsure of what career paths they are most interested in.

Psychologist John Holland developed a theory of career development known as **RIASEC** (realistic, investigative, artistic, social, enterprising, conventional). He theorizes that people fall into one of these six categories, which determines for which work environment they are best suited. Clients who would like to understand more about their personalities and what type of environment they have the potential to thrive in would benefit from this assessment. Please see Chapter 9 for more details.

The **Self-Directed Search (SDS)** is a formalized assessment based on Holland's career development theory. It is a self-directed assessment, making it ideal for independent clients who prefer to explore career possibilities on their own.

The **Kuder Occupational Interest Survey (KOIS)** is a normed survey that compares the client's scores of areas of interest with the scores of people currently in those fields. Known as "the Kuder," it is self-administered and can be interpreted at home. For clients who are concerned about how personality and interest fit within certain fields, the Kuder can help illuminate how similarly a client may feel compared to others in that field.

The **Career Beliefs Inventory (CBI)** is an assessment administered by social workers that is designed to help them explore the clients' areas of mental blockage, assumptions, generalizations, and beliefs about themselves and others that may be preventing them from exploring their full potential. It is ideal to use as an initial assessment for a client experiencing career difficulties, as it can provide important information for the social worker to explore with the client.

Finally, the **DiSC Assessment** groups people into four main personality profiles:

1. dominance (results-oriented, confident)

2. influence (relationship-focused, persuasive)

3. steadiness (cooperative, sincere, dependable)

4. conscientiousness (competence, clarity, accuracy)

The DiSC assessment can be used in the workplace, especially to analyze candidates and leadership qualities.

Practice Question

11. A client comes in concerned that he would not fit in well in his preferred career choice. Which assessment would BEST help the social worker determine the validity of that concern?
    A) Career Beliefs Inventory
    B) Kuder Occupational Interest Survey
    C) Strong Interest Inventory
    D) Self-Directed Search

Cognitive Functioning Assessments

Certain instruments and assessments are designed to measure psychological functioning. The **Rancho Los Amigos Level of Cognitive Functioning Scale (LCFS)** determines the level of brain function in post-comatose clients and clients with a closed head injury (including traumatic brain injury).

The LCFS focuses on eight areas of cognition (awareness), with each level representing a progression of improvement from brain trauma or damage:

1. No response (level 1)

2. Generalized response (level 2)—reacts inconsistently with no purpose

3. Localized response (level 3)—reacts specifically to various stimuli, with a different response each time

4. Confused-agitated response (level 4)—active but does not comprehend what has happened

5. Confused, inappropriate, nonagitated response (level 5)—less agitated, consistent reactions to basic commands

6. Confused-appropriate response (level 6)—motivated, highly dependent on others, more aware of self and loved ones

7. Automatic-appropriate response (level 7)—acts appropriately in the health care setting and at home; self-aware, oriented to place and time

8. Purposeful-appropriate response (level 8)—independently functions well within the world, has memory of how the past fits with the present and future

The **Mini-Cog assessment tool** is administered in three minutes to screen for cognitive deficiency in older adults. The Mini-Cog is used within the principal health care environment and mainly concentrates on recall abilities. An individual is asked to remember three simple words, is then intentionally distracted by the examiner, and is later asked to repeat the three words.

> **Did You Know?**
>
> The Mini-Cog instrument is widely used to assess memory recall for people with Alzheimer's disease.

The **Mini-Mental State Examination (MMSE)** is brief and used to screen for dementia and cognitive functioning. There are five sections on the MMSE:

1. orientation

2. immediate memory

3. attention and concentration

4. delayed recall

5. language

The MMSE is not to be confused with the mental status exam (MSE) used in clinical intake interviews.

The **Child Development Inventory (CDI)** is a 300-item screening tool that parents complete at home and provide to the social worker. It looks at the child's development in eight areas:

1. social

2. self-help

3. gross motor

4. fine motor

5. expressive language

6. language comprehension

7. letters

8. numbers

The CDI also includes the **General Development Scale** which investigates health, growth, vision, and hearing, as well as a child's developmental behavior.

Cognitive functioning can also be measured by **intelligence tests**. Special training is required to administer and score intelligence tests. Two main intelligence tests are

- the Stanford-Binet test
- the Wechsler test

French psychologist Alfred Binet wanted to develop a test measuring academic ability in order to determine which students are not learning well in the classroom and who might need special instruction. He assumed that intelligence increases with age and devised a "mental age" measurement. For example, if Bobby, an eleven-year-old, has a mental age of eleven, he is on par with his peers. If his mental age were nine, he would be behind. If his mental age were thirteen, he would be ahead.

Lewis Terman, a professor at Stanford University, used Binet's mental age system to create an **intelligence quotient (IQ)** that links intelligence to a number. To determine someone's IQ, the mental age is divided by the actual age and then multiplied by 100. So, if Bobby's mental age is twelve, his IQ would be 118.

To apply this method to adults, Terman set an arbitrary age of twenty for calculating all adult IQs. Terman developed the **Stanford-Binet IQ test** to determine IQ. Test takers are asked a variety of questions, the answers of which determine a single score.

The other major intelligence test was created by David Wechsler. It is also called an IQ test, although the resulting number is not actually a quotient. Instead, the test is standardized so that the mean (the average of the numbers) is 100, and the **standard deviation** (how spread out the numbers are) is 15 with a **normal distribution** (or bell-shaped curve).

A test taker's percentile (relative to the population of test takers) is determined, and the score is based on the number of standard deviations the percentile is from the mean. For example, if Shauna is in the sixteenth percentile, that places her at 34 percent below the mean (fiftieth percentile), which is one standard deviation to the left of the mean. Her IQ score would therefore be 85. The Wechsler test comes in three different forms:

- Wechsler Adult Intelligence Scale (WAIS)
- Wechsler Intelligence Scale for Children ages 6 – 16 (WISC)
- Wechsler Preschool and Primary Scale of Intelligence (WPPSI)

Each test is composed of different types of questions (e.g., verbal and performance on the WAIS). These yield subscores which, taken together, yield a total IQ score.

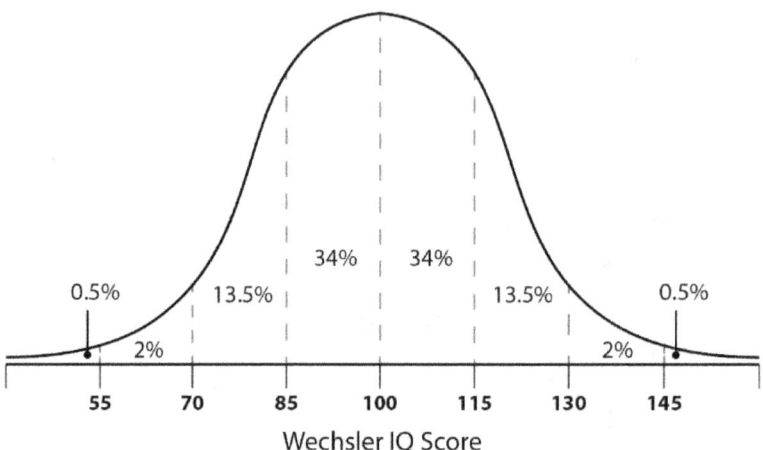

DISTRIBUTION OF IQ SCORES

Wechsler IQ Score

Practice Question

12. The first IQ test was developed to determine which of the following?
    A) entry into Mensa
    B) second grade readiness
    C) graduate school readiness
    D) possible intellectual disability

Criticisms of IQ Tests

There are several criticisms of the efficacy of intelligence testing of any kind. First, the tests focus heavily on verbal skills. While the Wechsler tests require more manipulation of objects and other such performance skills, the verbal components can skew the scores of those whose verbal skills may not match their intelligence.

Additionally, intelligence tests are often accused of being biased. The questions are constructed on certain cultural norms and are not universal. If the question references information not regularly available to a certain individual, it can unfairly skew the results of the test. Defenders of the test argue that the test has the same validity—and predictive power on, for example, college grades—for all cultural groups. Others claim that the bias runs much deeper, setting up certain groups for success on both intelligence tests and college success, while unfairly impeding others.

Practice Question

13. Why are IQ tests frequently criticized as being biased and not universal?
    A) The tests have high validity with GPA.
    B) They ignore domains like emotional intelligence.
    C) The questions assume certain cultural norms.
    D) The questions have low reliability.

Assessing Outcomes

Assessing outcomes is an important part of rigorous therapeutic methods. Outcomes are assessed using **pretest** and **post-test measures**. For example, a client who presents symptoms of PTSD is given the PCL-5 in the first session to determine the rate of her symptoms. After three months of weekly sessions, she reports having fewer nightmares and is better able to cope with triggers in the community. A new administration of the PCL-5 reveals that she no longer meets the clinical criteria for PTSD. This is considered a positive outcome as a result of treatment sessions with the social worker.

Pre- and post-test measures can also evaluate therapeutic effectiveness. Some social workers or clinics ask their clients to fill out a weekly, monthly, or termination evaluation that rates their perceptions of the social worker's efficacy. Common questions ask whether the client

- feels understood by the social worker
- perceives improvement in symptoms
- feels like the sessions are a good use of time.

Practice Question

14. Assessing a client's symptoms when she starts treatment and when she terminates with her social worker is known as which of the following?
    A) random sampling
    B) pre-test and post-test measures
    C) stratified sampling
    D) case study

Diagnosis

A **diagnosis** is an identified health condition that is based on an assessment by a trained professional. To make a diagnosis, social workers look at the client's symptoms and compare them to the symptoms listed in the *Diagnostic and Statistical Manual of Mental Disorders* (*DSM*-5).

Determining and Using Diagnosis

Because diagnosis is a key component of a client's medical records, clients have the right to know if they meet clinical criteria for a diagnosis. After learning their diagnoses, clients can make informed decisions about their treatments.

Social workers should use language the client can understand when discussing a diagnosis. For example, the way a diagnosis is explained to an adult will be different than the way it would be explained to a child.

Diagnoses are used to help guide treatment. Research has found that specific presenting concerns require different therapeutic approaches. For example, cognitive therapy will not be as effective as using dialectical behavior therapy (DBT) for someone living with borderline personality disorder.

Once a diagnosis is made, the social worker can determine whether additional treatment services would benefit the client. Medication management, as an example, can be an effective intervention for several clinical diagnoses.

Having a clinical diagnosis can significantly change the objectives and goals of a treatment plan. Treatment plans should be in place after the initial interview and continually be adjusted to reflect the client's progress.

Treatment plans allow for further specification and can include goals specific to a diagnosis. For example, clients struggling with obsessive-compulsive disorder (OCD) may learn new and effective coping skills for their obsessions in the early phases of treatment. Once those skills have developed, the treatment plan can progress to other approaches to respond to the compulsive behaviors that are present. The next chapter discusses treatment planning in depth.

After meeting with a client for an initial interview, the social worker should take time to consider possible diagnoses. The ***Diagnostic and Statistical Manual of Mental Disorders, Fifth Edition* (DSM-5)** contains twenty-one sections of similar diagnoses. A social worker should get a general idea of which section the client's diagnosis may be in, and then she can begin looking at the specific symptoms for this diagnosis. Every diagnosis has different requirements, all of which are explained in the "Diagnostic Criteria" section for the diagnosis in the *DSM-5*.

Many diagnoses within the *DSM-5* are rated on a mild, moderate, or severe scale, which is determined by the number of symptoms present. This is explained in the "Coding and Recording Procedures" section for each diagnosis in the *DSM-5*. Diagnoses may also have additional specifiers that would be listed in the same section.

The term ***co-occurring*** refers to the presence of a mental health diagnosis in addition to a substance-related disorder. Some people use alcohol and drugs to cope with symptoms resulting from a mental health condition. As a result, individuals who have co-occurring disorders need to receive treatment for both concerns for the best treatment outcomes.

Dual diagnosis refers to an individual who meets the criteria for two separate diagnoses. Symptoms for both diagnoses must be present at the same time. The term is usually used to describe the presence of a mental health diagnosis and a substance use disorder, but it can refer to other disorders as well. Dual diagnoses can be two mental health conditions, two medical health conditions, or one of each.

> **Helpful Hint**
>
> Social workers may come across dual diagnoses referred to as "co-occurring"

Comorbidity is similar to dual diagnosis, but it refers to the presence of more than one health condition. These can be medical or mental health conditions. Each diagnosis section in the *DSM-5* ends with a paragraph explaining the common comorbidities found with that particular illness.

Practice Question

15. A social worker is reviewing initial assessment paperwork before meeting with a new client. The client has been diagnosed with PTSD with dissociative symptoms and severe major depressive disorder. She received the PTSD diagnosis first. Three years later, she developed depressive symptoms that led to her second diagnosis. Which of the following would BEST characterize her diagnosis?
    A) co-occurring diagnoses
    B) dual diagnosis
    C) comorbid diagnoses
    D) clinical diagnosis

Levels of Care

Depending on their concerns, individual clients may require varying levels of care. There are a variety of options, each with its own benefits.

Residential inpatient care programs typically occur within a hospital setting. The goal is to stabilize clients so they can begin receiving treatment for their mental health concerns at a different location:

- Clients receive treatment that can include:
    - psychoeducation
    - individual therapy
    - crisis intervention
    - medication management
- Inpatient programs are appropriate for individuals who have safety risks, such as:
    - recent suicide gestures or attempts
    - homicidal attempts
- Inpatient programs are also suitable for clients who need a high level of care, including
    - medication management
    - drug/ alcohol detox and treatment

In **partial hospitalization programs (PHPs)**, the client attends a structured day program at a treatment facility:

- The program's structure resembles an inpatient program, but the client goes home at night.
- PHPs typically run five days a week for six to eight hours per day.
- PHPs provide clients with safety and structure for most of their day.
- PHPs are appropriate for clients who can safely live at home but still need a thorough treatment program.
    - A typical client might have severe mental illness, be compliant with medication, and learn how to manage symptoms behaviorally.

In **intensive outpatient programs (IOPs)**, the client attends structured programming for a few hours per day:

- IOPs usually treat addiction, eating disorders, and depressive disorders.
- IOPs typically have a psychoeducational component in addition to group treatment.
- IOPs are appropriate for
    - clients with mild disorders

- clients with mild and severe use disorders who have already completed residential treatment programs

Outpatient treatment (outpatient therapy) is usually recommended to build on what clients learned in other, more intensive programs:

- The duration of an outpatient program varies depending on the presenting concern.
- Outpatient treatment typically follows successful completion of an IOP or PHP.
- Outpatient treatment is typically fewer hours per day than an IOP or PHP.
- Outpatient activities include:
    - group therapy
    - individual therapy
    - medication management
    - specialized treatment
    - psychoeducation
    - family therapy
- Outpatient treatment programs address various mental health concerns, including
    - addiction
    - childhood behavioral and emotional concerns
    - mood disorders

Psychotherapy is individual therapy that

- is appropriate for individuals with a mild mental health concern
- allows complex clients to maintain a connection to a supportive professional after more intensive treatment
- includes high-functioning clients
- usually consists of weekly or biweekly individual sessions

Self-help programs generally refer to support groups run by peers rather than mental health professionals:

- Many self-help programs address addiction, but some address other mental health concerns. These include:
    - twelve-step programs (e.g., Alcoholics Anonymous, Narcotics Anonymous)
    - support for families of addicts (e.g., Al-Anon, Nar-Anon)
    - eating and weight management groups (e.g., Overeaters Anonymous, Weight Watchers)

- o some grief support groups
- Activity and attendance rate depend on the client.
- Self-help groups can be used at every level of care.

Treatment programs offer guidelines that can help the social worker decide which level of care to recommend to a client.

Practice Question

16. A client just completed a detox program and an inpatient addiction program to address opioid use disorder. The client has a history of trauma, anxiety, and depression. He has a safe home environment and believes that his mental health concerns triggered his substance use disorder. The inpatient program recommended that he attend treatment for a few hours a day, three to four days per week, while living at home. Which level of care is the client now entering?
- A) partial hospitalization program (PHP)
- B) intensive outpatient program (IOP)
- C) psychotherapy
- D) outpatient treatment

Answer Key

1. C: The systems approach recognizes the interconnection of those various levels of an individual's life as potential risk and protective factors related to the problem.

2. B: The social worker demonstrates genuineness and congruence by stating that she does not agree with the client's choices, shows nonjudgment by keeping the behavior separate from the person, and expresses positive regard by encouraging the client to work on making better choices.

3. A: Attending behaviors, like eye contact and other nonverbal signals, communicate that the social worker is present and paying attention to the client.

4. D: The client is in shock, not thinking straight, and needs to express these emotions. The social worker can demonstrate empathetic attunement by giving her time and space to feel what she needs to feel without judgment.

5. C: The client's statements suggest that he blames his failure on the school, professors, and peers—not himself; this demonstrates an external locus of control.

6. D: Refusing to interact with anything that may remind the client of the traumatizing event is a sign of avoidance.

7. B: The Car, Relax, Alone, Forget, Friends, Trouble (CRAFFT) is the only assessment that is endorsed for use with adolescents and screens for drug usage.

8. B: The first step in assessing for suicidality is to determine if the client has any suicidal thoughts.

9. B: When using the Suicide Assessment Five-Step Evaluation and Triage (SAFE-T), the social worker begins by identifying risk factors that can be changed to reduce the client's risk. Next, the social worker determines what protective factors can be increased to reduce risk. This is followed by a suicide assessment that looks at the client's thoughts, plans, behaviors, and suicidal intent. Once the social worker has all the information needed, the client's risk level can be determined and an appropriate response to ensure the client's safety can be formulated. After discussing recommendations with the client and developing a plan, the social worker should document the assessment of the client's risk level with supporting evidence discussed, the interventions used, and the recommended follow-up steps.

10. C: The Minnesota Multiphasic Personality Inventory-2 (MMPI-2) scores and assesses for negative personality traits associated with psychological disorders, including areas such as paranoia, antisocial behaviors, depression, and more.

11. B: The Kuder Occupational Interest Survey (KOIS, or "the Kuder") is normed against scores of people across ten respective fields, which is ideal for helping a client who wants to know if he has similar thoughts and feelings as other people in his chosen field.

12. D: Alfred Binet first developed his IQ test at the request of the French government to determine which students might have an intellectual disability as a basis to require separate classroom instruction.

13. C: The main criticism of intelligence quotient (IQ) tests not being universal is that the questions are culturally biased toward the test makers.

14. B: Using pre-test and post-test techniques determine if an intervention has caused a change in symptoms or behavior.

15. C: The client has comorbid diagnoses because more than one disorder is present. Option A can be ruled out because neither disorder is a substance use disorder. Option B is incorrect because the client received the diagnoses at separate points in her life. If she had developed symptoms of both disorders at the same time, then Option B would be correct. Clinical diagnosis (Option D) simply refers to an identified health condition as determined by professional assessment.

16. B: The client is entering an intensive outpatient program (IOP). A partial hospitalization program (PHP) can be ruled out because the treatment recommendation is only a few days a week. Psychotherapy is generally one or two short sessions per week and would not meet the recommended level of care from the referrer. Finally, the situation describes more intensive scheduling than a typical outpatient program. After completing the IOP, the individual would likely be encouraged to continue with outpatient treatment.

6. Concepts of Abuse and Neglect

Indicators of Abuse and Neglect

Abuse and neglect are defined by federal and state laws:

- **Abuse** means to treat another person improperly through cruelty and violence and can be physical, sexual, emotional, or psychological.
- **Neglect** is to withhold care or affection that is necessary for healthy development.

Both abuse and neglect fall within mandated reporting requirements. Some vulnerable populations, like children, rarely volunteer information about being abused or neglected.

Children are particularly vulnerable because they rely on adults to provide for them both physically and psychologically. In most cases of child abuse, family members or caregivers are responsible and give the children instructions to not speak about their mistreatment. Children may not understand that they are being abused or neglected. If they do understand, they often lack the words in their vocabulary to explain what is happening to them. There are several indicators that someone is being abused or neglected. These indicators are not all-inclusive but do provide a starting point for recognizing that something is wrong.

There are several physical indicators of the maltreatment of children:

- an unkempt or dirty appearance
- dirty or ill-fitting clothes
- an onset of physical ailments (e.g., stomachaches, headaches, bedwetting)
- noticeable bruises, scrapes, and/or other injuries
- sleep problems
- eating problems
- confirmed diagnosis of sexually transmitted disease(s)

Children may exhibit the following emotional indicators:

- an inability to regulate emotions
- inappropriate emotional expression
- needy, wanting attention all the time
- depression

Lastly, the following behavioral changes may indicate the maltreatment of children:

- social isolation
- increased anger, hostility, hyperactivity, or temper tantrums
- stealing, hoarding food, or comfort items
- not wanting to be around certain people

Adolescents can also be at risk of abuse and neglect. Though they have the capacity to ask for help, they may have reasons (e.g., guilt, fear, or shame) to keep it to themselves. Family members or caregivers are usually the most likely perpetrators of adolescent abuse. Dating partners, coaches, teachers, and other adults in positions of authority may also be maltreatment perpetrators. Technology and social media access bring their own risks by exposing teens to the harms of sexting, sextortion, and cyberbullying.

There are several physical indicators of maltreatment in adolescents:

- sleep disturbances
- appetite issues
- drastic changes in weight
- psychosomatic illnesses
- evidence of self-injury
- substance use
- sexually transmitted diseases

Adolescents may exhibit the following emotional indicators:

- emotional dysregulation
- overreaction
- the onset of anxiety, depression, phobias
- self-injury behaviors
- suicidal ideation

Lastly, the following behavioral changes may indicate maltreatment in adolescents:

- engaging in high-risk behaviors (e.g., substance abuse, promiscuity)
- changes in social groups
- social isolation
- changes in grades or school performance
- the avoidance of people or situations

While adults can face abuse in any number of forms, the most common is **intimate partner violence**, which is when a spouse, partner, or significant other exerts coercion and control over the individual who is being maltreated.

The following are physical indicators of abuse or neglect in adults:

- unexplained injuries
- frequent injuries
- the sudden onset of illness
- recurrent medical issues with fatigue, headaches, or GI issues
- the onset or increase of alcohol or substance use

Adults may exhibit the following emotional indicators of abuse or neglect:

- mood swings
- depression, anxiety, fear
- difficulties regulating emotions
- low frustration tolerance

Lastly, the following behavioral changes may indicate maltreatment in adults:

- not having freedom of movement
- needing permission to go out socially
- restricted or severed contact with family and friends
- not having access to money
- social isolation
- Older adults are a vulnerable population for abuse and neglect since many must rely on family members or professional caregivers in their daily lives. For that very reason, older adults with chronic health issues (e.g., dementia) are particularly at risk of abuse or neglect by family members or health care providers and organizations.

The following may be physical indicators of abuse or neglect in older adults:

- unexplained injuries
- not well-groomed
- unexplained weight loss or gain
- unsafe or unclean surroundings

Older adults may exhibit the following emotional indicators:

- depression

6. Concepts of Abuse and Neglect

- increased confusion
- anxiety or fear around certain people or locations

Lastly, the following behavioral changes may indicate maltreatment in older adults:

- social isolation
- missed medical appointments or treatment
- not seeing family and friends
- changes in spending or finances
- the appearance of new people in their lives
- a lack of desire to talk to anyone

Practice Questions

1. Why are children and older adults particularly vulnerable to abuse and neglect?
   A) They rely on others to provide for and care for them.
   B) They are more likely to use drugs and thus unable to fight back.
   C) They are not protected by legal status.
   D) They tend to be in risky environments.

2. Why are children unlikely to report neglect or abuse?
   A) They rely on their abuser for their physical and psychological needs.
   B) They fear punishment and repercussions from the perpetrators of their maltreatment.
   C) They are unable to understand they are being mistreated or lack the vocabulary to do so.
   D) They do not have enough contact with the outside world to find a safe adult to tell.

Types and Effects of Abuse

Physical, Sexual, and Emotional Abuse

Physical abuse is the use of physical force against another person. This type of abuse includes hitting, beating, shaking, holding someone underwater, or throwing things at another person.

Sexual abuse is coercive sex or sexual acts through the use of force or violence. It includes taking pictures of a person without permission, exposing minors to pornography, or behaving in a sexual manner with minors. Sexual abuse may also involve drugging victims or using emotional manipulation.

Emotional abuse involves using belittling language, name-calling, bullying, withholding love and affection, or manipulating self-worth to emotionally damage the victim.

Abuse causes many detrimental changes in victims, many of which overlap with possible indicators or warning signs. The following are the most common indicators, almost all of which are either psychological or physical changes:

- bruises or injuries that are not well explained
- burns, especially patterned burns that cannot be explained

- patterned injury marks as from a belt or other object
- unattended medical issues
- expressing fear or dislike of their parents/caregivers
- high fight-or-flight response to being touched
- bruising, bleeding, or pain around genitals
- pregnancy or STDs
- acting out sexually at a young age
- speech problems, emotional development delays
- depression, low self-esteem
- poor academic performance
- unexplained physical pain (e.g., headaches or stomachaches)
- poor hygiene
- missing a lot of school
- being underweight
- hoarding

> **Helpful Hint**
>
> Social workers have legal and ethical obligations to report any suspected child abuse or cases in which children witness domestic violence. It is not the counselor's duty to investigate to confirm child abuse—only to report it to the appropriate authorities.

Domestic violence, which was introduced earlier in this chapter as "intimate partner violence," is abuse within the home. It can be physical, sexual, and emotional abuse or a combination of all three. Couples do not have to be married for abuse to be classified as domestic violence. Domestic violence is not reportable unless witnessed by a child.

The effects of domestic violence do not stop with the trauma and damage done to the domestic partner—they also create a dysfunctional family dynamic. Children who witness this form of abuse experience symptoms of trauma, with adverse outcomes seen in their emotional well-being and other relationships, social or otherwise.

Regardless of the reporting requirements, the social worker can—and should—assist families as follows:

- safety planning
- helping the partners develop more effective relationship and parenting skills
- building emotional regulation
- any next steps that may need to be taken if an investigation is opened

Practice Question

3. Which of the following scenarios would require a counselor to make a child abuse report to the state?
   A) Freddie was pushed by a peer at school and has a bruise; he is afraid of the child who hit him.
   B) Marco has been pinching his mom every day when she picks him up from school; he says his mom is mean and does not like him.
   C) Suzie reports feeling sad and scared because she can hear her parents yelling sometimes after she goes to bed at night.
   D) Angie tells the counselor that her stepdad likes to take pictures of her in her bathing suit when they are alone.

Exploitation

Exploitation is the unfair and disparate treatment of someone else to create an advantage or benefit for the perpetrator. It is the misuse of power and authority in a way that keeps one person powerless and without resources. A poignant example of exploitation is slavery in any form, whereby an authoritative power forces people to labor with little to no compensation so that those in power can profit from that labor. However, there are other forms of exploitation.

Financial exploitation is taking advantage of someone who is vulnerable for the perpetrator's financial gain. It may involve withholding money, improperly using funds, or outright theft. The following populations are at risk of financial exploitation:

- those who require long-term care (e.g., foster children, older adults, persons who are disabled)
- people lacking family or strong social connections

These populations are at greater risk because they require extensive care and/or are too trusting. Financial exploitation may happen in one of two ways:

- The caregiver, in a position of authority to do so, may take the someone's finances for their own.
- Exploiters may ingratiate themselves to people who are vulnerable and convince them to grant access to their finances.

Exploitation of immigration status is leveraging the threat of deportation in order to benefit the exploiter. Employers in the US may engage in this practice since immigrants will often work for lower wages than citizens and may not understand employment law. This benefits the employer, who nets more profit when paying lower wages to employees. Workers may see longer hours at low-wage jobs as improvement over the conditions in their home-country. Employer's may also leverage room and board, deducted from the worker's salary, to extend their control over that worker's family.

Exploitation of immigration status may also be used in conjunction with domestic violence and abuse. A citizen in a relationship with an immigrant may help that person obtain legal status; however, in an unhealthy relationship, the citizen could exploit the immigrant by threating to report the person for deportation or withholding the person's participation in the process to gain legal status. The immigrant

may not be aware of the legal system in the US and may therefore remain under the control of the exploiter.

Sexual trafficking is a form of slavery whereby people are held against their will for the purpose of sexual exploitation and often transported from place to place. Victims are forced to perform sex acts or engage in the sex industry for money that goes to the exploiter. The trafficker often lures people who are vulnerable by lying to them, forcing them, or coercing them into participation. Those who are exploited sexually are held against their will and are usually involved in substance use either because they are forced to by the exploiter or because it helps them cope with their circumstances. Sex trafficking affects children, adolescents, and adults. Those most vulnerable to sex trafficking may have a history of maltreatment, sexual abuse, or neglect, with few social connections. Children who grew up in poverty, were part of the welfare system, ran away from home, and/or used drugs are more vulnerable to targeting by sex traffickers.

Practice Question

4. Which of the following individuals is most likely to be a target for exploitation?
   A) an employed, middle-aged woman involved in her community
   B) an single woman from Honduras who has no money and crossed the border illegally
   C) an African American female adolescent involved in athletics at her high school
   D) a White male college student involved in student government.

Characteristics of Perpetrators

Perpetrators come from every ethnicity, race, religion, and socioeconomic class. It is important to note that some perpetrators of child abuse and neglect do so intentionally; other times, they engage in these behaviors due to external factors that they cannot handle and thus displace their stress onto their children. Though they can look and come from very different places, people who engage in abuse neglect, or exploitation of others may share several characteristics. For example, many perpetrators of child abuse and neglect learned these behaviors by being abused or neglected themselves when they were children. Other shared characteristics include the following:

- poor or nonexistent parenting skills
- lack of relationship skills
- poor or nonexistent emotional regulation skills
- an inability to deal with stress
- low frustration tolerance
- not knowing how to properly discipline a child
- substance use or abuse
- being a victim of intimate partner violence
- poor self-concept and self-esteem
- a lack of empathy

- easily angered with no coping skills
- low intelligence or lack of education
- antisocial personality traits
- psychiatric disorders like personality and mood disorders
- impulsivity and poor self-control
- feelings of entitlement, narcissism
- rigidity of personality
- lack of problem-solving skills
- other external stressors like economic, employment, or relationship problems
- a lack of understanding of child behavior

Those who perpetrate exploitation use coercion and control techniques that may lead a person to volunteer or choose to be exploited. Much like those who perpetrate child abuse and neglect, those who exploit others tend to have been victims themselves. They also tend to want to control or manipulate others. In some cases, control and manipulation make them feel more powerful or better about themselves; in other cases, it may be a necessary function of survival. People who exploit others may have aggressive or violent tendencies, a history of criminal behavior, or involvement with gangs or other criminal organizations. Criminal organizations and gangs often exploit others for financial gain for the good of the group without caring for the individuals in the group.

Individuals who exploit other individuals and are not part of an organization may be motivated by external stressors like economic hardship; however, in order to exert power and control over another person, an individual will lack empathy, feel entitled, and expect others to fulfill their wants and needs. They may also not be able to relate to other people emotionally and thus only maintain superficial relationships. Mental illness may also be a factor in a person's willingness to exploit others.

Employers who exploit people for inexpensive sources of labor are motivated by greed and selfishness, placing the achievement of profit ahead of anything else. They may also feel entitled to circumvent the law due to feeling exploited themselves. Other times, gaming the system or exploiting the rules of a given system to achieve a benefit is considered a worthy risk in order to increase the reward for oneself.

Practice Question

5. Which of the following characteristics do those who perpetrate abuse, neglect, and exploitation usually have in common?
    A) involvement in criminal gangs
    B) strong social bonds
    C) lack of empathy
    D) poverty

Answer Key

1. A: Children and older adults are especially vulnerable to abuse and neglect because they rely on caregivers; caregivers are typically more likely to abuse or neglect those for whom they are supposed to care.

2. C: Children are too young to understand that their treatment is 'bad' or not normal. They may also lack the communication skills at such a young age to explain what is happening to them.

3. D: While all of the situations would benefit from monitoring for possible indicators of abuse, option D is the only clear indicator of an abusive situation.

4. B: This woman will be looking for any employment she can get and could become involved with a partner who will exploit her immigration status.

5. C: A lack of empathy is typically a characteristic shared by those who perpetrate abuse, neglect, and exploitation.

7. Indicators and Effects of Crisis and Change

Indicators of Traumatic Stress and Violence

Stress, trauma, and violence are all related in that they disrupt a client's physical response to danger. The human body is designed for survival, and the mechanisms within the body that react to stress, trauma, and violence are the same.

The **fight-or-flight response** is a complex system of the autonomic nervous system. This means it activates when danger is near in order for the body to react to the danger instinctively, thereby enhancing survival. This part of the nervous system operates by sensation, so any kind of stimuli registered by the senses can trigger it.

The sympathetic nervous system activates to prepare the body to engage: the pupils dilate, the heart rate increases, breathing becomes shallow, digestion stops, blood vessels constrict to bring blood to the body's core, and a flood of hormones gives the body energy to do what it needs to do.

When the danger passes, the parasympathetic nervous system engages, which essentially relaxes everything back to normal; however, that also needs to happen using the senses, which is why grounding is a good technique to use when someone's stress response is activated. Again, all of this happens without a person needing to decide to make it happen, which can cause mental health issues when it occurs at times when it is not necessary. For example, people who experience panic attacks are feeling this process in action but not in response to a real threat.

Stress refers to the internal and external signals that cause the autonomic nervous system to activate all the time. Over time, constant activation of the stress response can cause physical health problems, such as cardiovascular issues, immune system issues, and other chronic problems related to inflammation and oxidation.

Although **trauma** can refer to a specific event that threatens the life of the individual (e.g., violence), it can also refer to the consequences of this event. Those who experience trauma may become stuck in the trauma. If that trauma is not resolved, the body continues to react to cues and triggers related to the trauma as if it is happening again in real time. **Physical symptoms of trauma** include sympathetic nervous system activation like

- increased heart rate
- gastrointestinal issues
- shallow breathing
- feeling on edge

- an inability to relax
- sleep disturbances
- fatigue
- muscle heaviness.

The continued activation of these physical symptoms caused by hypervigilance, hyperarousal, and re-experiencing can create a significant physical toll on a person and lead to chronic health issues. There are some indications that conditions caused by chronic inflammation or oxidation may be related to the effects of unresolved stress and trauma. Stress and trauma can impact client systems in multiple ways, as described in Table 7.1.

Table 7.1. Effects of Stress and Trauma	
Biological effects	<ul><li>put a person at risk for physical harm in the moment (e.g., in cases of violence and trauma)</li><li>cause disruption in attention and focus (in the case of stress) that make a person more susceptible to mistreatment or accidental injury</li><li>can cause a person to disregard his own safety and engage in behaviors that are high risk for injury or death</li><li>can impact a client's long-term physical health and put her at risk for chronic health issues</li><li>can contribute to a person choosing to self-medicate with alcohol or substance use</li></ul>
Psychological effects	<ul><li>can cause or worsen mental health issues (e.g., anxiety, depression, panic disorder, social anxiety disorder, post-traumatic stress disorder)</li><li>contribute to emotional instability and feelings of not being in control of oneself</li><li>produce reactions to stimuli that are out of proportion to the stimuli (e.g., a short fuse or very low frustration tolerance)</li></ul>
Social effects	<ul><li>create interpersonal issues and increase tension in relationships</li><li>can cause a person to detach from others emotionally or to over-attach to others for protection</li><li>can cause a person to become unnecessarily fearful of others in the environment and see danger everywhere</li><li>may contribute to social isolation</li><li>in some cases, can cause an individual to become violent toward others</li></ul>

Practice Question

1. Which of the following statements could explain why a person cannot be talked out of a panic attack or extreme stress response?
   A) He will not be conscious of who is talking to him due to dissociation.
   B) The sympathetic nervous system is activated automatically and only responds to sensory information.
   C) It is best to just let the panic attack run its course.
   D) During a panic attack, the brain scrambles words, so the person may not understand.

Anxiety and Obsessive Thoughts

While the terms *anxiety*, *stress*, and *worry* are often used interchangeably in colloquial parlance, it is important to parse these terms out to better understand clients' experiences and provide them with the appropriate words to label their feeling states:

- **Worry** refers to thoughts that are often perseverative and project a negative outcome.
- **Stress** often accompanies worry and is described as the perceived experience of increased adrenal response:
    - physical agitation
    - tightness in the chest
    - elevated heart rate (tachycardia)
    - quickening of the breath (tachypnea)
- **Anxiety** refers to the combined experiences of ruminating thoughts and psychomotor stress.

These feeling states of stress, worry, and anxiety are often overwhelming. When combined and experienced over an extended period, certain psychological and physical effects are often measured.

A diagnosis of **generalized anxiety disorder (GAD)** includes criteria of prolonged and pervasive worry and anxiety that impede daily functioning. Specifically, a person must experience them for at least half a year, during which the majority of days are wrought with worry and anxiety.

The *Diagnostic and Statistical Manual of Mental Disorders* (*DSM-5*) requires that an adult have a minimum of three of the following symptoms to satisfy the requirements for a diagnosis of GAD. Children need to have one symptom:

- restlessness, feeling keyed up or on edge
- being easily fatigued
- irritability
- muscle tension
- sleep disturbances (difficulty falling or staying asleep or restless, unsatisfying sleep)

In conjunction with talk therapy models, pharmacologic interventions effectively treat GAD. These interventions include:

- selective serotonin reuptake inhibitors (SSRIs)
- serotonin norepinephrine reuptake inhibitors (SNRIs)
- benzodiazepines.

Obsessive-compulsive disorder (OCD) is perhaps most effectively treated with cognitive behavioral therapy (CBT). The layperson's understanding of OCD is that of a person who is particular about organization and cleanliness, but OCD actually requires a two-part diagnosis:

1. intense perseverations on unwanted intrusive thoughts

2. compulsive behaviors that function in response to the unwanted thoughts

A person with OCD often believes that these obsessive behaviors will alleviate the anxiety associated with the rumination on intrusive thoughts; however, the behaviors do not improve functioning, decrease anxiety, or curtail intrusive thoughts. The behaviors are often rigid and repetitive. In fact, they decrease the person's ability to function by taking time away from social interactions and work/family obligations.

Clients with OCD often benefit from high dosages of selective serotonin reuptake inhibitors (SSRIs) to decrease the level of neurological underpinnings that can cause intrusive thought patterns. In conjunction with medication, behavioral modifications and exposure therapy can be implemented through CBT or other models. These interventions allow clients to break their habituated and rigid patterns of behavior while challenging the cognitive distortions that allow them to continue using their maladaptive coping skills.

When someone's intrusive thoughts are memories of past experiences, specifically traumatic experiences, a social worker may consider a diagnosis of **post-traumatic stress disorder (PTSD)**. Certain memories can trigger physiological reactions that cause a person to dissociate, including:

- near-death experiences
- sexual violence
- serious injury

These dissociative reactions are called **flashbacks** and are a hallmark of a PTSD diagnosis. Individuals experiencing PTSD are debilitated by their attempts to avoid the triggers that cause their flashbacks.

> **Helpful Hint**
>
> A PTSD diagnosis differentiates between intrusive thoughts and flashbacks.

To address PTSD, a social worker must address the physiological dysregulation before focusing on the emotional and cognitive distress:

- Interventions such as CBT or dialectical behavior therapy (DBT) with a trauma focus must include a commitment to work on distress tolerance or relaxation skills.

- Without decreasing hyperarousal and physiological symptomology, the brain cannot function at the more executive levels necessary for emotional and cognitive reprocessing.

> **Did You Know?**
>
> Treatment models such as eye movement desensitization and reprocessing (EMDR) address the neurological underpinnings of a PTSD diagnosis while simultaneously treating negative cognitions and emotional dysregulation.

Practice Question

2. Which of the following is NOT a diagnostic criterion for GAD?
   A) compulsive rituals performed in an attempt to control obsessive thoughts
   B) difficulty concentrating
   C) perseverative negative thoughts that anticipate negative outcomes (worry)
   D) sleep disturbance

Fear and Panic

While the hyperarousal experienced with PTSD is a result of a tangible external trigger, individuals experiencing panic disorder, social anxiety disorder, and separation anxiety disorder have physical anxiety responses that are triggered by internal stimuli. The common thread among these three diagnoses is the fear around an invisible, often irrational, threat.

The treatment model involves the same therapeutic interventions and often the same pharmacology as GAD; however, the approach involves a greater focus on affect regulation. Individuals with these disorders, who often experience unpredictable fear and panic, benefit from learning how to identify their internal feeling states. These skills include:

- labeling feelings

- reporting on the severity of distress (e.g., using the subjective units of distress scale [SUDS])

- working on distress tolerance skills to use when feelings become overwhelming

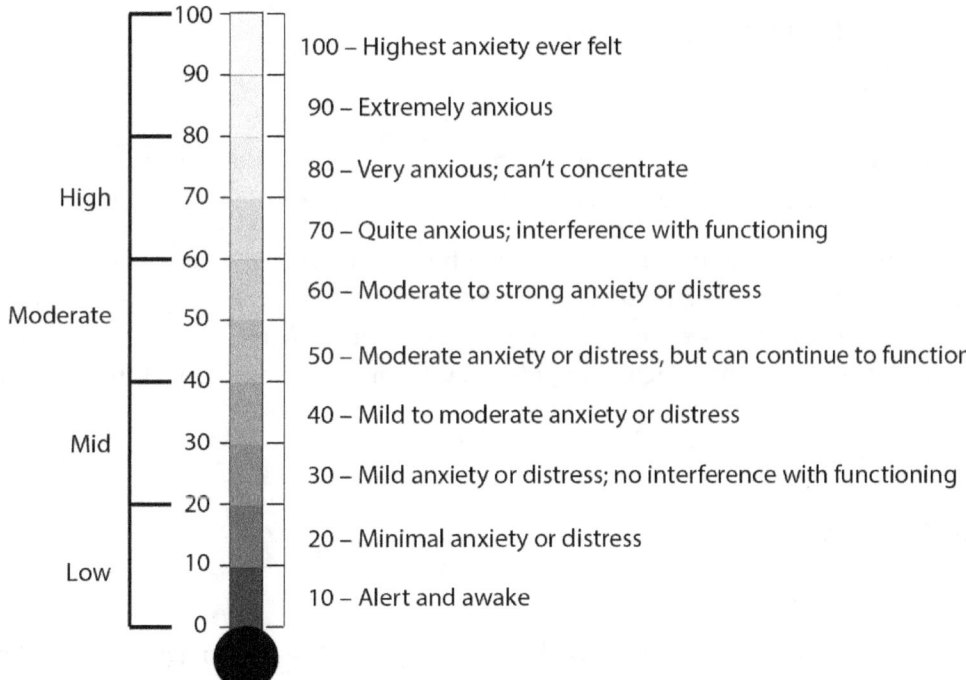

Panic disorder is characterized by sudden attacks of overwhelming panic along with constant anticipatory fear of experiencing an attack. Because these attacks are not related to external stimuli, they feel random and uncontrollable to the individual experiencing them.

To be diagnosed with panic disorder, clients must have a minimum of four of the thirteen physical symptoms present during panic attacks. Additionally, they need to have one month of persistent worry of more panic attacks OR have made significant changes to their behaviors to try to avoid future panic attacks. Their symptoms cannot be caused by drugs and/or alcohol, nor by other mental health concerns. The following thirteen physical symptoms are associated with panic disorder:

1. palpitations, pounding heart, or accelerated heart rate (tachycardia)
2. sweating
3. trembling or shaking
4. sensations of shortness of breath (dyspnea) or smothering
5. feelings of choking
6. chest pain or discomfort
7. nausea or abdominal distress
8. feeling dizzy, unsteady, light-headed, or faint
9. chills or heat sensations
10. paresthesia (numbness or tingling sensations)
11. derealization (feelings of unreality) or depersonalization (being detached from oneself)
12. fear of losing control or "going crazy"
13. fear of dying

Often, people with panic disorder change their lives to try to avoid having attacks but are unsuccessful. When they come for treatment, CBT/DBT and psychopharmacology are tried-and-true interventions.

Social anxiety disorder presents a similar set of issues wherein the trigger for anxiety is irrational and does not necessarily stem from adverse experiences in the person's past. Typically, there are limiting beliefs and negative cognitions at the root of these anxieties. Clients with social anxiety experience emotional dysregulation in response to feeling watched or judged by others in social settings. Treatment for social anxiety can include:

- exposure therapy
- affect regulation
- cognitive reprocessing.

Separation anxiety disorder is characterized by chronic worry about real or imagined separation from major attachment figures. The level of emotional dysregulation and distress that individuals experience at even the thought of separation is both developmentally inappropriate and disruptive to some major area of their lives. As with social anxiety and panic disorders, therapies to improve emotional regulation, such as CBT and DBT, can help the individual break unhealthy perseverations and obsessive thought patterns.

Family systems therapy and other interventions that involve the attachment figure in question are also useful for separation anxiety disorder. If a client presents with a need for family work, the social worker should discuss making a referral. If a client has been working with a social worker for a significant time as an individual, referring her to another practitioner for family work may be in her best interest. Serving as both an individual and family social worker can create dynamics within family sessions that threaten alliance and outcome.

Clients can engage their families in the necessary work by including them in individual therapy to complete assessments or facilitate difficult conversations. In this way, the social worker can empower clients while continuing to maintain the therapeutic relationship. Social workers can also coach their clients to have these conversations at home through role-play during sessions.

Practice Question

3. Which of the following BEST describes panic disorder?
   A) emotional dysregulation in response to feeling watched or judged by others in social settings
   B) being debilitated by flashbacks
   C) attacks of overwhelming panic and constant anticipatory fear of experiencing an attack
   D) chronic worry about real or imagined separation from major attachment figures

Stress

Many effective tools for stress management are widely available thanks to technological advances and cultural interest in mental health and self-care. Typically, **stress management** refers to increasing behaviors or skills that can be implemented throughout the day or at designated times to alleviate the symptoms of stress.

Stress management can help decrease elevated levels of cortisol. Decreasing cortisol is achieved by activating the parasympathetic nervous system and has the following outcomes:

- improved sleep
- the prevention of heart disease
- immune system boost

Relaxation techniques tend to center around cultivating the following:

- deep-breathing skills
- mindfulness
- meditation practices
- somatic relaxation (such as progressive muscle relaxation)

Practice Question

4. Clinicians can help clients decrease stress by teaching and coaching them to use skills such as the following:
    A) labeling feelings
    B) distress tolerance
    C) progressive muscle relaxation
    D) all of the above

Grief and Loss

Grief refers to the state of being that results from experiencing the loss of a meaningful person or relationship. While the ways an individual experiences grief can generally be defined by culture, personality, psychology, and spirituality, people ultimately express grief in intensely personal and varied ways. The widely accepted stages of grief are

- denial/shock
- guilt/pain
- anger/bargaining
- depression
- acceptance/integration

It was once believed that these stages occurred in succession; however, people tend to experience these stages in cycles that take various lengths of time and can repeat or restart. For example, an individual may jump from denial to anger, return to pain, move toward acceptance and then back to denial within a day. Or an individual may stay in denial for months at a time and experience other feelings subconsciously or in an otherwise repressed state.

Denial is a protective state that allows people experiencing overwhelming pain to feel a window of tolerance so they can function in their daily lives; however, denial can serve as a subterfuge and facilitate a lack of emotional awareness in other areas of life. Sometimes, those experiencing early stages of grief report feeling "fine" and do not feel they have changed since their loss. Still, spouses or family members may notice changes in behavior, such as increased isolation or mood lability.

If people in denial are truly struggling to experience and express their feelings, they can become defensive toward situations or people who encourage vulnerability. A safe space can feel like a threat when the feelings being denied are too painful. Denial can become a dangerous pressure cooker of resentment or fear that then motivates maladaptive coping skills or masking behaviors, such as using alcohol/drugs, misrepresenting feelings, and avoiding social connections.

Group therapy can be an effective treatment for those who share a common loss. For example, a group for recently divorced people or for parents who lost children can allow these individuals to process their grief together. Group therapy allows clients to create and maintain relationships in the aftermath of losing important connections.

Isolation results from the masking behaviors associated with denial in the grief process. In isolation, the other stages of grief can become harder to manage. Whether one is dealing with anger, depression, pain,

or guilt, connecting with others who are also experiencing similar stages allows those difficult feelings to be acknowledged and mindfully dealt with rather than ignored and perpetuated.

Complicated grief is also known as **persistent complex bereavement disorder (PCBD)** and can be diagnosed when the grieving process significantly impairs the individual's functioning six months after the loss. PCBD can result from a lack of supportive environment; in other words, an environment that promotes isolation and repression will likely extend the process of bereavement.

Traumatic losses, such as the violent death of a loved one, witnessing the death of a loved one, or experiencing multiple deaths in a short period can lead to PCBD. A history of mental illness or substance use can also interfere with the normal process of healing grief, which then results in complications. These complications can include symptoms that are typical in depressive episodes, such as suicidality, emotional numbness, and loss of interest in hobbies.

Practice Question

5. Which of the following BEST describes grief?
    A) Grief is the same for all human beings.
    B) Grief is best dealt with alone.
    C) Grief is easier to process when there is an underlying mental illness.
    D) Grief is the emotional experience that comes after loss.

Effects of Displacement

Out-of-Home Placement

Out-of-home placement can occur expectedly or unexpectedly; either way, it causes significant disruption in a client's life and on a client's system. The effects of the disruption vary. Some out-of-home displacements occur due to a traumatic event, so consideration for the consequences of that trauma needs to be added to the issues associated with out-of-home displacement. Additionally, the age of the person displaced also makes a difference in that children will experience different effects than adults. Regardless of the cause, the stages of grief and mourning will be associated with any kind of significant life disruption as well as the stress that goes along with it. What follows is a discussion of several types of out-of-home displacement and how they impact the client and client system.

Hospitalization

When **hospitalization** is planned, the client system is less disrupted than when it is unplanned or due to a traumatic accident, injury, or disease. The length of hospital stay and the severity of the injury or disease are also factors. Hospitalization disrupts the normal family routine, strains interpersonal relationships within the family, and causes significant financial worries. There is also the uncertainty of whether the hospitalized person will recover or not and whether the individual has made his wishes known through advanced directives and a living will. In addition to the stages of grief and emotional reaction to what is happening, there may also be religious and spiritual issues that need to be addressed by the individual and the family. This could be related to why physical suffering or death occurs and how to deal with it. Social workers can help families in these situations by providing therapy interventions, connecting them to social support, and helping them navigate the legalities and complexities of the health care and insurance systems.

Foster Care

Foster care is an out-of-home placement for children. One of the most common reasons for out-of-home placement in foster care is due to parental substance use. Other cases are due to child abuse or neglect. In most cases, the children placed in foster care are removed from unsafe, unstable homes and placed into safer, more stable homes. The children may have experienced trauma, and they may have difficulties trusting adults or caregivers, which can add a dynamic to the foster families that can make life challenging. Even if the children's homes of origin were unsafe or unstable, it was normal for them; foster care takes these children out of everything that is familiar to them and places them somewhere they are unfamiliar with, that is uncomfortable, and that is completely foreign to them. In some ways, foster care placement is double trauma for children and can cause significant changes in mental and emotional health as well as behavioral issues. This can impact children in terms of family and social relationships as well as academic achievement. Additionally, children placed in foster care are at risk of abuse within the foster system.

Foster care situations can involve reunification with the child's birth parents, adoption by the foster family, or aging out of the foster care system. Children who age out of the foster care system are more likely to have negative outcomes, whereas those who stay within foster families are more likely to have positive outcomes. Social workers are integral to helping children adjust to their new family environments as well as educating the family about how the out-of-home displacement affects children and how to help children adjust.

Residential Care

Residential care can include treatment for severe mental illness, eating disorders, substance use, or juvenile delinquency. Again, these can be planned or unplanned, for children or adults, with potential positive and negative outcomes. Either way, the family system becomes disrupted by the absence of the family member, and adjustment becomes necessary. There may also be changes in family dynamics and emotional connections.

Incarceration

Whether **incarceration** occurs to a juvenile or an adult family member, this causes significant changes in the family system that last far beyond the person's release. Changes to the system include significant disruptions in spousal and parent-child relationships. Furthermore, there is the social stigma attached to incarceration that can impact the ability of a family to secure housing and employment.

Practice Question

6. Which out-of-home displacement situation creates a double trauma?
   A) incarceration
   B) hospitalization
   C) residential care
   D) foster care

Out-of-Home Displacement

Natural disasters include hurricanes, floods, fires, earthquakes, and other disasters. Some result in death and injury. Displacement due to natural disasters affects clients and client systems in addition to the effects of trauma. For example, the loss of material possessions adds another dimension to the trauma of no longer having a safe space to call home, the damage to the community, and sharing the loss with others.

In some cases, the sharing of loss and the gathering of people who come to help can be a positive experience, but there is also the increased risk of people taking advantage of the vulnerable. People are also affected by the way in which governmental systems respond to the disaster and whether they are offered financial and economic assistance to rebuild.

Often, disadvantaged communities and low-income areas suffer the most because they are less likely to have insurance to cover their losses. When this occurs, there are issues related to equity, justice, and fairness.

If rebuilding is impossible, people must completely relocate to another geographic location. This can add a completely new dimension of stress and adjustment to an already stressful situation. Many people struggle with fear that a disaster will happen again and with the concept of not being in control and not being able to prevent natural disasters from happening.

Many people who are **homeless** have mental health or substance use issues that are left unaddressed either due to the client's choice or because of other circumstances. Furthermore, homelessness includes families who are living in hotels, motels, and with family or friends. While they may not be considered technically homeless, they do not have access to a stable and secure home environment, which is almost as stressful as living on the street.

People experiencing homelessness face stigma, discrimination, and oppression which can compound the stress related to not having a secure or stable environment. Children who are homeless are more likely to experience malnutrition and underachieve in school.

In **immigration**, people move to a new country—from an environment of familiarity to one that is completely foreign:

- Immigrants may not speak the language or understand the culture of the new country.
- For some immigrants, the process of moving is fraught with danger, including increased risks of assault, theft, sexual assault, and rape.
- Some immigrants fall prey to human trafficking.
- Women and children are more likely to experience domestic violence relationships.
- Some immigrants are separated from their family members who would normally fulfill the roles of social support.

Some immigrants, particularly those who are undocumented, fear reporting mistreatment or crimes to law enforcement or government entities because they believe doing so will lead to deportation. This means that employers can take advantage of immigrants who want to work.

Social workers who work with immigrants need to understand the immigration system so they can explain it to clients, and they need to articulate to clients what their rights are and what services are available to them. Immigrants are often unfamiliar with social services in the new country and will need assistance navigating them.

Practice Question

7. Which aspect of immigration creates a barrier between individuals who need help and the social services that can help them?
    A) work and transportation
    B) lack of health insurance
    C) separation from family
    D) fear of deportation

Trauma-Informed Care

Theories of Trauma-Informed Care

Trauma-informed care is a guiding philosophy and framework of service provision where the recognition of the pervasiveness of trauma is evident in all aspects of care. For example, it should inform how the physical environment is set up, the methods of assessment, the providers, and the interactions with clients and their supportive others. Additionally, a trauma-informed provider recognizes that there may be situations that could be triggering for a client or colleague and tries to avoid engaging in behaviors that could re-traumatize someone. In general, there are **six guiding principles** of trauma-informed care:

- safety
- trustworthiness and transparency
- peer support
- collaboration and mutuality
- cultural/historical/gender issues

The principle of **safety** refers to physical safety as well as mental and emotional safety. In the physical environment, this might be evident in certain factors:

- the security of the provider's location
- the availability of separate waiting areas for people who need them
- limiting the use of identifying information in public areas of the provider's location
- privacy in all aspects of care

In terms of assessment and therapy, this means making sure that the clients feel safe with the providers they are assigned to. If they do not feel safe with someone, the provider must have options available for them to easily request someone else.

Finally, safety in terms of interactions with the client and supportive others means strict adherence to confidentiality and transparency in terms of whom the information is shared with and how, as well as what is shared with others on behalf of the client.

The principles of **trustworthiness and transparency** intersect with safety. Organizationally, trustworthiness and transparency mean that the staff and providers conduct themselves professionally and honor the client's autonomy. The procedures used in the agency are transparent to the clients, and all providers abide by those policies. Honesty and integrity are important aspects of this principle.

Peer support highlights the importance of social support. Social support can occur in a therapeutic setting, or it can occur in an informal setting.

Collaboration and mutuality build on the general professional ethic of providing client-centered care and making sure that the client is involved in all aspects of treatment.

Empowerment and choice are derived from the assumption that people who have experienced trauma did not have a choice and were powerless when the trauma occurred. In the therapeutic setting then, it is imperative that the clients get the message that they are in control of what occurs and they can make choices for their lives as they see fit.

Finally, the provider and the agency understand that various **cultural, historical, and gender issues** contribute to the client's experience of trauma. This also means that during therapy, the social worker should bring attention to these issues if the client chooses to address them.

Agencies should give training and education to providers so they can stay current on trauma-informed care and other issues that may be relevant to their clients. Agencies should recognize the impact that trauma can have on their employees as well.

Working with clients who experience the consequences of trauma can be very stressful, emotionally draining, and challenging to manage. Many social workers experience symptoms of compassion fatigue and secondary trauma that can occur as a result of working with people with trauma histories. Symptoms of burnout include:

- decreased concentration
- sadness
- guilt
- anger
- shame
- sleep changes
- behavioral changes
- physical health issues
- increased irritability
- burnout toward work.

Helpful Hint
See Chapter 13 for more on self-care for social workers.

These symptoms mirror those of their clients and are a significant cause of social workers leaving the profession. Trauma-informed providers and agencies recognize the importance of looking for signs of these issues in each other, promoting self-care, and empowering providers to take time off when they need it.

The Substance Abuse and Mental Health Services Administration's (SAMHSA) six guiding principles to trauma-informed care are listed in Figure 7.2.

Practice Question

8. A woman who comes to therapy for help with a domestic violence situation does not want to press charges against her husband or leave him right now. Which trauma-informed care principle should the social worker apply in responding that the woman does not have to do that unless she chooses to?
   A) empowerment and choice
   B) cultural issues
   C) peer support
   D) safety

Methods and Approaches to Trauma-Informed Care

There are four basic components of a trauma-informed approach (the "four Rs"):

1. realization about trauma and how it can affect people and groups
2. recognizing the signs of trauma
3. responding to trauma with a capable system
4. resisting re-traumatization

Realization about trauma and how it can affect people and groups is an approach that requires social workers to be educated about the various types of trauma, how the types of trauma can impact people at various stages of development, and the current research about trauma.

Realization also means keeping updated on information about current events and trends in what people are experiencing and what may cause them to experience the consequences of trauma. Examples include:

- the increased rate of migration and human trafficking
- the increase in criminal activity like carjackings and riots
- the increased deaths related to substance misuse, especially fentanyl

In addition, there may be cultural differences in the way that people react to trauma, and social workers need to be informed about that. For example, some cultures expect people who served in the military to not be affected by killing or watching people die and believe that to admit symptoms of trauma is to fail as a human being, which adds another dynamic to the traumatic experience.

New research is always emerging about new methods of treatment intervention. Social workers need to keep updated on those methods as well as the research that provides data about the evidence for them. This also includes knowing what types of interventions are appropriate for which types of trauma or populations. For example, eye movement desensitization and reprocessing (EMDR) is an evidenced-based intervention; however, it not only requires additional training and certification to use it, but it is also not indicated for every type of trauma.

Social workers should **recognize the signs of trauma**. People deal with trauma differently and rarely present as a concise bundle of symptoms. Additionally, the different types of trauma that people experience will produce different types of signs and symptoms.

For example, PTSD related to combat will look very different from someone who endured years of sexual assault as a child. Both are traumatic, but the symptoms each client will present with will be very different. Social workers educate themselves about the different types of trauma and the problems they cause, including those that may be masked as something else.

Responding to trauma with a capable system means being able to offer clients the type of treatment and support they need by ensuring that the agency providing care is doing so in a trauma-informed manner.

A social worker who works with people who have experienced trauma will maintain referral connections with other agencies or providers that their clients might need, such as:

- domestic violence shelters where they can send clients who need immediate residential care
- substance use services
- physical health services
- psychiatric services.

Additional systems such as housing, employment, childcare, and criminal justice may also be within the social worker's network so that when clients need help from those other systems, referrals can be made without significant disruption to clients.

Resisting re-traumatization means minimizing the chance that engagement in services or therapy will make a person's trauma symptoms worse. Social workers should be attentive to

- client safety
- client autonomy
- client power.

For example, the social worker could silence her phone, preventing a phone alarm from sounding during a session and causing a client to startle or panic. Another example is not telling clients what to do about a situation, but instead educating them about their options and allowing them to choose. This also means doing therapy at the client's speed.

Finally, a social worker using a trauma-informed approach with these principles in mind will be transparent with clients and educate them about what they are experiencing. For example, a social worker can explain why a client with years of childhood sexual abuse feels like he cannot trust anyone by framing the trauma in developmental terms. Or a social worker can explain the different therapeutic interventions available, how they work, why they work, and then ask the client how she feels about that as an intervention.

Practice Question

9. A woman brings her 4-year-old child to therapy and says she cannot understand what is going on with him. He has regressed to bed-wetting, does not want to be left at grandma's house, and throws multiple temper tantrums per day. Which of the four Rs would be appropriate in this situation?
   A) resisting re-traumatization
   B) responding to trauma
   C) recognizing signs of trauma
   D) realization of trauma's effects

Crisis Intervention Theories

Conflict and Crisis

Constructive confrontation is a helpful therapeutic tool social workers use to call attention to the client's behaviors and feelings in the present moment, especially when there is incongruity. This method is useful to confront transference and defense mechanisms.

For example, if a client is talking about something distressing but is smiling or laughing, the social worker might stop the client and share his observation about her behavior. By confronting the client about the difference between the painful experience she is discussing and the outward emotional expression, the social worker can guide her to increased self-awareness and, possibly, some insight.

Everyone's interpretation of a crisis is different. Social workers cannot rely solely on their own judgment. Potential crisis situations can include:

- suicide risk
- self-harm
- danger to self
- danger to others
- interpersonal violence
- situational violence
- a health emergency for self or loved ones
- sudden changes in education, employment, or housing
- natural disasters

- accidents
- a sudden change in relationship status
- psychotic episodes
- substance use lapse
- sudden strong mood changes, such as mania or depression

Safety planning is a client-led process whereby the social worker and the client discuss

- what determines a crisis
- what the client will do in a crisis
- whom the client will reach out to in a crisis
- under what conditions outside help will be sought.

> **Helpful Hint**
>
> Risk assessment should occur at intake and periodically throughout the therapeutic relationship.

Depending on the client's situation, a safety plan will be put in writing so that the client and social worker can each keep a copy and the client can share the plan with others who will be involved in the plan. As clients progress through treatment, their needs will change, so safety plans should be revisited and revised over the course of treatment. Safety plans include the following information:

- how to tell if the client is in crisis
- whom to call when the client is in crisis
- whom not to call when the client is in crisis
- what supporters should do
- what supporters should not do
- under what circumstances to call for outside help
- which outside help to call
- how to tell when the client is no longer in crisis

> **Did You Know?**
>
> Social workers must establish boundaries in crisis planning; some clients use crisis situations to seek attention from social workers.

Social workers need to keep boundaries with clients and ensure that they understand when it is appropriate to contact the social worker when in crisis and when to call others. Most counties in the United States have a crisis hotline; some have hotlines specific to sexual assault and domestic violence. If a social worker is employed by a community mental health agency, the organization will likely have emergency and crisis policies in place for clients.

Practice Question

10. During a session, a client has tears in her eyes while discussing her mother. She screams at the social worker, "I don't care what my mother thinks!" What therapeutic tool can the social worker use to help the client process her outburst?
    A) summary reflection
    B) positive reframing
    C) constructive confrontation
    D) empathetic attunement

Conflict Resolution Strategies

Some strategies to resolve conflict include conflict avoidance, giving in, standing one's ground, compromising, and collaborating:

- **Conflict avoidance** involves not acknowledging the conflict.

- **Giving in** means acquiescing to the other party, thereby giving her what she wants or letting her have her way.

- **Standing one's ground** is a way of competing with the opposing party in the hopes that he does not win the battle.

- **Compromising** involves seeking out common ground as a stepping-stone to negotiating and resolving the conflict.

- **Collaborating** consists of actively listening to the opposing party's perspective, discussing areas of like-mindedness and common objectives, and confirming that both parties understand each other's viewpoints.
    - This strategy is sometimes difficult, but it can be rewarding when it is effective.

Practice Question

11. Jolie manages a department in a mental health clinic. Mary, one of her employees, is constantly at odds with Nicole, another employee. Mary has seniority over Nicole but is not her direct supervisor. Mary wants Jolie to write Nicole up for disrespecting her. Jolie listens to both sides but takes no action and goes about her work as if no conflict has occurred. What type of conflict resolution strategy is Jolie employing?
    A) compromising
    B) conflict avoidance
    C) giving in
    D) collaboration

Answer Key

1. B: The sympathetic nervous system is part of the autonomic nervous system which reacts to sensory stimuli to activate and thus requires sensory stimuli to deactivate.

2. A: Performing compulsive rituals to control obsessive thoughts is a diagnostic criterion for obsessive-compulsive disorder (OCD), not generalized anxiety disorder (GAD). Anxiety disorder may present with either obsessive thoughts or perseverative behaviors, but rituals that are specifically motivated by a misguided attempt to control anxiety are characteristic of OCD.

3. C: Panic disorder is characterized by sudden attacks of overwhelming panic and fear of having an attack.

4. D: Labeling feelings, distress tolerance skills, and progressive muscle relaxation are all techniques social workers can use to help clients decrease stress.

5. D: Grief is best described as the emotional experience that comes after loss. People manifest, process, and experience grief differently.

6. D: Foster care is considered double trauma because of the trauma the children endured in their families of origin plus the trauma associated with being placed with families unknown to them.

7. D: Immigrants perceive any organization or government agency as an entity that can get them deported, which prevents them from seeking services.

8. A: The social worker can walk the woman through her options, but the choice must be the client's; thus, the social worker upholds the principle of empowerment and choice.

9. C: In very young children, the behavior changes described can indicate the potential of sexual abuse.

10. C: The social worker can use constructive confrontation to draw the client's attention to the discrepancy between the words she is speaking and the visible emotion she is displaying.

11. B: Jolie is practicing conflict avoidance by pretending that no conflict has happened.

8. Intervention Processes

Planning Treatment Strategies

Evidence-Based Practice

Evidence-based practice describes methods and interventions used by social workers that are supported by research and professional best practices.

Evidence-based practice creates a standard of client care, beginning with a comprehensive assessment of the client's presenting problems. That assessment informs a diagnosis, which must be backed up with evidence that the client meets the criteria, including formal assessments and clinical interviews. The diagnosis then informs the treatment plan, which consists of a list of goals and objectives for addressing the symptoms associated with the diagnosis.

$$\text{assessment} \longrightarrow \frac{\text{diagnosis}}{\text{formal assessments + clinical interviews}} \longrightarrow \text{treatment plan}$$

Figure 8.1. Evidence-Based Practice

To meet the goals and objectives, the social worker uses evidence-based therapeutic interventions supported by research as valid approaches for that specific diagnosis.

Social workers are expected to abide by evidence-based practices while also ensuring they receive the proper training to implement the evidence-based interventions.

There are many evidence-based manualized treatments that target specific diagnoses and specific clients, which present treatment interventions with step-by-step modules that social workers can use with clients to ensure program fidelity or adherence to proper use of the intervention.

Evidence-based practice holds social workers to a professional standard of care. It also builds public trust between the therapy profession and potential clients. Social workers should therefore not use treatment intervention methods that are not supported by research for a particular diagnosis.

Practice Question

1. Evidence-based practice includes standards of care informed by research that begins with which of the following?
    A) comprehensive assessment of a client that yields a diagnosis.
    B) determining which treatment a client needs
    C) consultation with the client's previous providers
    D) researching available treatments for the client's diagnosis

Care Planning

Planning a treatment strategy is vital for achieving the client's goals. The social worker will use the list of needs discovered from the client assessment to create a care plan. A good **care plan** will include:

- the problem noted
- the goal to be achieved
- objectives for achieving the goal
- interventions the social worker will use
- a timeline for achieving objectives and goals
- an evaluation of the intervention.

The **main components** of a treatment plan include:

- a brief client background
- diagnosis
- problem list
- treatment goals
- objectives
- interventions
- timeline
- method of evaluation
- tracking progress.

The following **strategies**, which are plans for action, draw on and overlap with the main components of a treatment plan and drive treatment planning:

- The **diagnosis** acts as the anchor for the treatment plan. Every step in the treatment plan must address the diagnosis in some way.

- The **problem list** details the problems described by the client related to the diagnosis. There will likely be more than one, and there may even be multiple problems for each diagnosis. The problem list must follow the diagnosis.

- **Treatment goals** are the broad statements of what the client wants to achieve in therapy; they must relate to the diagnosis.

- **Objectives** are the steps taken to achieve the client's goals, as outlined in the treatment goals. Just as the goals directly relate to the diagnosis, so too do the objectives.

- **Interventions** are the clinical therapeutic techniques the social worker plans to use with the client. These must be evidence-based interventions appropriate for the diagnosis, such as cognitive behavioral therapy (CBT) for anxiety, dialectical behavior therapy (DBT) for borderline personality disorder, or exposure therapy for phobias. The social worker must be adequately trained to provide any chosen interventions.

- **Timeline** refers to the projected amount of necessary time expected to meet the objectives.

- **Method of evaluation** details how the client's progress will be measured.

- **Tracking progress** includes keeping notes related to the client's achievement of the objectives and goals in the treatment plan. If the client does not show progress, the social worker and client may consider adjusting the treatment plan.

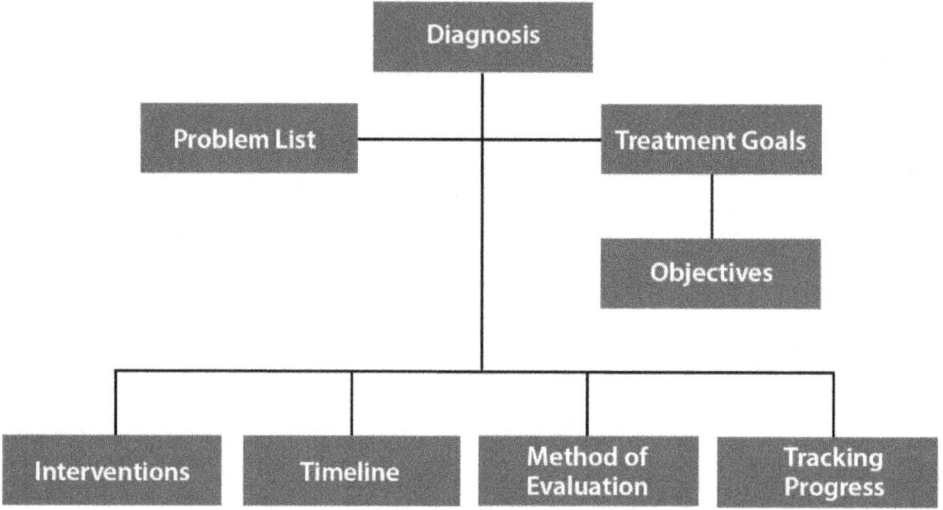

The treatment plan should be reviewed and revised regularly; the schedule and frequency for review depend on both the agency and state regulations. Some states require that agencies providing mental health services review and revise treatment plans formally every thirty days or every four to six sessions. Those reviews must be documented in the client's file. Additionally, some states require an agency's program directors to regularly review client files, sometimes as often as quarterly. This varies based on state law and the type of service provider.

If a state or agency does not provide these guidelines, it is up to the social worker to determine the review schedule based on the frequency of sessions and client needs. It is generally appropriate to review and revise every four to six sessions. Other circumstances may inspire a review and revision of the treatment plan, including

- if the client experiences a crisis
- a change in diagnosis
- if a new problem arises
- if the client solves a stated problem outside of therapy
- if the client is not making progress with current interventions.

Practice Question

2. Which component of the treatment plan acts as an anchor for directing the rest of the plan?
   A) diagnosis
   B) goals
   C) interventions
   D) timeline

Collaborative Care

Collaboration means working with clients, families, colleagues, and other care providers to support clients in meeting their goals. The goal of **care coordination**, or **collaborative care**, is to achieve safe, effective care through the deliberate organization of client care activities within the interdisciplinary team. Social workers may collaborate with medical staff or other professionals in a variety of contexts:

- inpatient treatment settings
- outpatient programs
- schools
- child protective services
- the criminal justice system
- drug courts
- mental health courts
- disability services
- housing case management
- veterans' services

Some examples of care coordination include:

- sharing knowledge within the health care team (in a clinical setting)
- aligning resources with clients' emotional and social needs
- setting clients up with community resources
- reporting on program compliance
- sharing client progress related to stated goals
- reporting effects of other interventions (e.g., medications or case management) that are reported in therapy

Collaboration with other care providers requires a client's written consent. Ethical conduct requires a social worker to be transparent about what is shared with other providers. Ideally, clients would be involved in any care collaboration meetings, but if they are not, the social worker should tell the clients what information was shared about them. Social workers should also collaborate with other providers and client support systems. A collaborative social worker

- is willing to be mentored, coached, or taught
- is open to team members' contributions
- participates in health care meetings to discuss practice issues/care activities
- reaches out to mentor others and continues self-learning by a willingness to be taught
- facilitates care delivery discussions and practice decisions
- optimizes diverse resources and promotes client/family outcomes through inclusivity
- cooperates in maintaining documentation and reporting
- participates in discussions regarding ethics and cultural competence
- educates other providers about the therapy process and the role of the social worker

During this process, the social worker should collaborate with the client to establish treatment goals and objectives. Clients should be involved in all care decisions.

Clients come to therapy with a presenting problem, but as the social worker conducts intake and assessment, it is important to check in with the client to confirm that the client agrees with the diagnosis. This ensures that the social worker is correctly interpreting what the client says. The social worker begins with the end in mind. Important questions to ask the client include the following:

- "How will you know when you are better?"
- "How will you know when the issue is no longer a problem for you?"

These questions give the social worker insight into what the client considers to be the goal and how the client will measure progress. As goals are discussed, the social worker should also outline other services or resources that could help the client achieve his goals.

For example, if the client is depressed because he is in a dead-end job, the social worker might ask him if he feels vocational assessment and training would be helpful. If the client agrees, the social worker can assist with a referral. Ultimately, the client must agree with treatment goals and objectives, or the treatment plan will not be effective.

When determining the treatment plan goals and objectives, an important topic is the integration and maintenance of therapeutic progress. In other words, how will the client and the social worker know that the client is making progress, and what steps can the client take to maintain that progress? Again, this should be an ongoing process.

A social worker's scope of practice is limited to psychological well-being; however, there may be times when a client's psychological well-being is impacted by factors that require concurrent treatment. As a social worker completes a thorough assessment, problems will be identified, including some that are not appropriate for a social worker to address but that impact a client's mental health. **Concurrent treatment** needs may include:

- psychiatric medication
- physical therapy

- vocational training
- occupational therapy
- housing therapy
- case management
- medical care.

Practice Question

3. A client asks for a specific type of therapy that one of her friends experienced. During the assessment, the social worker determines that the requested intervention is not appropriate for this client's diagnosis. How should the social worker respond?
   A) Do the therapy because the client requested it.
   B) Come up with a diagnosis that fits so the intervention can be done.
   C) Ignore the client's request and tell her that the social worker chooses interventions.
   D) Explain why the intervention is not appropriate for the client and suggest one that is.

Multicultural Considerations

A multicultural social worker keeps treatment focused on clients/client systems and their needs. Additionally, social workers pursue knowledge of cultural issues by learning about the populations they may encounter within their communities. This means that they learn about the general values, beliefs, and behavioral norms of each group. Acquisition of knowledge leads to awareness of:

- the social worker's own cultural biases
- the social worker's attitudes toward people of different cultural groups
- the attitudes of various cultural groups toward each other.

Acquiring knowledge enables the social worker to put knowledge and awareness into practice with clients by:

- asking about cultural issues during the assessment process
- creating a safe environment for the client to discuss cultural issues.

Refugees and both documented and undocumented immigrants face many challenges in their day-to-day lives. Knowledge of these challenges will help social workers provide adequate support for this vulnerable population.

Refugee and immigrant populations are extremely vulnerable to exploitation, which can take many forms: employment exploitation, forced criminal activity, or participation in sex trafficking—to name a few. This population may not speak English well enough to understand labor and employment laws in the United States. They may rely on someone who does not prioritize or value their best interests or quality of life.

Refugee and immigrant populations are also at risk of poverty and discrimination. They will, most likely, live in poor housing conditions, work low-wage jobs, and lack access to health services. They may be subject to discrimination due to the language barrier and the generally negative perception of undocumented immigrants in the US. The language barrier encourages immigrants to live together, so they

may form communities in which they feel comfortable; however, this further exacerbates the stigma surrounding immigrants.

These populations are least likely to have the means to access health care services. They are more likely to work low-wage or cash-pay jobs, where employer-sponsored health insurance is not provided. Without health insurance or discretionary income, they have no way of paying for healthcare, and thus are more likely to suffer significant health issues. Refugees and immigrants are also likely to struggle with trauma from their migration journey to the United States.

In some states, Medicaid and CHIP may be available for all who qualify as low-income, with no restrictions on immigration status. There is no federal law that guarantees this access; if there was such a law or program, it would likely be avoided by the populations that need it most. Fear of deportation encourages great distrust in government-associated programs.

Practice Question

4. Which of the following approaches could a multicultural social worker use to reach people in the community who are undocumented?
    A) advertise services on social media in the community's language
    B) partner with someone from that community who can act as a liaison
    C) go to the community and conduct a public workshop
    D) set up an information booth at a local hospital

Interviewing the Client

Initial Interview and Interviewing Techniques

The purpose of a client interview is for the social worker to collect relevant health information to determine if the client is appropriate for a particular level of care and to begin developing the treatment plan.

For the **initial interview**, the social worker will meet with the client individually. Before beginning, the social worker should discuss confidentiality and situations during which confidentiality might be broken. The underlying goal of any interview is to assess the client's concerns and work toward developing an appropriate treatment plan.

A key reason to conduct the **initial interview** is for the social worker to establish a rapport with the client. Establishing a **rapport** means building trust and understanding. A strong social worker-client rapport means that the client will feel more comfortable with the social worker and offer more information.

Asking **open-ended questions** allows the client to lead the conversation in a way that is specific to him and his experiences. Open-ended questions teach the social worker more about the client than "yes" and "no" questions. For example, asking a client, "Tell me about your family," will reveal more information than "Do you have any children?" Thoughtful, open-ended questions start a conversation.

Motivational interviewing (MI) strategies can be used with clients who are resistant and unsure about engaging in treatment. MI skills include:

- open-ended questions

- reflective listening
- summarizing statements.

Using these strategies can help create an environment where clients feel more comfortable talking about their concerns.

> **Helpful Hint**
>
> Social workers should be mindful of their body language while a client is sharing. If a client feels uncomfortable or as though she is being judged, she is more likely to stop sharing openly.

At the end of the interview, the social worker should summarize the gathered information and highlight important points for the client to ensure that nothing was missed. The client should be informed of the next steps, given an opportunity to ask questions, and given the social worker's contact information.

In behavioral health interviewing, the client may have amental disability that prevents productive interviewing. A family member or guardian may assist in obtaining all pertinent information to establish a care plan. This can also include children who need mental health treatment. The care plan will be the foundation to develop a treatment strategy with achievable goals for the client.

Practice Question

5. In which situation should a social worker use motivational interviewing strategies?
    A) The client is lacking external motivation for treatment.
    B) The client has been hesitant but is answering questions truthfully.
    C) The client is unsure if she needs to make a change in her life.
    D) The client sought treatment because he is concerned about his mental health.

Structured Clinical Interview

A structured clinical interview is part of a client's initial intake exam. It is primarily conducted through **client self-report**, which describes when the client describes his symptoms to the social worker based on questions the social worker asks.

There are some standardized structured clinical interviews, like the **Structured Clinical Interview for *DSM-5* (SCID-5)**. The SCID-5 is most commonly used in research settings to screen participants for certain diagnoses that would disqualify them from participating in the study. There are four main reasons to use the SCID-5:

1. to evaluate for all the major DSM-5 diagnoses
2. to select the population for a study
3. to identify current and past mental health concerns within a study's population
4. to help students and new mental health professionals improve their clinical interviewing skills

Currently, the SCID-5 is only approved for use with adults over the age of eighteen. Some clinics use the SCID-5 as part of their clinical intake; others use their own version of structured questions, or even use an unstructured format. In either case, the goal is to provide a set list of questions (some open-ended) that

can be used to screen for and rule out diagnoses and presenting issues in clients. There are ten core diagnoses covered in the SCID-5:

1. mood episodes, cyclothymic disorder, persistent depressive disorder, and premenstrual dysphoric disorder

2. psychotic and associated symptoms

3. differential diagnosis of psychotic disorders

4. differential diagnosis of mood disorders

5. substance use disorders

6. anxiety disorder

7. obsessive-compulsive and related disorders

8. feeding and eating disorders

9. externalizing disorders

10. trauma-and stressor-related disorders

The SCID-5 is a comprehensive assessment that can take anywhere from fifteen minutes to several hours. Because it primarily relies on self-report, it may not be an appropriate assessment tool for individuals with significant intellectual issues or an inability to self-report for other reasons (e.g., poor language ability or highly disorganized thought).

Helpful Hint

In general, it is not considered best practice to diagnose from only one meeting or assessment. Diagnosis can be ongoing, especially with more complex cases. A diagnosis can change if new information emerges.

During a structured clinical interview, the social worker relies on both formal and informal observations. A **formal observation** includes items like the content of the responses the client gives to questions.

Informal observations include the client's body language, affect, and the emotive quality of the client's behavior. Interactional dynamics are an important part of informal observations. **Interactional dynamics** can include not only how a client is interacting with family members during a session but also how she speaks about friends, colleagues, and family members, and even how she interacts with the social worker.

The goal of a structured clinical interview is not to determine a firm diagnosis but rather to have a working diagnostic theory, a good understanding of the client's presenting problem and any environmental factors contributing to the problem, and the foundations for building a treatment plan with the client.

Cultural competence is a key concern in structured clinical interviews. A client who has visions or hears voices that are related to religion or culture should not be diagnosed with hallucinations, especially when these are corroborated by the client's community. Knowing diagnostic standards for cultural differences and having a strong understanding of the client's background are essential for effective structured clinical interviewing.

Practice Question

6. Which of the following is key to a structured clinical interview?
   A) Collateral reports from family;
   B) Client self-report;
   C) Transtheoretical model;
   D) Client goals.

Other Types of Interviews

There are several specific types of interviews social workers can conduct:

- biopsychosocial interview
- diagnostic interview
- cultural formulation interview

Templates for guiding the interview and creating documentation exist for all these types of interviews.

> **Helpful Hint**
>
> During an initial interview, social workers can use any interview type.

A **biopsychosocial interview** studies the relationship between the client's biological, psychological, and social health:

- Biological effects can include medical health concerns, disabilities, and the effects of substance use.
- Psychological health refers to the client's mental health concerns and coping skills.
- Social health includes clients' relationships with others and their families.

A biopsychosocial interview shows the social worker how these three areas intertwine and impact the client's distress.

A **diagnostic interview** assesses specifically for potential mental health diagnoses. These interviews tend to be more structured to ensure that the necessary information is covered to make an accurate diagnosis.

The **cultural formulation interview (CFI)** is a sixteen-question assessment used to recognize the cultural impacts on a client while assessing for an appropriate diagnosis. The CFI uses open-ended questions to give the client space to talk about his concerns regarding the cultural norms he experiences.

An **unstructured interview** has no standardized questions. This allows the social worker to guide the interview in ways that the social worker believes will lead to the most relevant information. An unstructured interview often allows for a more open discussion about the client's concerns, goals, and motivations. The main topics covered in an unstructured clinical interview include:

- age and sex
- the reason for seeking therapy
- work and education history
- current social activities

- physical and mental health concerns, past and present
- current medications and any drug and/or alcohol use
- family history of mental health and physical health concerns
- the social worker's observations of client behavior during the session (e.g., anxious, detached, euthymic)

Practice Question

7. Which of the following is the BEST interview type to use with a new client in an outpatient mental health clinic?
    A) cultural formulation interview
    B) biopsychosocial interview
    C) diagnostic interview
    D) structured clinical interview

Establishing Goals

Breaking down the problem into meaningful parts helps demystify what clients experience and gives them the precursor to hope that their problems can be solved. The social worker guides clients in formulating a road map of where they are now and where they would like to be in the future. That road map becomes the client's goals. There are three main reasons to establish goals:

1. Goals offer hope to clients by creating a plan for what they want to achieve.
2. Goal-setting complies with the medical model of care.
3. Goals demonstrate how therapy will help a client with a presenting problem.

Setting Attainable Goals

Within the goal-setting process, the social worker helps clients identify **strengths** and resources that can help them attain their goals. Strengths are found at the individual, relational, social, and environmental levels.

Table 8.1. Client Strengths

Individual	Relational	Social	Environmental
positive self-esteem	supportive parent	belongs to a religious organization	lives close to services
willing to work hard	supportive significant other or friend	makes friends easily	access to the beach

Identifying **strengths** in the goal-setting process reminds clients of the resources that can help them achieve their goals. Some clients forget about these resources as they become overwhelmed by the presenting problem. Goals should be SMART: Specific, Measurable, Attainable, Realistic, Time Restricted. SMART goals are useful for clients for several reasons:

- They break problems into manageable pieces.
- Each goal includes actions to be taken.

- They set a client up for success.
- Success fuels hope, so as clients achieve each SMART goal, they feel empowered to pursue the next.
- They help clients track their progress.

Common client goals include the following:

- functional status (financial stability, employment)
- lifestyle factors (diet, exercise)
- relationships (improve communication, establish boundaries)
- coping skills (exercise instead of substances, journaling)
- changing thought patterns (gratitude journals, identifying cognitive distortions)
- managing emotions (controlling anger, allowing oneself to feel sad)

Table 8.2. Example of a SMART Goal	
Situation	A client worries all the time and excessively ruminates.
Diagnosis	generalized anxiety disorder
SMART goal	The client will reduce time spent on rumination from most of the day to thirty minutes per day within two weeks by writing in a daily worry journal.

Practice Question

8. A client presents for therapy because she is afraid of flying and must do so in three months to attend a family member's wedding. Due to family circumstances, she cannot skip the event. Which of the following represents a SMART goal?
   A) The client will process events from her childhood to find the root cause of her fear of flying.
   B) The client will participate in exposure therapy.
   C) The client will succeed in exposure therapy exercises once per week for six weeks.
   D) Over three sessions, the client will learn three relaxation skills that she can use to reduce her anxiety about flying from level 10 to level 4 or below.

Types of Goals

Short-term goals fall within a time frame of up to thirty days and build toward long-term goals. A short-term goal might be to download a mindfulness meditation app and use it once per day for a week to manage anxiety symptoms.

Long-term goals have an extended time frame of three months and beyond. For example, if someone has the aforementioned short-term goal, a long-term goal might be to reduce anxiety symptoms by 50 percent within six months based on the Beck Anxiety Inventory scores.

Short-term goals stack up to help the client achieve long-term goals, and all goals must be directly related to the diagnosis. The intake and assessment inform the social worker's collaborative process with the client to establish goals consistent with the diagnosis. For example, if the client presents with the problem of

anxiety that interferes with functioning, the social worker might have him take the Beck Anxiety Inventory (described in the section "Reviewing Progress"). Based on the scores, the social worker might ask him which symptoms he would like to work on first to set short-term goals based on his long-term goal of reducing anxiety.

Practice Question

9. A client needs to overcome her fear of flying to attend a family member's wedding in three months. Which of the following is a long-term goal?
   A) Use meditation apps once per day for one week.
   B) Attend all nine therapy sessions.
   C) Get on the plane and attend the family member's wedding in three months.
   D) Keep an anxiety journal for thirty days.

Reviewing Progress

Social workers understand that assessment and the **review of progress** of treatment goals occur at multiple levels:

- During the session, the social worker checks in with the client regularly to make sure she is comfortable with the intervention.
    - Client feedback will inform the social worker about the usefulness and appropriateness of the intervention as well as the client's reaction to it.

- At the end of each session, the social worker checks in with the client to determine
    - what the client got out of the session
    - whether it was helpful
    - what the client might do between sessions to continue the work

- Every four to six sessions or every thirty days, the social worker reviews the full treatment plan with the client to determine and document her progress.

- Each quarter or preauthorization period, the social worker reviews the full treatment plan with the client to determine and document her progress.

- At the end of the therapy relationship, the social worker and the client review progress and celebrate successes.

Assessment instrument results facilitate clients' decision-making by quantifying their symptoms. The Beck Anxiety Inventory (BAI) and the Beck Depression Inventory (BDI) measure symptoms of two common mental health concerns and are commonly used in mental health settings.

At intake, the client fills one out, and, based on the scores, the social worker and the client decide how to address the symptoms that scored the lowest. That serves as the starting point for goal-setting. (See Chapter 4 for more on assessment.) At the thirty-day review, the client takes the inventory again to determine how the symptoms have changed. If they have changed for the better, the client can see quantifiable evidence of her progress.

If, for example, the client scores very low on the sleeping pattern scale of the BDI at intake, the social worker may discuss with her how a short-term goal should focus on improving sleep. After thirty days of practicing the intervention, the client's BDI shows that the sleep pattern symptom of depression is no longer an issue, thus demonstrating that the intervention was successful.

Multiple **barriers** can affect the attainment of client goals:

- The client is mandated to treatment and resistant to change.
- The client lied about the problem and/or symptoms.
- The client is ambivalent about making changes to current behaviors.
- The client presents for one problem and does not want help with any others that may contribute to the presenting problem.
- Goals are too broad, vague, or unrealistic.
- Goals are not achievable or coordinated to help the client succeed.
- External factors in the client's life can interfere.
- The wrong intervention is used to help the client achieve her goals.

Practice Question

10. When should a social worker review a client's progress?
    A) on an ongoing basis and at regular review times
    B) at the client's request
    C) when the supervisor requests a review
    D) only at the end of treatment

Client Considerations

Understanding the Treatment Plan

Social workers use psychoeducation to **educate** clients about the value of complying with their treatment plans. **Therapy** is an evidence-based practice. Providing clients with psychoeducation helps to demystify the process and empower them to work toward recovery.

Many clients feel overwhelmed and helpless when they present for therapy. **Psychoeducation** helps to validate and normalize their experiences and gives them hope for recovery based on a clear plan. Methods for psychoeducation include the following:

- explaining to clients the purpose of the intake, clinical interview, and assessment process and how these relate to what will happen in therapy
- teaching clients about their diagnosis, what it means, and the evidence-based interventions that result in positive outcomes
- providing clients with a preview of how the interventions will work together to help them succeed with their treatment plans

- explaining how the treatment plan serves as a road map for them to see their progress over time

- following the treatment plan to help both client and social worker determine the effectiveness of interventions

- explaining to clients that treatment plans can be updated at regular review times

Practice Question

11. What purpose is served by educating clients about the value of complying with their treatment plans?
    A) It puts the responsibility of change on the client.
    B) It empowers clients by providing a clear plan for recovery.
    C) It releases the social worker from liability.
    D) It holds clients accountable.

Conditions for Learning

Adult learners have several distinct traits that social workers should consider while developing client education plans:

- Adult learners are **independent** and **self-directed**. Social workers should actively engage them in the learning process and encourage them to help develop their treatment plans.

- Adult learners are **results-oriented** and **practical**. Social workers should give them information that they can apply immediately.

- Adult learners may be **resistant to change** and will require justification for new behaviors.

- Adult learners may **learn more slowly** than younger learners; however, they may be more skilled at integrating new knowledge with previous experience.

Educational psychologist Benjamin Bloom described three domains of learning:

1. The **cognitive domain** includes collecting, synthesizing, and applying knowledge.

2. The **affective domain** involves emotions and attitudes, including the ability to be aware of emotions and respond to them.

3. The **psychomotor** domain relates to motor skills, including the ability to perform complex skills and create new movement patterns.

When educating clients, social workers should address all three learning domains. For example, a client who is learning about smoking cessation may need to be taught about the negative health impacts of smoking (cognitive domain), how to manage negative emotions related to quitting (affective domain), and how to correctly apply a nicotine patch (psychomotor domain).

To better educate, encourage, and advocate for clients, social workers should assess clients' sources of **motivation** in the context of managing their health:

- **Intrinsic motivation** is the desire to achieve a goal, seek challenges, or complete a task that is driven by enjoyment and personal satisfaction (like exercising because it is enjoyable).

- **Extrinsic motivation** is the desire to accomplish a goal that is driven by external rewards or punishment (such as exercising to prevent ill health).

> **Did You Know?**
>
> Client mental health literacy improves as clients become more involved in their own care.

Adult clients' **readiness to learn** can be shaped by many factors, including openness to new information; emotional response to illness (e.g., denial, anxiety); religious and cultural beliefs; and social support systems. However, just because a client learns the information does not mean her behaviors will change.

The social worker must assess the **functional status** of a client before developing an education plan for him. Doing so ensures that the plan aligns with the client's abilities and capacity to learn. Functional status is evaluated during the assessment with the Mental Status Exam.

Mental health literacy is the degree to which an individual can obtain, process, and understand basic information needed to make personal health decisions. Mental health literacy gives clients ownership over their recovery and empowers them to learn the skills necessary to care for themselves. People do not stay in therapy forever, so the more mental health literacy clients have, the better able they are to care for themselves after therapy ends.

Mental health literacy also helps clients communicate their needs to others who are supportive. For example, someone who improves his mental health literacy about his panic disorder can explain to a loved one how to help him if that person is present during a panic attack. Interventions for clients with low mental health literacy include:

- asking clients questions to assess their current knowledge
- using plain language and short sentences
- applying the knowledge to the client's situation
- limiting important points to three or fewer
- using visual materials, such as videos or models, where possible
- discussing issues in terms of short periods (less than ten years)
- simplifying procedures and regimens as much as possible

Practice Question

12. A person who struggles with depression explains how her significant other can support her during a depressive episode to help shorten the duration and under what conditions to call the social worker. Which of the following is this person demonstrating?
    A) mental health literacy
    B) treatment plan compliance
    C) incompetence
    D) emergency management

Cultural Considerations

Social workers should consider any cultural traits or factors that might affect an intervention plan. A client's cultural background will always inform and influence their perceptions about seeking help, assumptions of what that process may look like, and expectations for intervention.

Seeking help holds a certain stigma for most people, but that stigma or the perception of attending therapy will vary from culture to culture. Some do not consider mental health issues valid or requiring help and will therefore not seek help. Other cultures view mental health issues as spiritual or religious problems and might turn to a religious person within their community rather than a mental health professional. Others may view mental health issues as a physical problem and go to a physician for help rather than a mental health professional.

Assumptions about the therapy process also vary from culture to culture. There is general acceptance and knowledge of what a therapeutic relationship may look like in Western cultures. Other cultures may not understand that process, and a lack of understanding often breeds fear. Some cultures view mental health professionals with skepticism and suspicion, while others view them as an extension of the medical, doctoral field. This assumption, at least, puts the mental health professional in a position of authority. It places the burden of responsibility and leadership firmly with the social worker or therapist; however, that responsibility and authority come with the assumption that the mental health professional will only provide direction and instructions, rather than foster the true purpose of a therapeutic relationship. This plays heavily into a client's possible expectations for the interventions, which may also vary from culture to culture.

As mentioned previously, there may be a transactional expectation of therapy, whereby the client presents for help and expects the provider to give advice. There may be an expectation that a mental health provider can dispense medication to fix the problem. There may also be resistance to discussing certain topics in a therapeutic environment, especially if the client perceives the topics as irrelevant to the problem for which they have sought help.

Family members, and their defined role within their culture, may affect how a client receives treatment. For example, in some cultures, parents will not allow their children to be alone with a mental health provider. They will expect to be involved in every aspect of the child's care. In some cultures, a husband may not allow his wife to attend therapy on her own. In some cultures and religions, young women do not associate with young men unless accompanied by a family member or unless the purpose is dating in preparation for marriage. Some cultures have strict expectations of the roles of each gender, with consequences when those expectations are not met. In other cases, the family may be very concerned about confidentiality. Seeking mental health care could stigmatize the family and ruin social and community relationships.

Language barriers may present challenges over the course of treatment. The meaning and connotations to certain words may vary from language to language. Clarifying terms is important. In cases where the client does not speak English very well and the social worker does not speak the client's native language, a professional translator may be required.

> **Helpful Hint**
>
> Translators must comply with confidentiality policies and HIPAA, and clients must give permission for the use of a translator.

Body language is incredibly nuanced. The connotation or meaning behind eye contact and the use of touch may hold very different meanings from culture to culture. Both may be viewed as a positive or negative social cue depending on the client's perception of those actions. It is important to understand how the client may view body language. For example, in Western cultures, if a client does not maintain eye contact with a mental health provider, that might be recorded as a symptom related to anxiety or fear, yet in some cultures, not making eye contact is considered a sign of respect.

Another cultural consideration for creating an intervention plan is how resources are defined by the client. Each client's cultural background can either be considered a positive resource or a negative one. In other cases, there is a conflict between the client's cultural background and adjusting to Western culture. That conflict is often evident in families where the parents and older family members seek to remain culturally faithful to their country of origin and the younger members wish to adopt the cultural values of their new country. Therefore, the cultural and religious practices or traditions endorsed by the family could be protective sources of help for the client, or they can be sources of conflict. The social worker should discuss these issues with the client without bias to determine which are positive and which are not.

This knowledge of a client's cultural background will inform the way the social worker interacts with the client.

Practice Question

13. Which approach should a multicultural social worker use when working with clients with different cultural backgrounds?
    A) the same approach used for every client
    B) a psychodynamic approach
    C) a client-centered approach
    D) a cognitive behavioral approach

Working with the Client

Establishing the Therapeutic Relationship

Individual therapy follows a template:

- Assess client issues.
- Determine diagnosis.
- Set goals based on the diagnosis.

- Design an evidence-based plan of treatment for the diagnosis.

Everything flows together and relates back to the diagnosis. Even as new information emerges over the course of treatment, any changes to the treatment plan must still directly relate to the client's diagnosis. For clients to be correctly diagnosed, they must

- feel safe enough with the social worker to truthfully disclose information needed to form a correct diagnosis
- feel like the social worker is not judging them—embarrassment and shame often accompany mental health issues.

The importance of the **therapeutic relationship** can therefore not be understated. The therapeutic relationship is the most important factor that predicts treatment outcomes. For clients to accept the proposed treatments, they must first trust the social worker enough to be honest about their experiences and issues:

- Without trust, the client may not feel comfortable sharing everything with the social worker.
- If the client does not share openly, it can lead to the wrong diagnosis and the wrong plan of treatment.

For example, a person with depression who does not trust the social worker might not disclose a serious trauma, like childhood sexual abuse. Without that information, the social worker may make the wrong recommendations for treatment. While the client may experience some relief, he will not truly benefit from the treatment plan if therapy does not address the underlying issues.

The foundation of the therapeutic relationship is the therapeutic alliance. The **therapeutic alliance** is an unwritten agreement between the client and the social worker based on trust, boundaries, and mutual respect. It is not a friendship but rather a formal treatment relationship.

In the therapeutic alliance, clients feel safe to explore issues and be vulnerable with the social worker. At the same time, they know that the social worker will hold them accountable and maintain professional boundaries. Clients need assurance that the social worker will not judge them.

The therapeutic alliance is also an equalization of power between the client and the social worker. Often, clients enter into therapy viewing the social worker as a person of authority, much like many people view physicians. In that type of relationship, clients may expect the social worker to tell them what to do to get better. Unlike the client-physician relationship, however, the social worker in the therapeutic alliance

- makes it clear that clients lead the way and establish their own goals
- uses therapeutic techniques—not force or coercion—to help clients achieve their goals.

Practice Question

14. At her first appointment, a client asks the social worker for help with sleep difficulties that interfere with functioning. After talking about the sleep issues, the client says, "Okay, that's my problem, tell me how to fix it." Which aspect of the relationship should the social worker address to create a therapeutic alliance?
    A) Explain that therapy is client-focused and not social worker-focused.
    B) Establish the social worker's position as an expert and tell the client what to do.
    C) Question the client's experience and tell her there is nothing wrong with her.
    D) Explain to the client that the problem is all in her head and the issue is not really about sleep.

Client Education

Social workers should provide educational resources on relevant topics (e.g., stress management, assertiveness training, divorce adjustment). This type of education in the context of mental health is often referred to as **psychoeducation**, or education focused on sharing evidence-based information about a mental health issue and how to cope with it.

Psychoeducation is valuable because it helps clients understand the what, how, and why of what they are experiencing. For example, a social worker who diagnoses a client with generalized anxiety disorder would teach her about the diagnostic criteria for the condition, evidence-based causes for the disorder, the available options for treatment, evidence-based means of coping with the disorder, and the potential prognosis for the disorder based on research. Often this education can help clients understand that they are not alone in this experience, that their experiences are valid, and that there is hope for treatment. When seeking social support, it can also help when clients explain to other people in their lives what they are experiencing. Strategies for teaching include the following:

- **Lectures** (groups or one-on-one) are effective for conveying cognitive knowledge, particularly to auditory learners. A social worker uses this strategy to convey information on a specific subject to a client individually or to a group.

- **Group discussions** in which clients can ask questions and share information are effective for social learners and can help with affective learning (e.g., changing attitudes) and practicing skills in a safe environment.

- **Role-playing** is a good way to teach affective skills (e.g., responding to peer pressure) and to practice relational and communication skills in a safe environment.

- **Instructional materials**, like films or pamphlets, may be used as part of a larger education plan; however, they may be ineffective if clients are disengaged or the materials do not match the client's needs and learning abilities.

    o Social workers may provide instructional materials to clients within the context of treatment to support additional learning. For example, during a session, the client learns about healthy coping skills and discusses coping skills to try during the next week.

    o A social worker might give the client a pamphlet that defines healthy coping skills and provides a list of healthy coping skills to try.

Some specific strategies to engage clients in the learning process include the following:

- Link new information to current behavior; new learning is better received when it focuses on what the client already knows.

- Be clear, explicit, and specific.

- Suggest alternatives or adaptations that apply directly to clients and their situations.

- Be transparent about the goals of the learning process and why these are important.

- Involve other health providers (e.g.,. dieticians) to engage clients and reinforce learning.

- Invite people from the client's social support network to participate in the learning process.

Finally, technology can engage clients and connect them to providers and support communities. **Webinars** or **live events** are often available in the community and geared toward specific client populations (e.g., parents). When recommending these resources, the social worker should verify the credentials of presenters as well as the validity and quality of the information presented.

Practice Question

15. A mother brings her teenager to therapy because of significant mood changes and increased social isolation. During the assessment, the social worker diagnoses the teenager with PTSD due to recent bullying at school. How can the social worker use psychoeducation in a session with the mother and teenager?
    A) explain the symptoms of PTSD and ways to manage the symptoms during treatment
    B) refer the client to a psychiatrist for medication
    C) bring in another social worker to work with the mother
    D) tell the mother to keep the teenager home from school until symptoms subside

Treatment Termination

Discharge planning is the process of planning for the cessation of treatment. In an inpatient setting, it includes planning for the client's exit from services and preparing for aftercare. Discharge planning

- begins at intake

- considers under what circumstances or conditions treatment will be successful

- considers the achievement of client goals, including the ability to care for oneself independently, medical equipment or care needed in the home, referrals, available social support, available community resources, and what to do in case of a crisis

Discharge planning includes discharge teaching relevant to the client's treatment plan. Discharge teaching may include:

- an explanation of the diagnosis

- recommendations for aftercare

- tips for mental health

- when to consult with a mental health professional if symptoms get worse

The Termination Process

The termination process starts at intake and assessment. Social workers should explain to clients that therapy is finite and meant to end.

Part of the treatment planning process is estimating the number of sessions required to help clients achieve their goals. When the treatment plan is formulated with the client, the social worker and client agree on how many sessions it will take to complete treatment.

The social worker needs to consider the client's needs as well as how many sessions the client's insurance company will pay for before requiring preauthorization for more sessions. One way the social worker can do this is by asking the client questions:

- How will you know you are better?
- How will you know the problem is solved?
- What does recovery look like for you?

Each session should include some time to assess what the client has accomplished thus far toward his goals. As each session passes and the treatment plan review sessions occur, the social worker refers to the number of sessions left and decides with the client how many more sessions are necessary.

Session fading is a technique through which clients may start with one session every week, but as they progress in the treatment plan, they may have a session every other week. This strategy of adding more time in between sessions continues until the client may need only one session every six months until termination.

There are multiple reasons for termination. **Planned termination** may occur for the following reasons:

- The client has successfully completed treatment.
- The client requires a different level of care.
- The social worker is leaving and will not be working in the treatment setting.
- Insurance or the party paying for services will no longer pay.

Unplanned termination is characterized by the following:

- The client no longer shows up for treatment.
- Problems with the therapeutic relationship prompt a referral to another provider.
- The social worker or client experiences an illness or other emergency.
- The client or social worker dies.
- The client is incarcerated (e.g., following mandated treatment).

In situations of **social worker-initiated termination**, the social worker decides to terminate the therapy relationship. Common reasons include the following:

- The social worker is leaving the agency.
- The social worker lacks the expertise to meet the client's specific needs.
- The therapy process is stagnant.
- There is inappropriate conduct involved.

In these cases, the social worker must explain to the client the reasons for termination, document that conversation, and make every reasonable effort to help the client find another provider. If the client refuses the referral, that should also be documented.

In **client-initiated termination**, the client decides to end the relationship. Reasons for this may vary and include the following:

- The client does not like the social worker.
- The client can no longer afford therapy.
- The client does not feel like therapy is helping.
- The client stops attending sessions (unresponsive clients).

When the client terminates the relationship, the social worker should make a reasonable effort to determine the cause for the termination and document it as well as make a reasonable effort to refer the client to another provider.

Social workers should also make a reasonable effort to reach out to unresponsive clients, both administratively to enforce any policies related to missed or canceled appointments and to determine what barriers are keeping the client from participating in therapy. A social worker might be able to address some of these issues to help the client engage with the therapeutic process.

Premature termination occurs when a client stops attending sessions without completing the treatment plan. A social worker should make a reasonable effort to discover why the client terminated prematurely and provide referral information to the client.

Social workers can take steps to prevent premature termination by scheduling appointments in advance, offering reminders, and explaining the therapy process to improve client understanding of the importance of completing therapy.

Helpful Hint

Allowing for appointments over telehealth platforms or at hours more convenient to the client can reduce premature termination. Some social workers even offer in-home treatment

In some cases, **client resistance to termination** occurs. This may include asking for more sessions, asking for more time, or developing new problems beyond the presenting problem. A client's resistance to termination may indicate unresolved relationship issues. When a client becomes too attached to a social worker, an assessment may reveal additional problems for therapeutic intervention. It may also indicate that the social worker has not established and maintained professional boundaries with the client.

An **exit interview** is a final evaluation of the client's experience and includes the following:

- determining the client's progress through treatment and a review of what she learned

- assessing the client's experience in therapy
- evaluating the social worker's performance
- discussing how the client can address future issues on her own
- determining conditions under which the client might return to therapy
- reviewing what a client can do if she experiences a crisis
- discussing aftercare options (e.g., support groups, peer support, and community resource)
- celebrating the client's accomplishments
- scheduling a check-in session by phone or in person in three to six months

Practice Question

16. A client is progressing in the treatment plan and feeling better. The social worker suggests reducing sessions to once every two weeks, and possibly once a month thereafter. Which process is likely occurring here?
    A) Unplanned termination;
    B) Session fading;
    C) Client resistance;
    D) Premature termination.

Transitions in Group Membership

Transitions in group membership depend largely on the type of group. Some, like open psychoeducational or support groups, have a purpose that is not dependent on the relationships among group members. In open groups, membership changes frequently, and little attention is required for the members to adjust.

In closed groups, however, the therapeutic process depends significantly on the relationships among group members. Most closed groups have a session limit. For example, the group may meet for ten sessions and be finished at that point. For finite groups, termination is built into the group intervention, with the last sessions devoted to processing the members' feelings about the group ending, discussing if and how the members want to continue their relationships, celebrating accomplishments, reviewing the effectiveness of the group, giving ideas for how to continue using the skills they learned, and saying goodbye. There is also a review of the confidentiality rules that group members agreed on and how they apply after the group ends.

> **Did You Know?**
>
> Most states have regulations that outline the requirements for discharge planning and termination, including what efforts must be made to reengage client-initiated or unplanned terminations and how those efforts must be documented.

Other groups fall somewhere in between open and closed groups. The social worker facilitating the group needs to pay attention to the quality of relationships that develop among members and, if a member leaves, devote time to process how people feel about that. In cases where the group decides to ask someone to leave, the remaining members might need time to process what happened.

Practice Question

17. Which of the following types of group therapy would be MOST impacted by the unplanned departure of a group member?
    A) an open support group for people struggling with addiction
    B) a psychoeducational group about parenting skills
    C) a closed group about processing childhood trauma
    D) a twelve-session open anger management group

Follow-Up after Discharge

Follow-up with clients after discharge can be important for evaluating the efficacy of treatment for the client as well as the therapeutic process, customer service, aftercare, and education. Approaches for this include the following:

- **Efficacy of treatment evaluations** ask the client to evaluate the social worker and the treatment process after therapy has concluded. These evaluations may provide clients an opportunity to be more honest with their feedback because they are no longer receiving services.

- **Customer service evaluations** provide feedback about the clinic and administration.

- **Aftercare follow-up** may include providing referrals to resources for community-based groups, mental wellness events, or information on what to do in case of relapse.

- **Education** follow-up can include tips for maintaining good mental health or promoting mental wellness events.

Short-term follow-up tends to occur between one and four months after the client completes treatment. Examples of short-term follow-up include:

- efficacy of treatment evaluations
- customer service evaluations
- aftercare recommendations

Long-term follow-up takes place six months or more after the client completes treatment. Examples of long-term follow-up include:

- efficacy of treatment evaluations
- education
- community events
- newsletter items

Follow-up techniques may include:

- inviting the client to a follow-up session via text, email, or letter six months after termination

- reaching out to the client in a phone call, email, letter, or questionnaire
- sending clinic newsletters to clients

Practice Question

18. Which follow-up practice would social workers find helpful for improving their therapeutic techniques?
    A) a treatment evaluation sent thirty days after client discharge
    B) a customer service evaluation to rate the clinic's service
    C) an educational newsletter that goes out to clients every six months
    D) a community resource guide sent to clients after discharge

Answer Key

1. A: The first step in the process of evidence-based practice is conducting a thorough assessment of the client. Formal assessments and clinical interviews should be used to demonstrate that the client meets the criteria for a specific diagnosis. Once a diagnosis is made, then a treatment plan can be created.

2. A: Everything in the treatment plan must address the diagnosis.

3. D: The treatment intervention must be an evidence-based intervention that is appropriate for the client's diagnosis.

4. B: Due to the high level of distrust that many undocumented persons have, connecting with someone from that community will be the best chance a social worker has to identify the needs of that community and then educate them about the resources that are available to meet their needs.

5. C: Motivational interviewing (MI) is ideal for a client who is unsure about a life change. This client is in the contemplation stage of the transtheoretical model (TTM). Motivational interviewing could help the client find benefits to making changes in her life and encourage thoughtful communication about her hesitations. Option A might be an appropriate answer, but this client may have significant internal motivation. Someone with internal motivation and not external motivation will still be more open to making changes than the client in Option C. Option B describes a client who is actively participating in the interview, and Option D describes a client who seems to have internal motivation for treatment, which would encourage active participation during the interview as well.

6. B: Client self-report is the backbone of a structured clinical interview.

7. B: A biopsychosocial interview would be the best interview format to use when meeting a first-time client because it assesses physical health, mental health, and social life. This allows the social worker to determine areas of focus for the treatment plan as well as whether any specialized assessments or interview formats could also be used.

8. D: The goal is specific (learn three skills), measurable (reduce anxiety from 10 to 4), attainable (client chose level 4 as reasonable), realistic (not expecting zero anxiety), and time restricted (within three sessions).

9. C: The time frame for this goal is three months, which makes it a long-term goal. Short-term goals tend to include time frames of thirty days or less.

10. A: Reviewing client progress occurs at multiple levels, including at each session and at regularly set intervals.

11. B: Clients are empowered when they learn about how treatment plans will help them recover and the value of complying with these plans.

12. A: Mental health literacy is the ability to understand the basic information needed to care for oneself and make decisions. This person demonstrates an understanding of her depressive disorder and explains to her significant other how to help her.

13. C: A client-centered approach means that the social worker seeks information about cultural issues from the client—not from their own knowledge.

14. A: This client expects the social worker to be the expert professional and give direction, but the therapeutic alliance relies on equal power and trust between the client and the social worker.

15. A: Psychoeducation can help the teenager and the mother understand what the teenager is experiencing.

16. B: In session fading, a client progressing in the treatment plan reduces the frequency of sessions until termination.

17. C: Among the members of a closed group processing trauma, relationships are a significant part of the group process.

18. A: Clients may be more honest about the social worker's performance when they are no longer receiving services.

9. Intervention Techniques

Goals and Objectives of Case Management

Case management requires social workers to serve as client advocates. A **client advocate** ensures that the client receives the proper care and remains as safe and healthy as possible. Social workers will establish a care plan by assessing the needs of their clients. Based on those needs, the social worker can perform a wide range of job duties, including educating clients and their families, attending physician appointments, obtaining medical equipment for rehabilitation, and researching medication assistance funding. Case management for social workers involves work in a variety of health care settings. These settings include hospitals, doctors' offices, and behavior health facilities. Case management has four main goals:

- to improve the quality of care
- to reduce health care costs
- to coordinate care
- to encourage client engagement and self-advocacy

Improving quality of care is an important responsibility in social work. Social workers serve as another set of eyes for their clients. Medical care can be overwhelming to a patient, who may leave the hospital without understanding what to do upon returning home. The social worker will assess the hospital discharge summary and educate the client on follow-up medical appointments, medications, and treatment plans. Quality of care is achieved when the social worker successfully assists a client with information that may be lacking or misunderstood.

Health care costs may be reduced through intervention to help the client avoid hospitalization. For example, a social worker may observe that a client is not complying with her prescribed insulin usage. The client simply may not know how to inject the insulin and would have to return to the hospital with elevated blood sugar. Recurring demonstrations on medical equipment usage will ensure the client is using the equipment correctly. A patient may also need education on the importance and correct execution of behavior medications. Lack of education may require the patient to enter a behavioral facility.

With many medical professionals providing care for a single patient, care can be overlooked or misunderstood. The social worker may assist a client by communicating with all medical professionals involved to ensure that everyone is "on the same page" by coordinating care. Many clients may need services or medical equipment and may not know how to meet these needs. In this situation, for example, the social worker could help a mother obtain a wheelchair for her child at the most affordable cost available through research and communication.

Clients may need encouragement to achieve goals in the care plans created by their social worker. A client may wish to quit smoking, for example, but does not think it is possible. Researching community smoking cessation programs and being an extra resource for support may help a client become engaged with the

care plan. Working on short- and long-term goals may also be useful. A social worker who engages in these actions and observes medication administration will encourage client engagement and self-advocacy.

Practice Question

1. A patient underwent cardiac surgery and is given instructions from the physician to rest. Which of the following actions would NOT promote the goals of case management?
    A) completing a medical reconciliation against the discharge papers
    B) finding transportation for the patient for medical appointments
    C) allowing the patient to rest while the social worker meets with providers
    D) researching lower-cost medications

The Role of Case Managers in Different Settings

Social workers conduct case management in a variety of settings. Ensuring the client is functioning as well as possible is always the main goal.

A **hospital case manager** will focus on **discharge planning**. Where will the patient be going when she leaves the hospital? Will she have all the tools she needs to be safe and in optimum health at the new residence? Continuity of care is a priority and ensures there are no gaps in care.

Hospital case managers may also be trained in **utilization management**. This is a process that reviews services while the patient is in the hospital. In this clerical role, the social worker determines if the patient is in an appropriate setting with the highest level of quality care. The case manager will also review the services ordered by physicians and determine if the services are medically necessary.

A case manager in a **physician's office** setting is focused on the prevention of health-related concerns. This case manager may remind the patient about previously scheduled wellness exams and assist the patient with scheduling appointments. Case managers might also ensure that patients are properly educated regarding doctor's instructions and medication orders.

Palliative and **hospice care organizations** hire case managers as well. These case managers are unique in that they also provide hands-on, direct patient care. Frequent communication with the physician for medication instruction is part of this role, as the stages of the dying process advance. Often the patient is not able to communicate at this point, and a patient advocate is needed. The case manager will shine in this role.

Workers' Compensation case management is a growing field. The employer and employee wish to have the employee return to work as soon as possible after a work-related injury or illness. Coordination of care is still a priority in this setting; however, the communication involves additional professionals such as attorneys and claim adjusters.

Practice Question

2. What is the primary goal of a social worker in a hospital office setting?
    A) discharge planning
    B) the prevention of medical concerns
    C) communication with the client's employer
    D) utilization management

Evidence-Based Interventions

Social workers must be able to apply evidence-based counseling interventions. Ethical and competent social workers receive proper education and training before using these interventions with clients. Social workers must take care to use therapeutic techniques properly; the improper application of evidence-based interventions could harm the client.

> **Did You Know?**
>
> In some cases, third-party payers will not reimburse social workers for interventions unless they can provide documentation of authorized training.

Choosing an Intervention

Socials workers use several criteria to select intervention and treatment modalities:

- **Addressees clients' presenting problems:** Interventions should be evidence-based, requiring research that proves positive outcomes when used to treat a particular mental disorder.

- **Supported by data collected during intake:** Collected data forms the foundation for the diagnosis, which forms the foundation for treatment planning. If there is no data to support a diagnosis for anxiety, there is no data to support the use of an intervention aimed at anxiety.

- **Client and client systems:** If the client does not understand the modality or does not like the modality, then it will not be appropriate. The same is true for client systems. For example, the family and social relationships may or may not support some treatment modalities. It is no use to recommend family therapy if the client system includes broken family relationships.

- **Client abilities:** Social workers must weigh a client's ability to perform a treatment task before selecting it. This consideration can also apply to working with clients who struggle with language due to recent migration into the United States and those with various disabilities.

- **Client culture:** A client's cultural background and religious beliefs might make some interventions inappropriate or misunderstood by the client. Clients who do not understand the intervention will be less likely to participate.

    o Cultural values may preclude clients from telling providers that they disagree with recommendations, especially if the providers are viewed as authority figures.

    o Family, social connections, and religious communities play a role in recovery from mental health issues.

- **Life stage:** What a social worker recommends for a child or adolescent may not be appropriate for someone in middle age or older adulthood. Understanding the conflict or task that each life stage focuses on can help a social worker choose treatment interventions appropriate for the client's issue.

Practice Question

3. A 50-year-old man presents for therapy because he feels lost and depressed. He is unmarried and has spent his life thus far pursuing his career. The social worker recommends a treatment intervention where he mentors younger employees in his company. Which consideration has the social worker used in selecting this intervention?
    A) life stage
    B) culture
    C) client preference
    D) family

Cognitive Behavioral Therapy

Cognitive behavioral therapy (CBT) is based on the theory that thoughts and feelings influence behaviors. The theory further suggests that many of the thoughts that influence behaviors occur without a person's conscious knowledge.

The point of using CBT as therapy is to guide clients to become aware of those thoughts and identify the unhealthy ones. Clients can then learn to take control of their thoughts and separate the thoughts from their behaviors. Because several mental health issues are associated with negative thoughts and beliefs, the social worker can use this theory-based counseling intervention with clients who have a variety of diagnoses. The social worker's role in CBT is to

- help clients explore their thoughts and beliefs
- analyze where thoughts and beliefs originated
- evaluate the truth or effectiveness of thoughts and beliefs
- revise or create new thoughts and beliefs that help clients achieve their therapeutic goals.

Practice Question

4. A client comes to therapy with social anxiety that prevents him from having a social life because he thinks people are judging him. Which type of therapy would benefit this client?
    A) acceptance and commitment therapy (ACT)
    B) dialectical behavior therapy (DBT)
    C) eye movement desensitization and reprocessing (EMDR)
    D) cognitive behavioral therapy (CBT)

Dialectical Behavior Therapy

Dialectical behavior therapy (DBT) uses concepts from CBT but also considers the significant impact of strong emotions on thinking and behavior. As implied by the name, DBT suggests that opposing forces exist in a state of tension. For example, a person practicing DBT understands that she may feel very strong negative emotions, but her whole life is not ruined. Someone using DBT would understand that she might perform badly on an exam, but that does not mean she is unintelligent or that she has no future. The goal

of DBT is to help clients learn to balance between extremes and choose constructive or positive behaviors despite strong emotions. The therapy itself focuses on helping clients:

- learn mindfulness
- learn to regulate their emotions and tolerate distress
- identify dysfunctional thinking patterns
- choose healthy coping skills

Did You Know?

Dialectical behavior therapy was originally created to treat women with borderline personality disorder and high rates of suicidality.

Another characteristic of DBT is establishing and maintaining boundaries with clients to teach them how to do the same in their lives. Implementation of DBT interventions requires the social worker to engage in additional education and training.

Practice Question

5. Which of the following features of DBT distinguishes it from CBT?
    A) emotional regulation and distress tolerance
    B) identifying dysfunctional thinking patterns
    C) learning healthy copy skills
    D) developing healthy thinking patterns

Eye Movement Desensitization and Reprocessing

Eye movement desensitization and reprocessing (EMDR) is considered an evidence-based treatment intervention for clients with post-traumatic stress disorder (PTSD) and other diagnoses. This treatment is based on the theory of information processing. According to this theory, memories associated with traumatic events are not stored properly. The techniques used in EMDR employ bilateral stimulation while recalling a memory to store it properly in the brain and reduce the strong emotions attached to it.

Helpful Hint

Social workers should not use EMDR with clients until they are properly educated and trained by a qualified EMDR trainer.

To apply bilateral stimulation, a social worker may ask a client to hold two joysticks that vibrate alternatingly or to wear a headset that plays tones or clicks in one ear, and then the other. This therapy can be very effective for clients with the following diagnoses:

- PTSD
- phobias
- bipolar disorder

Practice Question

6. Which theory forms the foundation for EMDR?
    A) behavioral theory
    B) cognitive theory
    C) information processing theory
    D) social learning theory

Acceptance and Commitment Therapy

Acceptance and commitment therapy (ACT) is based on the theory that people can choose positive behavior even if their thoughts and feelings are negative. In other words, negative thoughts or feelings do not have to dictate a person's behavior. This therapy uses techniques such as:

- mindfulness
- changing the way a client thinks and behaves regarding strong feelings
- establishing values
- encouraging clients to take action consistent with those values

This therapeutic intervention can be used for clients with a variety of mental health issues. One example of its use is helping clients manage the discomfort of withdrawing from substance use or to manage the cravings involved in substance use recovery. The client may feel she needs the substance, and her thoughts tell her she needs it to curb the discomfort. The client can choose to exercise instead because she has the goal of remaining abstinent. Although there is no requirement to receive education and training to use ACT as an intervention, it is recommended.

Practice Question

7. Which of the following is a distinguishing feature of ACT?
   A) The intervention is shorter than most others.
   B) The therapist provides coaching and direction to the client.
   C) The client can choose positive behavior despite feelings to the contrary.
   D) It is the most effective addiction treatment intervention.

Solution-Focused Brief Therapy

Solution-focused brief therapy (SFBT) involves bringing attention to clients' internally held strengths and developing these into skills to solve their problem behaviors. SFBT is effective in three to ten sessions. SFBT is used for clients working on

- substance use disorders
- depression
- eating disorders
- anger management

SFBT interventions include:

- the miracle question (asking clients to envision an alternate reality where their problem does not exist)
- exception questions (focusing on when the client is not experiencing the problem)
- presupposing change questions (helping clients recognize change that has occurred in their lives)

- scaling questions (having clients rate their experiences or feelings on a scale of worst to best)
- coping questions (reviewing times clients have used coping mechanisms and shown resiliency)

Practice Question

8. Which of the following assumptions forms the foundation for SFBT?
   A) Clients do not understand what is best for them.
   B) Clients require intensive therapy to overcome challenges
   C) Clients have the skills and resources to solve their problems.
   D) The therapist must tell the client what to do.

Other Techniques

There are several other techniques used in social work intervention. **Partializing techniques** are used to simplify complex issues. For example, a client may present with several problems and significant functional impairments, including depression, substance abuse, housing issues, unemployment, and poverty. Partializing techniques allows the social worker to help the client identify the most important things to work on first by breaking down the big issues into smaller issues. The idea is to choose goals that a client can easily achieve at the beginning. This process is beneficial because as the client achieves the smaller goals, he feels more empowered to continue in recovery. As the client feels more empowered, the client can begin to work on more challenging goals.

Another intervention technique is **assertiveness training**, which includes teaching a client skills for behaving with more self-confidence, such as articulating wants and needs, identifying and maintaining boundaries, and making decisions about unhealthy relationships. For example, a client may be frustrated with a boss who continually makes her work late and tramples over her work-life balance boundaries. The client may feel depressed and hopeless about the situation. Assertiveness training can help the client identify her needs and wants related to work and learn ways to speak to her boss with respect while still advocating for herself.

A **task-centered approach** is another intervention technique. It focuses on solving a tangible problem. The social worker helps a client identify immediate problems and then creates a plan for what the client can do to solve those problems rather than using diagnostic techniques. For example, a client may be depressed because he cannot find a job. A task-centered approach would focus on solving the job problem by identifying what the client needs to secure a job rather than focusing on the client's depression symptoms.

Permanency planning assesses and prepares a child for long-term stable living arrangements. The process includes establishing goals and activities that bring the child closer to a permanent living situation. For example, permanency planning is often used in foster care to plan forever homes for children displaced from their families of origin. It is also used for families with children with disabilities who require institutional care to ensure that the children receive care when their parents are no longer able to provide it.

Mindfulness is the process of learning to observe and pay attention to one's thoughts, emotions, and behaviors in a nonjudgmental way and to focus on the present. There are multiple techniques used, depending on a client's comfort level, but the goal is to be open to what the person is experiencing. Formal mindfulness practice can include various forms of meditation and deep breathing exercises, or it can be less formal by remaining present and attentive during activities like exercise, creative arts, or everyday tasks. An example of mindfulness for a client with anxiety would be for the person to recognize her thoughts and feelings without judging herself and then use breathing exercises to calm her body.

There are also **complementary therapeutic approaches** that encompass a wide variety of activities that may be beneficial to clients. These can include massage, herbal supplements, and other physical activities like acupuncture or Chinese medicine. Other complementary therapeutic approaches can include things like art therapy, music therapy, or dance therapy. An example of using a complementary therapeutic approach with a client might be to recommend dance therapy for a client who feels out of touch with his body.

Practice Question

9. Which of the following would benefit a client who feels like everyone she dates uses her and then dumps her?
    A) permanency planning
    B) task centered approach
    C) partializing
    D) assertiveness training

Answer Key

1. C: Although the patient is supposed to rest, the social worker should promote autonomy and self-advocacy. The social worker should encourage the patient to play an active role in her health care management.

2. A: Social workers who work in hospitals focus on discharge planning.

3. A: The social worker recognizes the client's life stage where the primary conflict is generativity versus stagnation. By mentoring young employees, the client can pass his knowledge to others, thereby increasing generativity.

4. D: Cognitive behavioral therapy would focus on identifying and addressing the client's thoughts and beliefs related to how others view him.

5. B: In addition to using CBT techniques, DBT focuses on emotional regulation and distress tolerance.

6. C: Eye movement desensitization and reprocessing (EMDR) helps clients rearrange the stored memories of trauma through bilateral stimulation.

7. C: This intervention teaches clients to accept their negative emotions and commit to positive change anyway.

8. C: In SFBT, the role of the therapist is to help clients recognize their strengths and resources and how to use them to solve their problems.

9. D: Assertiveness training would help this client identify what she wants and needs in a relationship and how to articulate those wants and needs to a partner.

10. Use of Collaborative Relationships

Community-Based Intervention

Levels of Care

One of the functions of screening, interview, and assessment is to determine which **level of care** is appropriate for clients and their presenting concerns. There are a variety of options, each with its own benefits.

Residential inpatient care programs typically occur within a hospital setting. The goal is to stabilize clients so they can begin receiving treatment for their mental health concerns at a different location. Clients receive treatment that can include:

- psychoeducation
- individual therapy
- crisis intervention
- medication management

Inpatient programs are appropriate for individuals who have safety risks, such as:

- recent suicide gestures or attempts
- homicidal attempts

Inpatient programs are also suitable for clients who need a high level of care, including

- medication management
- eating disorders
- drug/alcohol detox and treatment

In **partial hospitalization programs (PHPs)**, the client attends a structured day program at a treatment facility:

- The program's structure resembles an inpatient program, but the client goes home at night.
- PHPs typically run five days a week for six to eight hours per day.
- PHPs provide clients with safety and structure for most of their day.

- PHPs are appropriate for clients who can safely live at home but still need a thorough treatment program.
- Typical clients might have a severe mental illness, be compliant with medication, and be learning how to manage symptoms behaviorally.

In **intensive outpatient programs (IOPs)**, the client attends structured programming for a few hours per day:

- IOPs usually treat addiction, eating disorders, and depressive disorders.
- IOPs typically have a psychoeducational component in addition to group treatment.
- IOPs are appropriate for clients with mild disorders and clients with mild or severe use disorders who have already completed residential treatment programs.

Outpatient treatment, also called outpatient therapy, is usually recommended to build on what clients learned in other, more intensive programs:

- The duration of an outpatient program varies depending on the presenting concern.
- Outpatient treatment typically follows the successful completion of an IOP or PHP.
- Outpatient treatment is usually fewer hours per day than an IOP or PHP.
- Outpatient activities include:
    - group therapy
    - individual therapy
    - medication management
    - specialized treatment
    - psychoeducation
    - family therapy
- Outpatient treatment programs address various mental health concerns, including
    - addiction
    - childhood behavioral and emotional concerns
    - mood disorders

Psychotherapy is individual counseling between a client and a social worker that

- is appropriate for individuals with a mild mental health concern
- allows clients with a complex diagnosis to maintain a connection to a supportive professional after more intensive treatment
- includes high-functioning clients

- usually consists of weekly or biweekly individual sessions

Self-help programs generally refer to support groups run by peers rather than mental health professionals:

- Many self-help programs address addiction, but some address other concerns:
    - twelve-step programs (e.g., Alcoholics Anonymous, Narcotics Anonymous)
    - support for families of people with an addiction (Al-Anon, Nar-Anon)
    - eating and weight management groups (Overeaters Anonymous, Weight Watchers)
    - grief support groups
- Activity and attendance rates depend on the client.
- Self-help groups can be used at every level of care.

Treatment programs offer guidelines that can help the social worker decide which level of care to recommend to the client.

Practice Question

1. Which of the following levels of care would be appropriate for a young man with an alcohol addiction who is going through a divorce and custody fight with his ex-wife but needs to remain employed?
    A) partial hospitalization
    B) residential inpatient
    C) intensive outpatient
    D) outpatient

Agencies and Community Resources

Social workers must understand the mission, function, resources, and quality of services offered by community-based organizations. Community-based organizations include:

- civic groups
- community groups/neighborhood organizations
- religious organizations
- governmental entities
- health and allied health care systems (managed care)
- criminal justice systems
- housing authorities
- employment and vocational rehabilitation services
- childcare facilities
- crisis intervention programs

- programs for people who have been abused
- mutual and self-help groups
- cultural enhancement organizations
- advocacy groups
- other agencies

Community resources exist to enhance the quality of life of community residents. Community resources include people, community services, and businesses. Older adult care services, for example, can provide meals to people over age sixty-five, help them maintain the structural integrity of their homes, and bring trusted professionals and community volunteers to their homes to perform chores. Other community resources include the following:

- **Religious organizations**, such as missions and youth groups, serve the community through meal programs, clothing/toy donation drives, and projects that may involve building houses for the homeless or providing medical care.
- **Government programs** often provide financial aid for communities. Just a few of these programs include:
  - Medicare and Medicaid
  - Housing assistance through the US Department of Housing and Urban Development (HUD)
  - grants and scholarships
- **Meal delivery programs** (e.g., Meals on Wheels and Nurture Life) deliver meals to older adults and children.
- **Pharmacy assistance programs** offer medication prescriptions at discounted rates and are an excellent resource for people with multiple prescriptions who are on a fixed budget.
- **Psychiatric assistance** and **hospitalization** may be appropriate for individuals who need detoxification, medication-assisted treatment, and/or prescribed psychiatric medications.
- **Psychological assistance and counseling** services in a hospital setting help to stabilize clients' mental health so that they can continue engaging with care on an outpatient basis.
- The **Substance Abuse and Mental Health Services Administration (SAMHSA)** helps people find treatment; provides grants for substance use prevention and treatment programs; and offers training, education, and research on behavioral health.
- **State and community health agencies** provide outpatient treatment services for individuals

> **Helpful Hint**
>
> Some clients may resist inpatient treatment programs due to a negative stigma associated with being in a mental health hospital setting. Additionally, many individuals are concerned about their ability to pay for inpatient treatment programs.

who use government programs like Medicare and Medicaid, increasing access to care for those in low-income and rural areas.

- **College and university health agencies** often offer students prevention education, intervention strategies that address student substance use and misuse, and counseling services, which increase access to care.
  - These programs are not designed to provide treatment for individuals who have a substance use disorder, but they can help students locate appropriate treatment providers.
- **State and local departments of family services** (e.g., child and adult protective services) can help individuals who are dependent on someone who is struggling with a substance use disorder.
- The **National Council on Alcoholism and Drug Dependence, Inc. (NCADD)** provides education and information to local communities, individuals in recovery, and concerned loved ones about addiction.
  - Additionally, the NCADD offers assessment and referral resources to individuals who are interested in treatment services.
- The **National Institute on Alcohol Abuse and Alcoholism (NIAAA)** is an independent institute within the Alcohol, Drug Abuse, and Mental Health Administration (ADAMHA).
  - The NIAAA researches alcohol use and its impact on public health and well-being.
  - NIAAA findings provide guidance in prevention and outreach efforts across the community.

There are multiple ways for a social worker to assess the availability of community resources:

- Social workers can use an informal survey of the services already provided in a geographic area by looking at readily available materials, such as:
  - the phone book
  - government agencies
  - online resources
- A **community needs assessment** collects data on the services that already exist and determines if there are needs in the community that are not currently being met. A community needs assessment is comprehensive and measures the strengths and weaknesses of each service offered. This is done through aggregated, quantitative data that has been collected through the following types of surveys:
  - those of the general population
  - those of people who work in the profession
  - those of people who are in government

- Interviews with people who work with various community populations can help provide information about the needs that are and are not being met by those populations.

- Census records and public health records can provide social workers with

  o demographic information

  o socioeconomic information

  o information on how the data has changed over time

> **Did you know?**
>
> In Illinois, New Mexico, and Louisiana, psychologists can become authorized to prescribe medications.

Practice Question

2. What is the purpose of a community needs assessment?
   A) to provide data to justify pay raises for social workers
   B) to identify which services are needed in a community
   C) to generate customer service reviews
   D) to show that no action is required

Other Health Care Providers

The social worker may collaborate with many different health care providers. This section describes the roles of these providers in treating clients.

Physicians include general (family) practitioners and specialists. Physicians spend a minimum of ten to twelve years in medical school and training/residency to earn a degree in medicine, and then they must take certification exams to practice medicine legally. They can diagnose conditions, order procedures, and treat and write medication prescriptions for illnesses. Physicians usually see clients in their office.

Physician assistants (PAs) assist a physician. They can operate within the same scope of practice as a physician but with limitations contingent on their education and professional experience, state regulations, office policies and procedures, and clients' needs. Physician assistants may collect a comprehensive medical history, perform a physical head-to-toe assessment, diagnose illnesses, prescribe medications, and establish care plans.

Nurse practitioners (NPs) possess a master's (or higher) degree in nursing and function in a similar capacity as that of a physician. They may diagnose and treat illnesses; they can also write prescriptions.

Clinical nurse specialists (CNSs) have advanced education and training in a specialized field, such as psychiatric care, women's health, or critical care. Clinical nurse specialists have graduated from an accredited school of nursing, earned a master's or doctoral degree in nursing, and passed a specialized certification exam. They can make diagnoses, develop treatment plans, and provide care. They are often in leadership roles in which they supervise other nurses.

Registered nurses (RNs) and **licensed vocational/practical nurses (LVNs/LPNs)** typically do not have advanced degrees. They will carry out orders from a physician, physician's assistant, or nurse practitioner; collect medical histories; perform assessments; develop a nursing diagnosis and treatment plan; implement the treatment plan; and evaluate client outcomes.

Nurse technicians provide care for patients under the supervision of an RN or other more credentialed health care provider. There is no official certification or scope of practice for nurse technicians, but some nursing coursework is usually required. Nursing techs are often students working toward a nursing degree or recent graduates looking to gain work experience.

Behavioral health care providers dedicate their lives to supporting and preserving the mental/emotional health and well-being of individuals with mental illness. A **psychiatrist** is a physician who has attended medical school, earned a degree in medicine, and chosen to specialize in psychiatry. Psychiatrists can write prescriptions for anti-anxiety medications and antidepressants, among other medications.

Psychiatrists are not to be confused with **psychologists**, who must undergo training and an internship to secure an advanced degree in psychology. While psychologists may have a doctoral degree, they are not medical doctors and, therefore, most cannot prescribe medications. They offer focused counseling services that can assist in the diagnosis and treatment of medical and mental health issues.

Licensed professional counselors (LPCs) possess a master's or doctoral degree in counseling and will, within their scope of practice, offer collaborative, therapeutic counseling to individuals who seek professional guidance to promote emotional, behavioral, and mental health well-being.

Licensed clinical social workers (LCSWs) are licensed to practice in a clinical or therapeutic setting and work directly with clients to diagnose and treat mental, emotional, and behavioral issues. These professionals will also often focus on public health and develop or implement new and advanced measures to facilitate and promote communication within the community.

Community vendors provide goods and services to the entire community. One such example is a **community health fair**. During the fair, health care professionals will talk to individuals about their health and ways to promote a healthy lifestyle. They will also often record vital signs and weight.

Another type of community vendor is a **community-based day program**. Community-based day programs include after-school activities for children and outpatient behavioral management programs.

> **Did You Know?**
>
> While the overarching goal of all health care providers is to promote a healthy lifestyle and healthy outcomes, each provider's scope of practice is very different. Social workers should consider which medical professional is appropriate to

Practice Question

3. If a social worker suspects that medication may be appropriate for a client to manage his depression, which of the following providers would be appropriate?
   A) licensed professional social worker
   B) psychologist
   C) psychiatrist
   D) nurse technician

Consultation Approaches

Case Consultation and Working Relationships

The social worker's role is to advocate for clients' interests. As a **client advocate**, the social worker's

attitude should be one of professional concern. When consulting with other providers, social workers should appreciate incremental changes and recognize relapse as an opportunity for growth rather than as a failure.

In **case consultation**, social workers consult with service providers and other relevant stakeholders to monitor assessments, develop or modify treatment plans, or review client progress. **Working relationships** with other providers, such as physicians, psychiatrists, case managers, and social workers, can enhance the quality of care for the client.

Consultants and service providers should always maintain respect for clients, their right to privacy, and the privacy of the information shared by them and their significant others. When interacting with service providers on behalf of the client, social workers should maintain a respectful and nonjudgmental attitude. **Consultation** with other professionals helps secure a high quality of care by ensuring a review of

- the treatment plan
- the client's progress
- any problems that inhibit progress

Consultation enables the social worker to gather feedback and adjust the treatment plan as appropriate. Consulting social workers must have a strong knowledge of assessment procedures and the following methodologies:

- assessing the client's biopsychosocial status (both past and present)
- social systems that may affect the client's progress
- methods for ongoing assessment of the treatment plan and modification if necessary

Consulting demands a deep understanding of teamwork and appropriate behaviors within a professional group setting. Social workers must be knowledgeable about related disciplines, including

- their various functions and any unique language/terminology used
- the primary roles of other team members within their own disciplines

In the collaborative professional setting, social workers must always demonstrate respect for the interdisciplinary nature of consulting work by showing interest in professional collaboration with partners. Social workers should be at ease sharing information and asking questions. They should always remain appreciative of the contributions of other team members and respect their professional roles and backgrounds.

Practice Question

4. What is one benefit of consulting with another professional on a client's treatment progress?
    A) to make the process easier for the social worker
    B) to prepare the client for referral to another provider
    C) to ensure that the social worker is competent to provide therapy
    D) to identify factors that may be hindering progress

Referrals

During the clinical evaluation and/or treatment planning, the social worker and client identify the client's needs. As a result, the social worker may provide a **referral**, which is a way to guide the client to other available resources and support systems to meet those needs.

Social workers determine whether a referral is appropriate by interpreting assessment, treatment planning, evaluation, and client feedback data. Referrals address client needs and service gaps by connecting clients with

- agencies
- governmental bodies
- civic groups
- other treatment professionals

Like other elements of care, referrals should be collaborative. Social workers should work with clients with decision-making and respect their capabilities in taking ownership of the referral (initiating and following up). Maintaining an attitude of collaboration and respect promotes the client's needs and positive self-determination. Social workers should educate clients on the referral process and motivate them to initiate the referral process and follow through with recommendations and commitments:

- **Readiness and education** include motivating clients to actively participate in the referral process.
- In **active participation**, the client is responsible for following through on the referral and following up.

When making a referral, social workers should keep the client's cultural influences, appearance, presentation abilities, and defenses in mind. All of these factors can affect follow-through on referrals. Some examples to consider include the following:

- If clients are legally obligated to participate in treatment, they may present with limited engagement and have difficulty developing therapeutic rapport. Additionally, they may struggle to find sources of intrinsic motivation.
- There may be a language barrier among clients whose second language is the social worker's native language; this can impact the ability of clients to communicate their thoughts and experiences effectively.
- Some clients may not have a working knowledge of different emotions and feelings. This can make it difficult for them to communicate how their emotions, thoughts, and feelings impact their use and recovery.
- The socioeconomic status of clients can impact their grooming patterns. It is important to differentiate this reason for changes in grooming patterns from those that result from clients' addiction or other mental health concerns, such as a major depressive episode.
- Clients who had a negative experience in a previous treatment setting may be hesitant to participate and engage and may struggle to develop a therapeutic rapport with their social worker.

The social worker must ensure that the client has the necessary access and logistics to follow through on referrals. For instance, a client who has no phone or internet access will need assistance to make medical appointments.

Social workers measure follow-up with the client by using specific processes and instruments and reporting information accurately. Social workers must be able to understand how referrals relate and contribute to progress in the overall treatment plan.

Practice Question

5. What is the purpose of a referral to another service provider or organization?
   A) to meet the client's assessed needs that are outside the social worker's scope of practice
   B) to test the client to see if she is really willing to do the work necessary for therapy
   C) to keep the client busy and engaged in the constructive activity
   D) to lighten the burden on the social worker and have someone else help with the client

Referral Best Practices

Not every client is appropriate for every social worker, and vice versa. A social worker should provide a referral in certain situations:

- The social worker does not have adequate training to work with the client's issues.
- The social worker and client cannot establish a productive therapeutic relationship.
- An ethical issue (e.g., a dual relationship) precludes a social worker from working with a client.
- The social worker experiences an issue that would disrupt the client's treatment.
- The social worker is resigning, retiring, or otherwise leaving the organization or profession.

When providing referrals, there are several **best practices** recommended for social workers:

- Give the client plenty of notice, if possible.
- Provide the client with several choices for other providers and offer to facilitate the transfer.
- Ask if the client wants a joint session or a phone introduction with the new provider.
- Ask if the client wants the social worker to share information about him with the provider; if so, discuss what information to share.

Social workers must know and adhere to local, state, and federal confidentiality regulations, client consent procedures, and other standards guiding the exchange of information. Still, a social worker should **provide information to third parties** as required by law. These generally include:

- insurance companies
- health care professionals
- legal guardians

Social workers should remain aware of their own potential **biases** toward or against referral resources. Examples of biases that social workers could unintentionally experience include the following:

- Social workers who do not have a spiritual or religious foundation in their lives may have a hard time encouraging religious and spiritual aspects of recovery.
    - Peer support groups such as Alcoholics Anonymous and Narcotics Anonymous have a spiritual component to their recovery programs.
    - Without personal experience, it is important for social workers to educate themselves about the role that spirituality and religion can have in a person's recovery so that they can provide support to clients who could benefit from having a spiritual or religious component in their recovery.
- Social workers who grew up in a home environment with a parent or guardian who struggled with an addiction may have unintentional bias toward clients who are parents or guardians.
    - Social workers are often drawn to this career path from a desire to help others, which can be a result of a history of personal challenges.
    - Being mindful of the role that past experiences have in their motivation can help social workers understand more about their personal biases.
    - Clinical supervision can help the social worker provide nonjudgmental and empathetic care.
- Similarly, social workers who are in recovery may have unintentional bias toward or against clients who are struggling.
    - Such biases could impact the social worker's ability to provide empathetic support and the quality of care needed.
    - Supervision is a useful tool to keep social workers' biases in check.

Practice Question

6. A social worker has been working with a client weekly for six months. The social worker is diagnosed with an illness that will require him to leave work for at least three months. Which action should the social worker take?
    A) Assure the client that he can keep up with weekly sessions.
    B) Coordinate with the client and refer her to another social worker.
    C) Tell the client that the social worker will be out for three months and will contact the client when he returns.
    D) Have the receptionist cancel the client's appointments and schedule with another social worker.

Roles and Responsibilities of the Social Worker

Collaborative Processes

Therapy is a collaborative process. As such, social workers may find it necessary to clarify their roles and responsibilities, as well as the role of the client and client system within the intervention process. There are several methods for doing so.

At the macro level, the National Association of Social Workers (NASW) and federal and state laws create guidelines that delineate the scope of practice for social workers. The licensing guidelines set forth by each state govern the roles and responsibilities of social workers in various specifications. For example, the macro-level scope of practice allows social workers to provide therapeutic interventions when properly licensed but not prescriptions for mental health medications.

At the meso level, a social worker's role would be clarified by the agency or environment in which they work. For example, if a social worker provides services in a child welfare setting and the agency's scope of practice is only child and family intervention, then the social worker would not be allowed to provide substance abuse treatment within that agency. If the social worker wants the role of providing substance abuse treatment, she will have to work in an agency or organization that is appropriately licensed to provide those services. Therefore, even if a social worker has experience and competence as a substance abuse treatment provider, her role would be limited to the scope of practice dictated by the agency in which she works. Agencies and organizations will provide social workers with policies and guidelines they are expected to follow while employed. Social workers are ethically bound to professional competence in that they are only allowed to fulfill roles and responsibilities for which they have received proper training.

At the micro level, the social worker and client roles are determined within that relationship and within the services the social worker is able to provide. This level also includes determining the role of the client systems (e.g., family, social relationships, and referral sources). During the assessment and goal-setting processes, the social worker and the client may have a conversation about the resources the client has access to and whether those resources are appropriate. That conversation should include defining the role and responsibility of the social worker and the client, as well as those invited by the client to participate in the intervention. There are multiple methods of care team collaboration:

- **Interdisciplinary team collaboration** involves working with people outside of one's field.

    o For example, a social worker's expertise might be in providing mental health treatment, which puts his field of expertise within the behavioral health profession. However, it may be beneficial for the client if the social worker invites a physician or community-based mentoring organization to consult on the client's case. The physician could provide a medical perspective on issues that the client deals with and the community-based mentoring organization could offer a perspective on how to get the client more involved with community activities.

- **Intradisciplinary team collaboration** is consulting with other professionals within one's field.

    o For example, psychiatrists, licensed professional social workers, and social workers are all part of the mental health field; however, each can offer differing perspectives on a client's situation because they have different backgrounds and training. When social workers consult with a supervisor or other social workers, this is also considered intradisciplinary collaboration.

Formal power structures are those organized and recognized by a particular profession or organization that creates a chain of authority. In agencies and organizations, there are supervisors, managers, and directors, for example, that create a formal power structure within that organization. Formal power structures provide formal rules and guidelines that must be adhered to in the decision-making process

Informal power structures, on the other hand, are those without a formal title, yet one person holds power based on personality or character traits. An example of an informal power structure is an informal group of people who form social connections based on a shared interest and exert influence over each other. Informal power structures can exert more influence than formal power structures. For example, the formal power structure may require a client to participate in an intensive outpatient treatment program based on his care needs, yet the client's family and friends who form the informal power structure in the client's life may have more influence over the client's decision to participate.

Practice Question

7. What is it called when a social worker consults with professionals outside the mental health field?
   A) interdisciplinary collaboration
   B) teamwork
   C) intradisciplinary collaboration
   D) referral

Accommodations

Clients with **disabilities** should be accommodated. Most health care organizations have policies and procedures in place to accommodate clients with disabilities. For instance, clients who are deaf, hard of hearing, blind, or who have low vision should be offered interpretation services or other assistance as appropriate. Whenever possible, the social worker should ask the client what his preferred method of communication is.

> **Helpful Hint**
>
> It is a good idea to review with the client what information will be disclosed.

Cognitive impairments can often result from trauma or injury (e.g., a stroke). In these cases, clients may not be able to speak due to motor impairments, or they may have neurological conditions that prevent them from processing communication. The social worker should ask the client or the client's representative which method of communication works best and remain aware of changes in the client's cognitive status.

The **Americans with Disabilities Act (ADA)** prohibits discrimination against individuals who are determined to be disabled. The ADA defines disabilities to establish which individuals need to be protected under the law. These individuals must have a mental or physical impairment that substantially limits one or more major life activities. The person may have a record or history of such impairments or may be perceived by others, such as an employer, as having such limiting impairments.

Most compliance with the ADA is initiated at the organizational level. Still, social workers must adhere to the ADA in their physical practices by providing

- sufficient space for wheelchairs or other assistive devices

- ADA-compliant furniture that can accommodate people of various weights and body types
- materials in alternative formats if requested (e.g., large-print forms)
- frequent breaks to support cognitive challenges

Part of the assessment process will include asking the client if she requires any accommodations. Persons with disabilities may require **accommodations** adjustments in their job duties or environment. Employers must provide these accommodations as long as they are reasonable and do not cause "undue hardship" to the employer, such as high expense or difficult installation.

Social workers may be called on to provide documentation of a client's disability. First, the social worker must get the client's written permission to share the information. The social worker must then limit documentation to issues covered within the therapeutic relationship.

If the client has cognitive challenges and the social worker has assessed the client for that, then the social worker can provide supportive documentation for that issue. However, if the client is requesting accommodation for a physical disability, the social worker cannot provide supporting documentation for the client's physical condition. The social worker could, however, provide information about how the physical disability impacts the client's mental health.

> **Helpful Hint**
>
> The social worker must always communicate with the client, not with the interpreter.

Language barriers can occur when a social worker does not speak the client's primary language or speaks it as a second language. Social workers who do not speak the client's language have options:

- The client brings someone he trusts to act as an interpreter. The interpreter will have to sign confidentiality forms.
- The social worker can use professional interpreting services. Many health organizations have relationships with professional interpreting services. Being under contract, interpreting services agree to abide by HIPAA and confidentiality rules.

It is important for the client to feel comfortable with the interpreter. The social worker is responsible for checking in about this and ensuring that the client understands that he can ask for someone else.

> **Helpful Hint**
>
> In the spirit of client-centered practice, the client should choose the translation option.

Conducting therapy sessions with an interpreter present can be challenging for both the client and the social worker, so social workers may wish to undergo additional training on providing these services with compassion and empathy.

Practice Question

8. A client gave a social worker permission to disclose confidential information when filling out a disability accommodation request form for his employer. The human resources director left the social worker a message requesting more information. What should the social worker do?
   A) Obtain written consent from the client to speak to the human resources director and agree on what information the client will allow the social worker to share.
   B) Return the call to human resources to provide the needed information as quickly as possible.
   C) Call the client and let him know the social worker will be returning the call to human resources to answer these questions.
   D) Ignore the voicemail message and do not mention the call to the client.

Answer Key

1. D: An outpatient program would be the best choice for this client because he cannot devote the hours required to attend intensive outpatient treatment.

2. B: Community needs assessments identify the services that exist and what the population needs that is not already provided.

3. C: A psychiatrist can prescribe medication for a client.

4. D: Another professional perspective may detect factors in the process that the social worker can use to help the client progress through treatment.

5. A: An assessed client need may include job training or vocational rehabilitation. If the social worker does not provide those services, it makes sense to refer the client to an organization that does.

6. B: When a social worker will be unavailable for any length of time, it is best practice to refer the client to another provider to continue the same level of care.

7. A: Consulting outside one's field is known as interdisciplinary collaboration.

8. A: The social worker may only speak or disclose information to other parties after receiving written permission from the client; otherwise, it is a breach of both confidentiality and the Health Insurance Portability and Accountability Act (HIPAA). If the client only provided written permission for the social worker to fill out a form, the social worker must receive written permission to talk to the human resources director, as it is a separate instance of sharing the client's personal information. Some states and organizations also require social workers to discuss with their client's what information will be disclosed and why. Even when it is not required, this is considered best practice to maintain trust between the client and the social worker.

11. Professional Values, Ethical Issues, and Documentation

Defining Professional Ethics, Values, and Principles

Ethics are moral principles, values, and duties. Whereas laws are enforceable regulations set forth by the government, ethics are moral guidelines established and formally or informally enforced by peers, the community, and professional organizations. Ethics include norms and duties:

- **Norm** is short for *normal*, a term used for a behavior or conduct that is valued and usually expected.
    - Norms are also often described as aspirational ethical principles because they are not enforceable by law.
    - Social workers aspire to the highest ethical standards to maintain trust between the public and their profession.
- **Duties** are commitments or obligations to act in an ethical and moral manner.
    - Duties fall under the minimum ethical standards and are usually part of the state regulations.
    - Social workers can be held legally accountable for violating ethical standards.

The National Association of Social Workers Code of Ethics

The **National Association of Social Workers (NASW)** is a professional organization providing resources, advocacy, and guidance to social workers. The NASW has a Code of Ethics. A **code of ethics** is a statement of the expected behaviors of its members. This code may also set standards and disciplinary actions for violations, including suspension, censure, fines, or expulsion.

There are core values central to the NASW Code of Ethics[1]:

- **Service:** This value encourages social workers to put the needs of others before their own. The NASW Code of Ethics likens this value to the principle of helping others in need and working to fix social problems.
    - Service is fulfilled in the clinical setting by placing the client's needs above the social worker's needs. It is fulfilled in the community by using social work skills to create positive change for social problems.

---

[1] "NASW Code of Ethics," National Association of Social Workers website, accessed July 19, 2023, https://www.socialworkers.org/About/Ethics/Code-of-Ethics/Code-of-Ethics-English

- **Social Justice:** This value calls attention to the vulnerable and the oppressed. The NASW likens this value to the ethical principle that social workers act to work toward social justice.
    - To fulfill this value, social workers are expected to be aware of the way social forces interact to create unfavorable social conditions like poverty, unemployment, and discriminatory systems. Once they are aware of these injustices, they are expected to educate others about them and help the vulnerable and oppressed access the services they need.

- **Dignity and Worth of the Person:** This value sets the tone for the way social workers interact with others. Every person, regardless of background or cultural identity, is worthy of respectful treatment and empathy.
    - This value is fulfilled when social workers respect the autonomy of clients and seek to empower clients to make changes in their lives. This value also informs the social work approach of ensuring that individuals are treated with dignity and respect within the community.

- **Importance of Human Relationships**: The NASW states that social workers are to view human relationships as a vehicle for change. There are many levels of relationships, which include the therapeutic relationship, the relationships within families, communities, and society in general. Thus, the power of relationships forms the bedrock of a healthy society.

- **Integrity**: Social workers must perform their duties in an honest and trustworthy manner. Not only should they consistently present themselves with integrity, they are also expected to represent the profession in a responsible and ethical way.

- **Competence**: This value describes the knowledge and skills used by social workers and how they are applied in their work. Social workers are expected to only practice within the realm of what they have received proper training to do, and to be honest about that with clients. Additionally, social workers are expected engage in professional development.

Social workers who have ethical concerns are encouraged to contact the NASW for advice. When addressing ethical concerns with a client case, the social worker should consult with a supervisor or colleague and document in the client's record the ethical decision-making process used during the consultation.

Practice Question

1. A client tells the social worker that he wants to try EMDR to work on anxiety. The social worker is not trained in EMDR. What should the social worker do?
    A) refer the client to a qualified practitioner
    B) suggest avoiding EMDR and instead focus on techniques the social worker is trained in
    C) explain that EMDR will be discussed later in treatment
    D) ask her supervisor for guidance

Nonmaleficence

Nonmaleficence is the principle of not doing harm. It requires social workers to consider the impact of their actions (and inactions). The potential for nonmaleficence in social work includes referrals. A social worker should refer a client to another provider if:

- the client's treatment progress seems stagnant
- the social worker does not have the expertise to treat the client's particular condition

A social worker might have good intentions in wanting to continue working with a client, but by not referring the client, he is actually harming her since another social worker might be able to help the client progress through her issues more quickly.

Another example of nonmaleficence application in clinical practice is hospitalization, especially **mandatory psychiatric treatment**. Some states have a provision that stipulates a person can be committed to a psychiatric facility against his will for a minimum period, often seventy-two hours, if he presents a danger to himself or others. While this may sound like a positive action to save someone's life, it must be considered whether that forced commitment will harm the client.

If a client shows signs of suicidality, proactive measures (e.g., developing a crisis plan) can be instrumental in providing the client with the help she needs without resorting to a potentially traumatic experience.

In any type of ethical dilemma, a social worker needs to balance state laws and agency policies with the principles of beneficence and nonmaleficence. Consultation and documentation are vital in these situations for the reasons previously noted.

Practice Question

2. A client presents for therapy with a medium risk for suicide. Although a crisis situation is not imminent, the client may experience a crisis at some point. A social worker practicing nonmaleficence would do which of the following?
    A) work with the client to develop a crisis plan that includes family and friends for social support
    B) explain to the client that any crisis situation will land him in the psychiatric hospital
    C) avoid discussing the problem until the client actually experiences a crisis
    D) continue with therapy interventions and do not discuss suicide any further

Dual Relationships

The clinical therapeutic relationship requires the social worker to refrain from any type of **dual relationship** with clients. A dual relationship is when the social worker has both a social work relationship with the client and a relationship outside the clinical setting.

Avoiding dual relationships reduces the chance of a social worker exploiting a client or conveying the perception of power and authority. For example, if a social worker has any type of personal relationship

with a client outside of the treatment setting, it is unethical for her to provide services to that client. In general, social workers should avoid:

- any sexual or romantic relationship with former or current clients
- a social work relationship with someone with whom the social worker had a previous sexual or romantic relationship

Any social worker who becomes aware of another social worker engaged in dual relationships or of sexual harassment or exploitation is obligated to follow procedures for reporting the legal and ethical violation.

A dual relationship can also apply to business relationships. In some states, business relationships are permissible with clients; however, these relationships are still unethical. For example, if a client is a carpenter and the social worker needs work done on her home, it is unethical to hire that client as a carpenter. Business relationships such as these have the potential for exploitation and the expectation of favors.

Practice Question

3. A client comes to therapy but explains that he does not have the money to pay for therapy. He has a house-cleaning business and offers to trade services by cleaning the social worker's house and office in exchange for therapy. How should an ethical social worker respond?
   A) accept the offer of trading services
   B) accept the offer but limit the trade to cleaning the office
   C) decline the offer
   D) explain the law to the client and refer him to a clinic that offers free mental health services.

Legal Aspects of Social Work

Social workers are vulnerable to legal action. There are multiple situations that may result in legal system involvement, including:

- disability evaluations
- workers' compensation evaluations
- workplace accommodations
- school accommodations for children
- custody disputes
- divorce disputes
- abuse and neglect cases of children, adults, people with disabilities, or older adults
- the use of therapeutic interventions that are not evidence-based or are unlawful
- criminal cases involving mental illness or substance abuse
- duty-to-warn cases
- complaints against a social worker to the licensing board

Social workers must be aware of and understand:

- state laws
- regulations
- standards of care
- agency policies
- the differences between subpoenas and court orders in their state
- the procedure for responding to subpoenas and court orders

Consistent supervision and consultation on client cases and thorough documentation of this help protect the social worker by showing that she followed policy and regulations. Social workers should seek advice from a supervisor or legal representative in these cases. Agencies usually have policies for handling these situations, but legal requirements will determine how a social worker must respond to requests for information by attorneys.

Not every state requires a social worker to provide records to a subpoena. Furthermore, when presented with a request for client records by someone within the legal system, it is important to discuss this with the client and document what and how the information was shared. Therefore, two rules of best practice apply to protect social workers in legal situations:

1. If it is not documented, it never happened.
2. Consult, consult, consult.

Many clients are referred for treatment by courts or systems affiliated with the courts. For example, child protective services may require that families or individuals engage in services. Also, mental health courts and drug court programs are becoming more widespread as incarceration diversion efforts. In these cases, there are special considerations for documentation requirements and sharing information with the courts and the rest of the client's care team.

> **Did You Know?**
>
> Complaints against a social worker can be made against both the agency and the individual social worker, including HIPAA violations related to clinical negligence. Therefore, social workers should carry professional liability insurance to protect their interests. They should not rely on their employer to do so.

Social workers should take extra care during the informed consent process to not only meet the needs of the referring system but also protect the privacy and confidentiality of the client to preserve the therapeutic relationship.

Practice Question

4. A social worker has been working with an adult client for several months. Without warning, the social worker receives a letter from an attorney working on behalf of the client's spouse, requesting the client's mental health records. What should the social worker do?
   A) send the attorney a letter clarifying which records are being requested
   B) consult with a supervisor or legal representative to determine the next steps
   C) ask the client what the attorney's purpose is in requesting the records

D) fax a copy of the client's records to the attorney

Principles of Documentation and Record Management

The Elements of Client/Client System Reports

Social workers use accurate, timely documentation to prove they have complied with standards of care and practice, which is important for professional advancement and a possible legal defense. Social workers should:

- only document facts—opinions do not belong in the official documentation
- record details of the client/client system visit as soon as possible after the visit
- always record if the client/client system agrees or refuses case management, interventions, or other types of care
- record all communication with people or organizations involved in the client's care, including the client's family, medical providers, employer, and insurance companies
- document the care plan, including assessments, interventions, evaluations, and the outcomes of each
- document all instances of consultation about the client with supervisors and colleagues, including what was discussed and with whom, and recommendations
- document modifications of the care plan, the rationale for the changes, and whether the client agreed
- include all legal documents, including advance directives and informed consent forms
- document discharge plans and client education

Many organizations require documentation and regular review by the clinic director to ensure compliance with state law.

Progress notes are the official record of a session and tend to follow a **SOAP note** format:

- **s**ubjective information about the client/client system and what they are experiencing
- **o**bjective findings from assessments or observation
- **a**ssessments that include findings of the client's diagnosis or evaluations of how the client/client system is progressing in the treatment plan
- **p**lans that include next steps, both therapeutic and otherwise

Progress notes may be shared with others:

- Insurance companies receive progress notes when determining reimbursement.
- Progress notes may be included in client records requests from other providers.
- Progress notes are subject to inspection by agency quality control personnel and government regulators.

> **Helpful Hint**
>
> When writing progress notes, keep them clinical and focused on the client's treatment plan.

When clients request a copy of their records, these are the notes that are included. When the courts request records, these are the notes that are subject to a subpoena.

The second type of notes, **process notes**, are considered a social worker's private notes. Process notes are not required to be part of the client's official record. Process notes generally include:

- hypotheses
- theories
- the social worker's thoughts regarding client treatment
- questions to address during supervision.

Process notes are considered privileged and are not generally accessible to the client or other parties except in certain circumstances:

- If a client is involved in a legal action, it is possible that the social worker's records, notes, and documentation will be shared with the court.
- When a social worker leaves an agency, the documentation stays with the agency; the social worker's notes will influence how future providers interact with that client.

Not all social workers use process notes. Still, social workers should consider the impact that any piece of documentation will have on a client.

Practice Question

5. A client with severe anxiety frequently talks about other people in session, especially his family members, because he believes his anxiety is all their fault. Which of the following would be included in a well-written progress note?
   A) the social worker's observations of the client's anxiety symptoms
   B) specific unpleasant remarks made by the client's mother to him
   C) actions the client's brother takes to bully him
   D) what the client said about his last social worker

Objective and Subjective Data

Robust and proper social work documentation includes two types of data: objective and subjective.

Objective data is information that is not influenced by a person's thoughts or feelings—only what can be measured or observed. Objective data is only the facts without any opinion involved and leaves out a person's bias. There are two types of objective data used in a clinical social work setting: assessments and observations.

Assessments can be formal or informal, self-reported by the client, or obtained through questioning by the social worker. Formal assessments include evidence-based measures of mental health disorder symptoms, memory or cognition tests, and questionnaires regarding treatment. The following are commonly used assessments:

- Beck depression inventory
- PHQ-9
- Beck anxiety inventory
- perceived stress scale
- trauma symptom checklist
- addiction severity index

Observations are objective data, as noted by the clinician, that serve as a means to conceptualize the client's problem. These observations can be collected formally with a standardized assessment or more informally by recording observations in a progress note. Observations include:

- noting how the client appears physically
- what emotions the client appears to portray during the session
- whether those emotional expressions are congruent with what the client reports
- what the client's body language indicates and whether the client appears tense or relaxed
- the tone and quality of speech
- behaviors that appeared bizarre or that are worthy of more formal assessment

Subjective data is information that is not measured or observed but rather is the opinion of the person recording the data. It includes:

- personal views
- thoughts, feelings, and reactions
- the social worker's hypothesis about the client's issues
- theories related to treatment interventions that may work for the client
- thoughts and ideas about what the client experiences or what he may need
- areas to explore in the future

Areas to explore with the client may also include notes about discussions for referral sources or additional resources that can help the client. Subjective data is influenced by a person's lived experiences and biases.

Recording subjective data in client documentation should be considered in terms of whether it is appropriate as a progress note or a process note. When used in a progress note, the formulation of it should be focused on therapy. For example, a social worker might record subjective data about a client's resistance to change by stating that the client's resistance may be due to not having a social support system available. A less appropriate piece of subjective data would be the social worker's commentary on why the client hates her mother. All aspects of documentation should be focused on treatment and include careful consideration of what goes in the client's record.

Practice Question

6. Which of the following statements represents subjective data?
    A) The client speaks hurriedly, jumping from one topic to the next.
    B) The client scores 18 on the Beck depression inventory, indicating moderate depression.
    C) The client changed the subject when asked about family, indicating this might be a problem area.
    D) The client hugs her knees during the session and refuses to make eye contact.

Answer Key

1. A: The social worker is not trained in the technique the client wants to try, so she should offer to refer him to a qualified practitioner. Practicing EMDR with the client would violate the NCC's Code of Ethics, which says that NCCs may only provide services for which they are qualified. It also violates the principles of veracity, nonmaleficence, and justice. Postponing the conversation (option C) could also cause harm by preventing the client from accessing the treatment sooner. The social worker should not need to ask her supervisor for advice; she should understand these ethical principles.

2. A: Social workers understand the risk associated with suicidality and the potential for a traumatic experience in mandatory psychiatric treatment. So, a social worker practicing nonmaleficence will work with the client to create a crisis plan that will help mitigate a crisis without requiring mandatory hospitalization.

3. D: While the social worker should decline the offer, an ethical social worker would explain the conflict related to dual relationships and refer the client to a clinic that offers free services.

4. B: The client's confidentiality and privacy are paramount. Depending on state law and agency policy, the social worker may not be required to turn over any records. Social workers should always consult with a supervisor or legal representative and document the consultation before taking action.

5. A: Progress notes include objective observations of the client's symptoms and progress through treatment. While the other options listed may influence the client's symptoms, the details are not relevant to the treatment progress; instead, a social worker might note, "client's anxiety increases due to mom's verbal taunts."

6. C: This option includes a subjective opinion about a problem area that can serve as another area to explore with the client.

12. Confidentiality

Confidentiality

Confidentiality in Practice

Confidentiality means that the social worker will keep the client's personal information confidential according to state and federal law. The social worker must also explain to the client when and under what circumstances confidentiality may be broken. In general, confidentiality requires that social workers must not disclose client information to anyone not authorized by the client.

Confidentiality is a vital aspect of the social work relationship and is protected not only by professional ethics but also by law. There are several **limits to confidentiality** that are usually explained in writing in the informed consent process:

- Client information will be shared with clinic personnel for record-keeping and billing purposes.
- Client information may be shared with a clinical supervisor or colleague for the purposes of consultation for the benefit of the client.
- Client records may need to be included in state or federal auditing procedures.
- Client information may be shared if the client expresses a desire to hurt himself or someone else.
- Client records may be shared in the case of a medical emergency.
- Records may be shared if the client discloses that she has experienced abuse or that she perpetrated abuse that falls under the requirements of mandated reporting.
- If the client brings someone else to the session and grants the social worker permission to waive confidentiality, client information may be shared.
- A court order may require a social worker to break confidentiality.

Social workers should abide by the principle of sharing the least amount of information needed to get the job done. Furthermore, it is best practice that any breaches of confidentiality be shared with the client either before or immediately after the breach, including what information was shared. Also, the social worker should document the incident, along with the personal information disclosed, in the client's records.

Social media and electronic communication should be considered risks for confidentiality breaches. Information posted on social media is not private, as the platform owners can access a person's data at any time. Therefore, social workers should be careful what they post about themselves on social media.

Some social workers use social media as a professional referral opportunity that includes a business page with how to contact them; however, connecting with clients as friends on social media is unethical. Also, communication with clients via social media is not recommended due to the confidentiality risks.

It is not ethical for social workers to look up clients on social media to learn more about them. Electronic communication may be used for setting appointments, but it is recommended to only use electronic communications for therapeutic purposes if that is part of an agency's protocols for conducting telehealth or distance social work.

Communicating with clients on social media outside of the social work relationship would ethically be considered a dual relationship unless it is conducted outside of the legal time allotted. States set the rules about this period. In some cases, a social worker may have to wait two to five years before engaging in a dual relationship with a client, and that includes social media friendships.

Practice Question

1. A client collapses during a therapy session, and the social worker needs to call an ambulance. Since this is an emergency, what can the social worker reveal to the emergency medical personnel?
   - A) The client's history of childhood sexual abuse and how it causes significant distress.
   - B) The reasons why the client is in therapy.
   - C) No information because he does not have permission from the client.
   - D) The client's name, how the client collapsed in session, and any physical conditions that may have contributed to the collapse.

Consent

Client **consent** is required for treatment. A client must provide **informed consent** for a social worker to perform a treatment or procedure, or if he is going to take part in a research study. For informed consent to be valid, the social worker must cover key elements:

- a description of procedures
- risks
- benefits
- alternatives

The social worker must also assess **client competency** to provide informed consent. A competent client understands:

- the procedure or practice
- the risk and benefits involved
- the possible consequences

> **Did You Know?**
>
> Informed consent forms may need to be updated once per year to remain valid.

Finally, the client must acknowledge having provided consent. Most states have regulations for practices that include having a signed informed consent form for each client.

State regulations vary regarding the age of consent. The age of consent to sign informed consent documents ranges from fourteen to sixteen. Regardless of the legal age of consent, a good way to establish trust with adolescent clients or with clients unable to provide legal consent for themselves is to gain the client's assent for treatment. Obtaining **assent** means:

> **Helpful Hint**
>
> To obtain assent, many social workers use a document similar to the informed consent form.

- going through the entire informed consent process with the client
- explaining the role of the social worker
- making sure the client understands the therapeutic process
- ensuring that the client agrees to participate freely

Obtaining assent helps establish trust with clients and engages them in the therapeutic process. This can be especially powerful for those who may feel they are being coerced into treatment.

Practice Question

2. While obtaining informed consent is required by law, obtaining assent is not. Why is it a good idea to obtain assent anyway?
   A) Clinic administrators want documentation that everyone involved in therapy has signed the proper forms.
   B) Parents will probably not tell their children what the process of therapy will include.
   C) Even if clients are not of legal age to consent, it is important to the therapeutic relationship that they understand the process and agree to participate.
   D) It protects the social worker from future legal action.

Electronic Health Records

The **Health Information Technology for Economic and Clinical Health (HITECH) Act** was written to encourage the use of electronic health records (EHRs) and related technology. The Centers for Medicare and Medicaid Services (CMS) have several objectives for using EHRs:

- Electronic exchanges of summary of care: An **exchange of summary of care** (also referred to as a discharge summary) refers to the movement of a client from one setting to another. For example, the exchange of summary of care is used when a client is discharged from an inpatient facility to an outpatient facility.

- There is greater ease of sharing records with supervisors and other members of a client's care team.

- Documentation compliance is improved.

- Clients can access an online portal to check on appointments and reminders.

Practice Question

3. A provider wishes to use electronic health records. Which objective BEST helps to eliminate gaps in care?
    A) reporting specific cases
    B) structured electronic transmission of laboratory test results
    C) the use of electronic prescriptions
    D) electronic exchanges of summary of care

Privacy Issues

In the age of social media, privacy is of particular concern for social workers and clients. Clients may share personal information in a public forum, but it is unethical for a social worker to use social media, technology, or other resources to find information about clients without their written permission.

Social media privacy is also appropriate to address in group therapy. Group members may have access to information about other members. Group rules should stress not only the importance of confidentiality but also of privacy.

Social workers consulting with supervisors or other care team members about the client should consider the client's privacy and only provide information relevant to his treatment plan.

> **Helpful Hint**
>
> If the social worker decides it is appropriate to accept a gift, the reasoning should be documented.

Social workers should also avoid accepting gifts from clients except in cases of cultural significance or therapeutic significance. Gift exchanges can create confusion about the nature of the therapeutic relationship, and the social worker needs to consider that as well as the impact that nonacceptance could have on the client's well-being.

Practice Question

4. When is it acceptable for a social worker to look up a client's social media presence?
    A) when a client is mandated to treatment by the judicial system
    B) never
    C) Before the first session so the social worker can get to know the client
    D) if a client makes comments in session that make the social worker uncomfortable

Referrals and Confidentiality

It is imperative to understand and follow confidentiality procedures concerning referrals and consulting. Social workers and consultants must know and understand all local, state, and federal confidentiality laws and regulations and know how to apply them when sharing information and documentation regarding clients. They must also be aware of client rights and responsibilities; furthermore, they should know the ethical and professional standards applicable to confidentiality.

Information provided to insurance companies and other health care professionals is regulated under state law and the Health Insurance Portability and Accountability Act (HIPAA), with those policies outlined in the informed consent. A social worker should share the minimum amount of information necessary to honor the confidentiality of the client. For example, to get reimbursement for services rendered, the social worker may need to disclose the diagnosis and treatment plan objectives to an insurance company;

however, the social worker should not include process notes that contain intimate details of the client's session. Those are not required to secure payment and should therefore remain confidential.

Within the comprehensive care model, organizations often encourage social workers to consult with a client's physician or case manager. This should be discussed with the client and included in the informed consent discussion. When social workers share information with other members of the care team, they should let the client know when and what information was disclosed. For example, the court usually requests progress reports for clients who are in court-mandated treatment. These reports may include attendance records and progress toward goals, but they should be limited to the required information only.

When the social worker provides services to a client with a legal guardian, some information may need to be disclosed to the guardian. Again, that information should be limited. The social worker should discuss the disclosure of other information with the client and get permission to disclose it; the information can then be shared in the client's presence.

For example, an adolescent client may not want the full extent of her substance use shared with her parents. The social worker is not required by law to tell the parents but feels it would be therapeutic for both the client and the family. The social worker may rehearse the disclosure with the client and then facilitate a family session in which the adolescent discloses the substance use to her parents. It is not the social worker's responsibility to tell the parents unless required by law to do so. Disclosing this information without the client's consent could damage the therapeutic relationship and harm the client.

Practice Question

5. What is the best practice model for sharing client information with referral sources?
    A) to share everything known about the client
    B) to not share anything and let the referral source assess the client as needed
    C) to send a copy of the client's file and allow the referral source to take what is needed
    D) to discuss with the client what should be shared, and then share the minimum amount necessary

Answer Key

1. D: In a medical emergency, the social worker may reveal confidential information about the client, but only enough to help the emergency medical personnel do their job. Therefore, the client's name, a description of how she collapsed, and any known physical conditions that could impact her medical treatment are appropriate to disclose. Following the incident, the social worker should document the incident, including what was disclosed in the client's record, and share this information with the client when she is stabilized.

2. C: Obtaining assent from underage clients makes them feel part of the process, helps them understand the social worker's role and how therapy will work, and establishes trust with the social worker.

3. D: Electronic exchanges of summary of care improve coordination of care.

4. B: It is unethical for a social worker to use social media, technology, or other resources to find information about a client without his written permission. Doing so constitutes an invasion of privacy.

5. D: A social worker must get permission from the client to share confidential information, but it is good practice to discuss with the client what he wants or feels comfortable sharing.

13. Professional Development and Use of Self

Social Worker and Client/Client System Relationship

The social worker in a treatment setting should demonstrate empathy while maintaining a level of clinical detachment. This is the basis for a therapeutic relationship.

The **therapeutic relationship** exists to benefit the client—not the social worker. Within a therapeutic relationship, the social worker

- limits self-disclosure
- establishes boundaries with clients
- focuses sessions on the client's treatment goals.

Building trust with a client in the therapeutic relationship involves

- honesty
- empathy
- boundaries
- communication
- client-led care.

In **client-led care**, clients set the agenda guided by the social worker. The social worker does not engage in coercive behaviors, such as forcing a client to participate in a particular type of therapy. Instead, the social worker explains the recommended therapies for a particular issue and allows clients to choose what will work best for them.

When clients present for treatment, they enter the therapeutic relationship with less power than the social worker. The social worker must be aware of this and equalize the power dynamic by consistently **monitoring the therapeutic relationship** and building trust as needed.

The social worker can use the following techniques to monitor the therapeutic relationship:

- Determine how the client feels about the relationship and the therapy process by asking what is working and what else is needed.
- Reestablish a rapport with the client, as necessary, based on client feedback.
- Observe and assess the client's behaviors and nonverbal communication in session.

A client who starts to close up and become quiet may be losing trust in the social worker, and the social worker must call attention to the change and switch gears to reestablish trust. This might mean stopping the work of therapy and establishing common ground again. This can be done by providing the client with standardized assessments at various intervals before a session in order to let the client rate his interaction with the social worker.

Client rights and responsibilities are often listed in the mental health regulations of the state in which the social worker practices. These rights and responsibilities generally fall into one of the following categories:

- high-quality care
- client-centered practice
- informed consent
- confidentiality
- right to records

High-quality care ensures that the client can expect prompt service from adequately trained professionals in an environment of physical and psychological safety:

- If the client feels she is not receiving high-quality care, she has the right to complain and request a referral to another provider.
- The client will not be subject to unnecessary or unending treatment.

In **client-centered practice**, the social worker must inform the client of all treatment options and allow him to choose his goals and treatment methods:

- The client has the right to ask questions about treatment, including methods and finances.

Clients must provide **informed consent** for treatment. To obtain informed consent, social workers must:

- disclose to the client their training and expertise
- explain how the therapy process works and what the client can expect
- describe the boundaries of the therapeutic relationship

Social workers may not conduct treatment interventions they are not trained for.

Clients have the right to a level of **confidentiality**. The social worker will keep the client's personal information confidential according to state and federal laws and explain to the client under what circumstances confidentiality may be broken.

Clients have the **right to records**. The social worker should explain

- how sessions are documented
- why sessions are documented
- how clients can access their records

Since many clients may not understand their records, social workers can go over the records with them.

Although this is usually covered in the first session, the social worker should make a practice of reminding clients of their rights periodically throughout therapy. The first session is usually stressful, so it is irresponsible to expect the client to remember everything that was said.

Practice Question

1. Which of the following BEST describes client-centered practice?
   A) A social worker tells a client how many sessions she will have.
   B) A client wants to focus on anxiety, so the social worker recommends therapeutic interventions.
   C) A client with depression asks the social worker to disregard his history of self-harm.
   D) A client asks to have ninety-minute sessions instead of the usual sixty-minute sessions.

Transference and Countertransference

Conflict in the therapeutic relationship can generate insight and provide beneficial therapeutic moments. **Transference** describes a situation in which the client interacts with the social worker as if the social worker were someone else in the client's life. These interactions can be positive or negative, but either way, they are unhealthy:

- A positive example of transference might be treating the social worker as if she were a friend.

- A negative example might be directing anger at the social worker when the client is angry at his spouse.

In either case, the social worker's skill at bringing awareness to the interaction and processing it with the client can be a constructive therapeutic moment. For example, if the client behaves toward the social worker in anger, the social worker can direct the client's attention to the emotion of anger. The social worker could ask the client to describe what she is feeling in the moment and determine the cause and object of that anger. Also, the social worker might invite the client to engage in a dialogue in which she imagines the social worker is the object of her anger, which allows her to process the emotion through role-play.

When discussing transference, it is also appropriate to bring attention to **countertransference**, which is the social worker's transference toward the client transference. For example, a client treats the social worker as if he is a friend, perhaps telling him that he reminds her of her friend, and then discloses a painful experience. The social worker reacts to the client's transference by sharing a similar painful experience instead of simply listening to the client. That disclosure is countertransference and often happens without the social worker realizing it, which is another reason social worker self-awareness and self-reflection are important:

> **Did You Know?**
>
> Social workers cannot serve clients well if they are not taking good care of themselves. In fact, social workers who do not practice self-care become more at risk of harming their clients either through ignorance or negligence.

- Countertransference can shift the focus from the client's therapeutic needs toward the social worker.

- It also compromises the social worker's objectivity because the professional boundary has been blurred by the disclosure of personal information.

Practice Question

2. Which of the following attributes of the therapeutic relationship is affected by both transference and countertransference?
   A) trust
   B) empathy
   C) professional boundaries
   D) intervention

Self-Care Principles and Techniques

Being a social worker can be a challenging, stressful job. Social workers often work with clients who are dealing with illness, death, or financial hardship. The emotional toll of managing these clients can be immense.

At the same time, social workers may also have to navigate complex systems like hospitals, insurance companies, and government agencies. The impact of these stressful situations cannot be underestimated.

Because of these strains, social workers should not overlook their own **self-care**. The first step in practicing self-care is practicing **self-awareness**. Understanding one's limits and the signs of strain can let the social worker know when it's appropriate to engage in self-care.

Social workers who work with clients who have experienced traumatic events are subject to **secondary trauma**, a condition that mimics the symptoms of PTSD. Although less severe than PTSD, secondary trauma interferes with the social worker's ability to function. Furthermore, when stress is left unattended for too long, social workers can suffer from burnout. **Burnout** is one of the primary reasons social workers leave the profession. Signs of exhaustion, stress, and burnout can include the following:

- increased anxiety
- worrying about clients after hours
- taking work home
- difficulty concentrating
- sleep disturbances
- emotional lability
- social isolation
- increased irritability

Social workers should develop proactive practices for self-care and self-awareness. This may include regularly scheduled activities to promote health and happiness. There are many ways a social worker can fulfill the goal of being healthy and happy:

- routine exercise
  - eating a well-balanced diet
  - getting adequate sleep

- enjoying hobbies
- relaxing
- spending time with friends and family
- refraining from overuse of alcohol or other substances

The social worker should also set physical and emotional boundaries with clients and be willing to ask for assistance when confronted with unmanageable tasks. A crucial boundary for social workers is the one between work and personal life. While social workers should check in with themselves, it is also recommended that social workers in an agency setting check in with each other. Social workers should also talk with spouses, partners, or family members about signs of stress and let them know how to point out those signs when they notice them. Sometimes others will notice the signs of stress before the social worker does.

Practice Question

3. A positive, proactive method for managing stress and burnout in social work might include which of the following?
    A) scheduling lunch away from the office and leaving work right at closing time
    B) taking on as many clients as possible to keep busy
    C) talking to colleagues about stressful clients
    D) refusing to work with difficult or complex clients

Self-Awareness

As an objective participant guiding a therapeutic process with clients, a social worker must practice clinical detachment while conveying empathy. This requires awareness of self. **Awareness of self** is a practice of reflection and observation both in and outside of the moment.

Awareness of self in the moment is a skill whereby the social worker notices his own thoughts, beliefs, emotions, and behaviors without judgment and recognizes how these impact the client. By noticing and evaluating, the social worker can adjust based on the client's reactions. For example, a social worker may find himself reacting emotionally to a client:

- The client may react with surprise.
- The social worker can then choose how to handle the situation without judging his own emotional reaction.
- Sharing an emotional reaction with a client may increase trust.
- The social worker may react negatively to a client's disclosure.
- In practicing self-awareness, the social worker can recognize a negative reaction, evaluate it, and put it aside so the client does not feel judged.
- The social worker may choose to share the process of self-awareness and invite the client to do the same.

Another aspect of self-awareness is the practice of self-reflection on one's own or in consultation with others. Before meeting a client of a significantly different cultural background, for example, the social worker might reflect on her values and beliefs about the client's culture and how those beliefs could impact the client in the session. By practicing self-reflection beforehand, social workers can:

- check whatever bias they may have
- educate themselves about the culture
- meet the client without bringing that bias into the session

The social worker's verbal and nonverbal communication impact clients in both positive and negative ways. Clients can tell if something is not right with the social worker, and that may interfere with building a therapeutic relationship. Therefore, the social worker needs to remain self-aware in sessions and must read the client's cues to understand the client's reaction and make adjustments as needed.

> **Helpful Hint**
>
> Social workers can also practice self-reflection with a supervisor or other colleague to help bring awareness to any bias or prejudice that could adversely affect the client relationship.

Practice Question

4. During a session with a client, a social worker makes a statement and notices the client flinch. What is one thing the social worker can do in the session to demonstrate self-awareness?
   A) continue the session as if nothing happened
   B) ask the client what he got out of the session when it is over
   C) point out the client's reaction and seek understanding from the client
   D) discuss the situation with a supervisor at the next supervision meeting

Self-Assessment

Social workers must continually **assess their competency to work with a specific client** through a process of self-awareness and objective evaluation. Choosing to work with a client when not qualified to do so violates professional ethics and could potentially harm the client:

- Social workers must be honest about the education and training they have received.
- Social workers should pursue continuing education and additional training to keep up with best practices.
- When meeting a client for the first time, social workers must objectively evaluate whether they are qualified to work with the client based on the client's presenting problem.

Being forthcoming about training and education usually applies to certain interventions with clients. For example, if a social worker has not received training and certification to perform EMDR, she must disclose this to a client requesting EMDR and offer another method of therapy or refer the client to someone who is trained.

Self-evaluation of competency to work with clients is more complicated. For example, if a client presents with severe addiction and the social worker is not trained in working with addiction, he must disclose that to the client and refer the client to someone who is qualified. Finally, consultation with a supervisor can help the social worker evaluate his effectiveness and competencies, including creating plans for professional development.

A prominent adage among social workers is, "When in doubt, consult." Social workers who work in community mental health clinics or organizations have access to an on-site supervisor, clinic director, or someone who acts as the senior therapy professional. **Supervision and consultation** are not just for inexperienced social workers; they provide support to all levels. A social worker should seek supervision or consultation in specific situations:

- difficulties with client assessment, diagnosis, and treatment planning
- when a client's progress appears to stagnate
- when a client is in crisis
- when presented with an ethical situation
- when faced with a court order or other legal issue

A significant benefit of seeking supervision and consulting with a colleague when dealing with a client issue or an ethical issue is documented evidence that additional help was requested with an incident. Documentation ensures that the proper procedures were followed and, in legal situations, can act as a level of protection.

When consulting with a supervisor or colleague within the organization that employs a social worker, client confidentiality should be honored, but those consultations tend to fall under the confidentiality exception that clients agree to in informed consent. Social workers in private practice who establish a consultation relationship with another colleague should also disclose to clients the potential for consultation and explain how the social worker will keep the client's information confidential. Consultation and supervision should be limited to issues pertaining to the therapy process, not gossip or the disclosure of client information that is not relevant to treatment.

Practice Question

5. Why is it inappropriate for a social worker to provide treatment using methods on which she has not been fully trained?
    A) The client will not know to ask about the therapy.
    B) An untrained social worker could harm a client.
    C) The client will not receive any benefit from it.
    D) The social worker could make money from referring the client elsewhere.

Group Practice

In **group practice**, the therapeutic relationship between social worker and client changes. The "client" is the group as a whole, rather than each individual member.

Different types of group therapy have their own best practices; however, the general rule is that the primary mode of therapy is the interaction among group members and the social worker as the facilitator. Ultimately, group work focuses on the members working together.

The social worker clarifies how groups work at the first session as well as when new members join (if the group is an open one). The social worker explains her role as facilitator and helps establish group rules with the full participation of members.

The **social worker-client role in group therapy** is a little different than it is in individual therapy. The social worker establishes group work **expectations** like attendance requirements and other administrative policies set forth by the organization and state laws.

In group work, the social worker is required to maintain the confidentiality of the group members, but individual members are not bound by confidentiality rules. Therefore, it is up to the members to create a confidentiality agreement among themselves when establishing group rules.

Group rules, in group therapy, are most effective when the members both set and agree to them. While there may be organizational policies and state laws that apply to group work, members should set a majority of the working rules. These may address:

- confidentiality
- how group members should treat each other
- the extent to which the members want the facilitator involved
- whether someone can be removed from the group for disrespectful behavior

The group should also discuss and agree on the process for member removal. Once the rules are established, they are usually posted in the room and revisited each time someone joins the group.

Termination criteria depend largely on the type of group:

- In **open-ended groups**, members come and go as they please; termination is not necessary.
- Curriculum-based or **closed groups** have start and end points, so termination occurs when the group curriculum is finished.

> **Helpful Hint**
>
> Some groups are open-ended but require clients to attend a certain number of sessions. In these situations, termination occurs once the requirements are met.

Another criterion for termination is the violation of group rules. If a member violates rules after agreeing to comply with them, she will be asked to leave. Such situations should be documented.

Practice Question

6. It is the first session of a closed group therapy meeting. There will be fifteen sessions focusing on dealing with childhood trauma. The facilitator should do which of the following FIRST?
   A) Explain to group members that any confidentiality breaches will lead to removal from the group and could result in legal actions.
   B) Ask group members to share their childhood trauma stories.
   C) Explain the differences between group and individual therapy and guide the group in creating rules.
   D) Invite the organization's administrator to the first group to explain the rules members must abide by.

Statistical Concepts and Methods Used in Research

Social workers must stay current on research trends in mental health and understand the statistical concepts and methods used in research. Research involves a combination of qualitative and quantitative research. Some studies use mixed methods.

Qualitative research addresses how and why things happen. This research relies on interviews, focus groups, and other open-ended evaluation techniques. Qualitative research generally uses fewer participants in an effort to explore a topic more deeply. While this research can lead to statistical results, it is important to review the methods used to achieve these results before applying them in practice. Often, the results of qualitative research can lead to more questions.

Quantitative research relies more on numbers and data points that can be measured and quantified. This form of research relies more on standardized assessments and methods of measuring behavior. It may involve experimental conditions. Quantitative research presents results using numerical data.

To inform the practice, it is best practice to ask several questions when reviewing research:

- **How old is the research?** It is important to consider when the study was conducted as well as when it was published. There is often a significant period between the actual study and the publication of the results, which may influence the applicability of the results. For example, a study published in 2020 that was conducted from 2013 to 2015 may not be relevant due to social and cultural changes that may have taken place since the study was done.

- **How many participants were involved, and what were their characteristics?** Studies with few participants tend to be less generalizable than those with large groups of participants. Furthermore, characteristics such as age, race, gender, geographic location, and socioeconomic status of participants can impact results. A social worker looking for research about depression treatment in adolescents from a particular cultural group would not find relevant information in a study about the elderly in a different cultural group. When deciding whether the research applies to their clients, social workers should consider if the participants are representative of their client population.

- **What methods were used in the research?** If a study reports significant positive results but does not compare the methods to a control group, the results may not be as positive as they seem. Or, if a study purports to be about children with ADHD, it is important to understand how the researchers determined that the participants have ADHD. Examination of the methods of the study will help social workers determine if the study presents results that make sense.

- **What are the limitations of the study?** Limitations presented at the end of the study will reveal flaws in the research and researchers' comments about how their study could have been improved. This may call attention to issues that might have limited the research in some way, such as a small number of participants or a focus on only one cultural group. Research can be stated in terms of statistically significant results and clinically significant results. Statistically significant results do not always mean that the results are clinically significant or clinically appropriate.

- **Over how many months or years did the study take place?** The period over which a study is conducted can impact the validity of the results. For example, a study on addiction treatment may only evaluate the results for the duration of the treatment and for a short time following the treatment. Addiction, however, can be a lifelong challenge, so a social worker should question whether positive results after a short period could be sustained after a longer period.

- **What other studies support the research?** Strong research is that which has been replicated under either the same or different conditions. When deciding between two evidence-based practices, the one with fifteen different studies will likely be more valid and reliable than the practice with only two studies.

Practice Question

7. A social worker is considering several group therapy treatment options while planning an intervention group for women with addictions in prison. Using knowledge of statistical concepts in research, which of the following would present the strongest research picture?
    A) one research study of a group intervention that evaluates women with addiction in an urban setting over ten years
    B) multiple studies that evaluate the intervention of women with addictions that took place seven years prior with no further research conducted
    C) a study of a group that used a similar intervention in one women's prison located in a foreign country
    D) several research studies of an addiction group intervention evaluated in several women's prisons over the past five years that include follow-up studies after the women were released

Advocacy

Social workers are in a unique position to advocate for professional and client issues. Because social workers are privy to the needs, causes, and consequences of mental health issues, that knowledge can be useful for public policy, health care policy, and prevention programs. **Professional advocacy** may occur in several forms:

- lobbying for laws that protect the liability of social workers in client safety situations
- advocating for changes in licensure requirements
- asking for credentialing requirements for joining insurance panels

Social workers should join professional organizations to stay informed about issues pertaining to the profession.

Social workers advocate on behalf of clients to help them secure services. Advocating for a client's needs may include connecting them to a vocational rehab organization to help them find a job.

Social workers also advocate for clients on a broader social level. For example, social workers can be instrumental in advocating for public policy that increases client access to mental health services.

While advocacy is an honorable endeavor, a social worker advocating on behalf of clients must consider whether that advocacy is appropriate and ethical. If advocacy might result in a breach of confidentiality or create a dual relationship, it may not be appropriate.

Practice Question

8. Which ethical issue must a social worker consider before advocating for a client?
    A) the amount of time required
    B) whether the client issue is important
    C) whether it would pose a breach of confidentiality
    D) the social worker's qualifications

Answer Key

1. B: In client-led care, social workers provide guidance, but clients determine the agenda.

2. C: Both transference and countertransference are indications that the relationship is no longer professional but rather focused on projecting a personal aspect onto the relationship.

3. A: Proactive boundaries and time away from clients can help social workers balance work stress and life.

4. C: A self-aware social worker will read the client's nonverbal feedback immediately, recognize something is wrong, and address it in the session as soon as possible to maintain a good therapeutic relationship with the client.

5. B: Without proper training in a given technique, there is a significant risk that the social worker could inadvertently harm a client.

6. C: The social worker's role is group facilitator; the group is the client. Therefore, the social worker needs to guide the group in establishing rules of conduct not otherwise covered.

7. D: This option includes several best practices in research, including studies on the same population with whom the social worker works, the same setting, multiple studies with a large number of participants, and an evaluation of how well the treatment serves the clients after they leave prison. Not only is this collection of studies valid for the application the social worker is considering; it also shows positive results over a long period, thus increasing the likelihood that the social worker's clients will benefit from the intervention.

8. C: Advocating on behalf of a client might risk breaching the client's confidentiality.

Practice Test 1

1. A counselor introduced play therapy to a withdrawn child at a children's day hospital, but the child has not been responding and seems disinterested. What is the counselor's BEST course of action?
    A) continue the treatment
    B) review the treatment with her supervisor
    C) ask a medical professional to review the case
    D) find a counselor with a different treatment style that may help the child

2. Anxiety disorders can develop when an individual's response to normal events is heightened, which can feel overwhelming and interfere with a person's daily life. Medication and psychotherapy can help treat this disorder. Anxiety becomes a severe problem when
    A) it interferes with problem-solving.
    B) thoughts turn to self-harm.
    C) it alerts one to a problem.
    D) it lasts for a short time.

3. A **21**-year-old client is seeing a social worker due to housing issues. She is currently living with her boyfriend, who has become physically abusive. What is the BEST option for the social worker?
    A) report the boyfriend for domestic violence
    B) refer the client to a domestic violence shelter
    C) assess the client's current social supports for possible housing options
    D) offer the client emergency temporary housing in the social worker's home

4. Your client, Marcus, has been struggling with grief since the death of his brother, who was diagnosed with cancer at a young age. Marcus has experienced some of the stages of grief, such as denial, but he is currently struggling with anger. Marcus's anger is directed toward God because he does not understand how God could allow this to happen. Which of the following would be an empathetic response to Marcus's grief?
    A) It sounds like you're angry with God.
    B) It sounds like this is hard for you to navigate.
    C) How does your anger impact your spirituality?
    D) How can you cope with your anger?

5. You are working in private practice and meeting with a new client. A brief review of the categories on his intake forms reveals issues with his social life, medical health, history of mental health concerns, and important relationships. Based on this information, what type of interview should you conduct?
    A) biopsychosocial interview
    B) diagnostic interview
    C) cultural formulation interview
    D) intake interview

6. Which of the following behaviors helps an ethical counselor stay informed of best practices?
    A) group supervision
    B) additional certifications
    C) case conferences
    D) continuing education courses

7. Studies reveal that alcoholism has negative effects on interactions with a person's family, friends, and society. What is a counselor's primary responsibility when working with clients with a history of alcoholism?
    A) finding the point of origin of the drinking problem, formulating a diagnosis, and creating a viable treatment plan
    B) providing clients with addiction psychoeducation to help them understand how their addiction affects their loved ones
    C) encouraging clients to consider a family therapy program so every family member can receive help
    D) helping clients get their family, friends, and other associates to be supportive of their recovery efforts

8. Jean is a thirty-two-year-old woman who began seeing a counselor three years ago when she became suicidal. In therapy, Jean has learned that her depressive symptoms are connected to her history of trauma. Previous counselors have tried using DBT and CBT without lasting results. Which of the following would be the BEST approach to try with Jean?
    A) motivational interviewing
    B) exposure therapy
    C) EMDR
    D) solution-focused therapy

9. When meeting a reluctant client for the first time, what is the counselor's BEST approach?
    A) set firm conditions for the client and get him involved
    B) take the initiative to tell the client about your personal background and beliefs so that you can put him at ease
    C) enable the client to express his feelings and ideas, while discerning that time and effort are required to build relationships
    D) get the client to agree with your ideas so that no problems arise

10. You are meeting with a young adult who was referred by her school counselor. The paperwork identifies concerns about periods of high energy, lack of sleep, and risk-taking behaviors, followed by a period of low energy, suicidal ideation, and feelings of worthlessness. Based on this information, which interview should you conduct?
    A) biopsychosocial interview
    B) diagnostic interview
    C) cultural formulation interview
    D) intake interview

11. Which of the following accurately describes qualitative research?
    A) It relies on data that can be measured.
    B) It is not intended to be applied in practice.
    C) It uses many participants.
    D) It investigates how and why things happen.

12. A **30**-year-old woman who recently immigrated to the US from India is seeing a social worker for assistance with getting a new job. Her English is highly proficient, but she does not have experience with the job market and interview expectations in the US What is the BEST term to describe the client's cultural comfort in the US?
    A) racial discrimination
    B) assimilation
    C) acculturation
    D) melting pot

13. You began working with John when he started struggling with anxiety. He experiences panic attacks and feels anxious throughout the day. John denied having a history of any mental health concerns, including anxiety, until he was diagnosed with prostate cancer six months ago. His symptoms have negatively impacted his job, which is what led to him meeting with you. He reports becoming "consumed" with fear about his treatment and how his family is being impacted by his health. Based on the information, what anxiety diagnosis is appropriate?
    A) panic disorder
    B) generalized anxiety disorder
    C) anxiety disorder due to prostate cancer
    D) panic attacks

14. You are meeting with a forty-eight-year-old Black man with suicidal ideation. He was recently discharged from an inpatient psychiatric program and given a major depressive disorder diagnosis. He shares that since he has been home, his mood has improved, and he has more energy than before. He lives with his wife of twenty-seven years, and his children are independent. He works in construction about sixty hours per week. Before he was discharged, he struggled to identify protective factors and was asked to sign a no suicide contract form. What suicide risk factors should you pay close attention to?
    A) He is at a higher risk of suicide because of his work schedule.
    B) The client is Black and therefore, statistically, has a higher suicide risk.
    C) Having adult children who have moved out of the home puts him at a higher risk.
    D) He is unable to identify protective factors.

15. A counselor is working with a client who has similar problems as several other clients. Which action is MOST appropriate for the counselor to take?
    A) let the client know she has problems that many others have
    B) try to learn if this client's problems have any significant differences
    C) talk about this situation with a coworker
    D) handle it like any other case

16. A counselor meets with a client whose son has been diagnosed with childhood diabetes. The client is disturbed and anxious about her child's condition. What is the BEST way to help this client?
    A) focusing on how the client can help her child
    B) completing a psychological assessment of the client to determine if she can care for the child
    C) referring her to a better paying job
    D) telling the client to calm down because if she is in a hysterical state, she will not be any help to her child

17. A client's value system may differ from that of the counselor. Which statement BEST exemplifies this?
    A) Clients are always immoral; that is why they are in therapy.
    B) Counselors tend to be more educated than their clients.
    C) Counselors should not try to get clients to conform to their values.
    D) Clients' value systems are inferior, which is why they need counselors.

18. You are meeting with a new client who is a teacher at your child's school. She has not taught your student, and your child is past the grade she teaches. What is an appropriate concern to discuss during her intake session?
    A) how to handle seeing each other in public
    B) concerns for your child's current teacher
    C) the school's attendance policy for students
    D) where the teacher can park for therapy

19. You are conducting an intake session with a new client at an IOP addiction counseling center. Clients are asked not to wear clothing referencing alcohol, such as a Bud Light T-shirt. How can you apprise the client of this policy?
    A) briefly touch on the policy during the intake session
    B) give her a printout instead of discussing the policy
    C) discuss the policy and ask if she has questions about it
    D) address it if the client comes to group wearing something restricted

20. Toby has lived with depression his whole life. He has tried psychotropic medications and has worked with several counselors and doctors who recommended that he attend therapy to investigate his thought patterns and how they influence his depressive feelings. By analyzing his thoughts, he can learn to replace them with new thoughts that positively impact his feelings. What kind of therapy should Toby attend?
    A) psychodynamic therapy
    B) Adlerian therapy
    C) cognitive behavioral therapy
    D) person-centered therapy

21. Which of the following factors is associated with an individual who has a higher risk of suicide?
    A) being a female
    B) being a male and living with family
    C) having a history of suicide threats
    D) feeling hopeless

22. What should a counselor do when a client complains of medical problems?
    A) ignore such problems because they are beyond the scope of her responsibilities
    B) inform the client that she recognizes his problems but will not address them
    C) recommend that the client suspends therapy and visits a physician instead
    D) make referrals to the proper sources for treatment

23. A client at the local domestic violence shelter is seeking assistance with gaining custody of her children. She left the father after enduring years of physical abuse, but he is claiming custody over their two sons. The client reports feeling scared and hopeless that the father will gain custody. What is the BEST response the social worker should give?
    A) reassure the client that the father will not win in a case like this
    B) explore the client's feelings of fear and hopelessness
    C) create a case plan for the client to prove her efficacy as a parent
    D) assess the client's current safety

24. You have been working with a client for several months and feel that you could improve the treatment plan by making it more person-centered and taking into consideration the client's customs and traditions regarding her presentation. Which interview could help you better understand how the client's experiences tie into her struggles?
    A) biopsychosocial interview
    B) diagnostic interview
    C) cultural formulation interview
    D) intake interview

25. You are meeting with a new client for an intake assessment. What is the main goal of this session?
    A) assess for a mental health concern
    B) assess for suicidal ideation, plan, and intent
    C) determine if the client is appropriate to work with
    D) understand the client's concerns and develop a treatment plan

26. What is the BEST way for an interviewer to secure reliable data and reduce the possibility of misunderstanding?
    A) use casual, undirected conversation, enabling interviewees to talk about themselves
    B) ask direct questions
    C) obtain the desired information from interviewees by putting them on the defensive
    D) explain to interviewees the information desired and the reasons for needing it

27. Which of the following behaviors could demonstrate genuineness to a client?
    A) warm and open body posture
    B) closed posture
    C) inconsistent eye contact
    D) fidgeting in chair

28. A counselor can exhibit which of the following characteristics to show genuineness?
    A) appropriate curiosity
    B) appropriate pity
    C) appropriate empathy
    D) appropriate interest

29. You are meeting with a new client who was referred by her primary care physician. Ann is a twelve-year-old female who has been lashing out verbally at teachers over the past year. Ann's parents report similar behaviors at home and explain that they do not know how to help her. Ann's mother says that there are usually four to five outbursts each week between school and home. Even when Ann does not have an outburst, she is irritable. Ann's mom feels like she is "walking on eggshells" when Ann returns home from school because she never knows how Ann's mood will be. Based on the information, which diagnosis will you investigate?
    A) borderline personality disorder
    B) disruptive mood dysregulation disorder
    C) attention-deficit/hyperactivity disorder
    D) bipolar disorder

30. The *DSM-5* permits certain diagnoses for mental disorders to be made even though the symptoms may not completely adhere to *DSM-5* criteria. These diagnoses are typically modified by which word?
    A) transitory
    B) provisional
    C) limited
    D) temporary

31. You are running a group therapy session that focuses on relapse prevention skills for individuals in early recovery. Some group members have just completed an inpatient rehab program; others have recently relapsed. Some individuals will be in this group longer than others, and new members will be joining. Which therapeutic approach would work BEST for your group?
    A) motivational interviewing
    B) cognitive behavioral therapy
    C) solution-focused brief therapy
    D) behavioral therapy

32. You are getting ready to meet with a new client and are deciding which version of the Structured Clinical Interview for *DSM-5* (SCID-5) to use. How many choices are there?
    A) three
    B) five
    C) six
    D) seven

33. The idea of congruence is associated with which therapeutic approach?
    A) cognitive behavioral therapy
    B) solution-focused brief therapy
    C) person-centered therapy
    D) family therapy

226   Practice Test 1

34. You use cognitive processing therapy with your clients who have a history of trauma. One client has not responded to this treatment. She has formed a therapeutic relationship with you and does not want to see a counselor who uses a different therapeutic approach. Which statement is MOST true about using a therapeutic approach you are not trained in?
    A) The client's insurance can elect not to pay for the sessions.
    B) The client's outcomes will be the same no matter which counselor she sees.
    C) You will not need supervision if the approach was covered in your education program.
    D) You do not need to tell the client that you are not trained in the other approach.

35. A counselor works in a psychiatric program at a hospital with a physician, a social worker, and several nurses. What is this approach called?
    A) collaborative care
    B) holistic care
    C) group practice
    D) inpatient care

36. A social worker has an older adult client who has been having trouble maintaining her finances. She recently moved in with her son, who is unemployed, to get some help keeping track of her expenses and doctor appointments. On her most recent visit, she stated that the son is wearing expensive new clothing and reported that several hundred dollars in cash she stashed in her drawer had recently gone missing. What is the BEST course of action for the social worker?
    A) report the son for suspected elder abuse
    B) conduct a family session to establish better boundaries between mother and son
    C) confront the son about where he purchased the clothes
    D) ask the client if she may have misplaced the cash

37. Jeremiah is a sixteen-year-old male who was arrested for destruction of property. His parents are concerned because this is not the first time his rage has led to him breaking things. When told he could not go out with his friends, he began throwing plates from the dinner table. Before his arrest, Jeremiah got into a disagreement with a stranger at a store. He did show remorse for breaking items in the store; however, his anger has lingered. The judge on Jeremiah's case enforced a mental health assessment as a condition of his release. Based on the information, which diagnosis will you investigate during your initial interview?
    A) antisocial personality disorder
    B) conduct disorder
    C) intermittent explosive disorder
    D) borderline personality disorder

38. You are conducting an initial assessment with a client who identifies with a different ethnicity and religion than you do. How would you proceed?
    A) refer the client to a colleague who shares his ethnicity
    B) cancel the appointment
    C) conduct the initial assessment
    D) speak with your supervisor for guidance

39. A couple requests help in improving their seven-year marriage. When the counselor asks them about their goals, they begin to argue almost immediately. The husband says that his wife nags him too much about chores. The wife says her husband is lazy. What should the counselor do?
    A) assist them in establishing treatment goals so they can learn to improve their communication and resolve conflict
    B) recommend that they attend sessions individually to set separate goals to work on until they are ready to work together in a session
    C) assist them in setting a goal to help them resolve their arguments about household responsibilities
    D) recommend that they receive individual treatment to help them work on individual issues

40. A couple requests help to improve their seven-year marriage. When the counselor asks them about their goals, they begin to argue. The husband says that his wife nags him too much about chores. The wife states that her husband is lazy. What should the counselor do?
    A) assist them in establishing treatment goals to help them learn to improve their communication and resolve conflict
    B) recommend that they each attend individual sessions with you to set separate goals to work on until they are ready to work together in a session
    C) assist them in setting a goal to help them resolve their arguments about household responsibilities
    D) recommend they receive individual treatment to help them work on individual issues

41. One of your current clients sent you a friend request on social media. How should you proceed?
    A) block the request
    B) ignore the request
    C) wait until your next session
    D) consult with your supervisor

42. You are meeting with two new clients, Thomas and Derrick, for a couples counseling session. Thomas and Derrick have been in a committed relationship for four years and are planning to marry in the fall. They have wanted to come to counseling for a while but could not due to financial constraints. After meeting with them, you recognize that Thomas takes on a caretaking role with Derrick by trying to fix his problems and ensure he is taking care of his responsibilities. This causes Thomas to neglect his own responsibilities. Thomas has begun feeling resentful toward Derrick because he feels that Derrick does not acknowledge all that he does for him. What would you begin to focus on in sessions?
    A) improving communication patterns
    B) decreasing codependency patterns
    C) establishing time management skills for Derrick
    D) determining what led to their delay in seeking help

43. A counselor is telling new clients how she can be contacted and gives them a phone number and email address. What should clients know about exchanging emails?
    A) Counselors are available 24/7 via email communication.
    B) Emails will be received by an automated service.
    C) Clients should not email personal or confidential information.
    D) Emails are not documented in a client's chart.

44. Regarding goal setting, what is the counselor's role when working with clients?
    A) let them know what has worked for the counselor personally
    B) allow them to identify their own goals
    C) explain what would be appropriate
    D) provide an objective perspective

45. Jerry is a 22-year-old client who is seeking help managing his school and workload in college. His family pressures Jerry to help pay bills while maintaining his GPA and applying for graduate school. Which of the following systems is the BEST choice for the social worker to examine with Jerry?
    A) church system
    B) political system
    C) academic system
    D) family system

46. You have a session with a twenty-four-year-old male who was referred by his school counselor. He has been struggling with anxiety symptoms and shares that he has become very close with his male best friend. He is worried that his feelings of friendship are romantic interest. He explains that his parents are openly against being gay, and he is worried that they would disown him. Which characteristic would be the MOST helpful for your client?
    A) consistency
    B) patience
    C) bias
    D) unconditional positive regard

47. Terry is about to complete his sixty-day inpatient treatment program for opioid abuse disorder. His clinical team recommends that he continue engaging in addiction treatment since this was his second time at the inpatient rehab. He is being referred to a higher level of care that depends on having a safe and sober home environment. He will attend treatment for six to eight hours each day. Terry lives with his wife, who doesn't use any substances, and their three children who range from six to nine years old. Terry has a great network of sober friends, including individuals with whom he attends Narcotics Anonymous. Which level of care would be an ideal fit for Terry?
    A) outpatient treatment
    B) detoxification
    C) partial hospitalization program
    D) aftercare programming

48. You are working with Lucia, a forty-two-year-old female, for her depressive concerns. Lucia's elderly mother moved into her home so that Lucia could provide support for her. In Lucia's family, this is a norm, and she has been expecting this to happen for some time after noticing her mother's mobility declining. Lucia's husband does not agree with this transition and feels that Lucia should move her mother into a nursing home. Which of the following could help Lucia with her husband's resistance?
    A) telling Lucia that you can only provide emotional support for her, not her mother
    B) encouraging her to do what feels right
    C) encouraging a couples counseling session
    D) encouraging her to move her mother into a nursing home

49. You are discussing with a colleague why you prefer the SCID-5 to other assessment tools. Which reason could you give to support your preference?
    A) It is required when giving a diagnosis using the *DSM-5*.
    B) It streamlines the intake process.
    C) It saves time.
    D) It ensures that counselors are checking for the most common diagnoses.

50. You run a support group at a college counseling center for students with social anxiety. During your first group session, members establish their rules. What is a benefit of group rules?
    A) Establishing rules can make members feel more comfortable.
    B) Rules are meant to be used as criteria for discharge.
    C) Rules are more of a guideline for group members.
    D) Making rules can be an icebreaker activity.

51. Mary is a thirty-eight-year-old client who has recently decided to find a new career opportunity. She has been experiencing a depressed mood, unplanned weight loss, insomnia, and an inability to concentrate. Mary believes that her depressive symptoms are tied to being dissatisfied with her job at an elementary school and that events during and after the COVID pandemic changed the environment. She talks about making progress toward her goal of finding a new job opportunity and expresses interest in developing short-term goals to work toward the big goal of finding a new job. What is the time frame associated with short-term goals that Mary should be aware of?
    A) sixty days
    B) fourteen days
    C) thirty days
    D) ninety days

52. A social worker is leading a women's support group focused on empowerment and self-actualization. A client in the group shares an experience she had in a recent job interview, where she was asked if she had adequate plans for childcare for her children. Which of the following terms BEST describes the woman's experience?
    A) discrimination
    B) stereotyping
    C) ethnocentrism
    D) consciousness raising

53. A social worker has a 21-year-old male client who is seeking help with his relationship with his boyfriend. They have been seeing each other for six months, but the client is experiencing some distress. The partner's family will not meet him because he is gay. What should the social worker do NEXT?
    A) invite the client to bring his partner into the session to better understand the partner's side
    B) teach the client some emotion regulation techniques to use when meeting his partner's family
    C) explain to the client that every family has different norms and expectations and to be patient
    D) actively reflect the client's distress and reassure the client of the validity of his feelings

54. You have continued working with Mary to develop short-term goals that can help her work toward her long-term goal of finding a new career path. Mary is not sure what she would like to consider for her new career and has only ever thought about being a teacher. What would be a helpful short-term goal for Mary?
    A) using bibliotherapy
    B) completing the self-directed search
    C) developing a list of interests
    D) identifying a desired salary range

55. You are a high school counselor checking in with the seniors at the beginning of the school year to discuss their graduation plans. You just met with Muhammad, the oldest of four siblings. He is in the top 10 percent of his graduating class and is planning to attend law school. His father is a practicing lawyer and has told Muhammad how proud he is that he wants to be in the same field. You realize that Muhammad has a hard time saying no and establishing boundaries with others. He said he has no time for leisure activities because he has been busy with soccer and studying. Which family role has Muhammad taken on?
    A) protector
    B) scapegoat
    C) hero
    D) mediator

56. You offer a family therapy program in your addiction treatment program. As part of this, you provide psychoeducation about the disease concept of addiction, recovery, communication, and healthy boundaries. A common boundary concern is when a person takes on a caretaker role with a loved one who is struggling with an addiction. This role may involve some enabling. How would you describe this relationship pattern?
    A) codependency
    B) gaslighting
    C) controlling
    D) dependence

57. You have been meeting with the Smith family for one month with a focus on improving communication, creating boundaries, and promoting healthier relationships. You have noticed that the middle child, Lulu, appears withdrawn, anxious, and shy. Her participation in family sessions has been limited. How would you describe Lulu's role in the family?
    A) scapegoat
    B) lost child
    C) mascot
    D) family hero

58. You have been working with Richard for approximately six months regarding his concerns with his marriage. Richard shares that he and his wife argue frequently and have been unhappy with their marriage for over a year. He would like to work through this tough patch and has been trying to understand his wife's perspective, be an active listener, and avoid blaming. Richard feels that these strategies have positively impacted his relationship. What skills has Richard been using with his wife?
    A) coping skills
    B) dialectical behavior therapy skills
    C) conflict resolution skills
    D) communication skills

59. You are working with a member of the First Nations who has been struggling with depressive symptoms. You do not share your client's cultural background. She shared that her family moved from Canada to New York in the 1960s after learning that a family member was being treated badly in a reform school. The client does not feel comfortable living in New York but does not feel like she belongs in Canada either. What would be the MOST culturally sensitive way to proceed?
    A) discuss your knowledge of reform schools
    B) suggest medication-assisted therapy
    C) explore and process her experience
    D) encourage her to focus on the present moment

60. You are working with Dan, a thirty-two-year-old male complaining of restlessness, inability to concentrate, and sweating. You suspect anxiety and want to use a short assessment of twenty-one questions. Which assessment would apply?
    A) Hamilton Anxiety Rating Scale
    B) Beck Anxiety Inventory
    C) Zung Self-Rating Anxiety Scale
    D) appearance anxiety inventory

61. You have continued working with Dan for several weeks since administering the BAI to assess the severity of his anxiety symptoms. Since then, you have suggested Dan use behavioral treatments like meditation, mindfulness, and CBT when he feels anxious. When would be the BEST time to readminister the BAI to assess for progress?
    A) fourteen days after initial administration
    B) thirty days after initial administration
    C) forty-five days after initial administration
    D) sixty days after initial administration

62. A client reports increasingly frequent bouts of dizziness and seeing bright lights. At times, the lights are so bright that the client cannot see. The client reports that these experiences often happen after stressful situations. What is the BEST course of action for the social worker to take?
    A) explore the mind-body connection with the client regarding the stress levels
    B) offer to reschedule the session for a time when the client is feeling less stress
    C) assess the client for any possible visual or auditory hallucinations along with the bright lights
    D) refer the client to a physician to determine if there are any medical causes

63. Which of the following is necessary for a client to give informed consent?
    A) must be physically present for the practice or study
    B) must understand the associated risks of participating
    C) must receive financial compensation for participating
    D) must give verbal consent, not written

64. You have suggested that Richard try an "I statement" strategy, explaining that this can keep him from placing blame on the other person, which can lead to a better outcome. Which of the following is an example of an "I statement"?
    A) "I feel sad when you leave. I worry you're mad at me."
    B) "I feel sad because you leave. It feels like you're mad at me."
    C) "I am sad because you left. I feel like you don't care."
    D) "I am sad when you leave. I get scared you won't return."

65. Which of the following mental health concerns commonly uses spirituality in treatment approaches?
    A) bipolar disorder
    B) substance use disorder
    C) post-traumatic stress disorder
    D) depressive disorder

66. You are studying for an exam in your developmental psychology class and remember that the initial version of the family life cycle was developed by whom?
    A) Bernice Neugarten
    B) Erik Erikson
    C) Evelyn Duvall
    D) Alfred Adler

67. A counselor is meeting with a new client for the first time. Nader shares that he has never been in counseling and appears uncomfortable: he cannot sit still, is bouncing his leg, and says he is having trouble concentrating. The counselor takes a few moments to explain what Nader can expect from his session and how it can help guide the counselor's work with him. Which intervention is this?
    A) normalizing the client's experience
    B) validating the client's experience
    C) psychoeducation
    D) therapy road map

68. The cycle for the intact middle-class nuclear family has how many stages?
    A) five
    B) six
    C) seven
    D) eight

69. Mark is a sixteen-year-old boy with depressive symptoms. He does not share much in therapy and appears uncomfortable. His mother brought him to counseling after his teachers told her about an essay he wrote that appears to glorify suicide. Which of the following could help build trust with Mark during sessions?
    A) using open-ended questions
    B) reflecting on his mother's input
    C) providing suicide psychoeducation
    D) family sessions with his mother

70. You have been working with Samantha, a thirty-two-year-old female who has been struggling with anxiety. She recently started a new job and is hoping to improve her confidence during interactions with her colleagues. Which of the following exercises would help Samantha work toward her goal?
    A) the empty chair technique
    B) role-playing
    C) the miracle question
    D) journaling

71. A family has adopted a seven-year-old boy who previously experienced severe neglect. The adoptive parents are meeting with a counselor because he continues to hoard food. The parents often find food under his bed, and he sneaks extra food into his backpack for school. What should the counselor recommend?
    A) The parents should take away privileges each time they discover that he is hoarding food.
    B) They should install locks on the cupboards and refrigerator so they can better monitor his food intake.
    C) The parents should ignore the behavior, as it will likely go away on its own once the child realizes that the family has plenty of food.
    D) They can provide the child with a food basket where he can keep his healthy snacks, and they can refill the basket when it is almost empty.

72. You are working in an outpatient addiction treatment program and are meeting with a new client, Sam, who recently completed a local inpatient addiction rehab program. You learn that Sam does not have sober support: his close family and friends struggle with their own addiction issues. Sam would like to find other options for support. What is an appropriate recommendation?
    A) social media connections
    B) group therapy
    C) Alcoholics Anonymous
    D) a dating app

234 Practice Test 1

73. Elaine and Joey have been married for about two years and have begun to argue more. They explained that this change began around the time they learned they would need to have medical supports to conceive a baby. Since then, they argue about every aspect of their lives, including their finances, hobbies, careers, and family relationships. Since meeting with you, they have been working on their ability to cope with their challenging emotions, which has had a positive impact on their arguing habits. How would you describe the resolution Elaine and Joey have reached?
    A) acceptance of their inability to conceive a child
    B) acceptance that they need IVF
    C) decrease in the frequency of arguing
    D) improved emotion regulation skills

74. You are working in an addiction treatment program and met with Nathan, who shared that he came to his appointment after his parents gave him an ultimatum. To continue supporting him financially, they want him to be in therapy and stop drinking. Nathan feels his drinking is sometimes a problem, but he does not think he needs to make any changes. He shared that he is only there to appease his parents. Which of the five stages of change is Nathan in?
    A) precontemplation
    B) contemplation
    C) preparation
    D) action

75. Elijah and Mary are developing a blended family. Both are divorced, have had time to process and move on from their divorces, and have children from their previous relationships. They are working on defining new roles, boundaries, and expectations within their blended family. Which stage of Carter and McGoldrick's stages of Remarried Family Formulation are they in?
    A) entering the new relationship
    B) conceptualizing and planning a new marriage and family
    C) moving into the same residence
    D) remarrying and reconstituting a family

76. A client is seeking testing accommodations for her learning disability at her university. What is the NEXT thing the social worker should do?
    A) create an action plan with the client to address the steps needed to secure testing accommodations
    B) assess to determine what steps the client has taken to secure accommodations so far and what steps she must next take
    C) educate the client on the steps she must take to secure testing accommodations
    D) call the disability center to advocate for the client's right to accommodations

77. Person-centered therapy should take place in a supportive environment created by a close personal relationship between counselor and client. The general direction of the therapy is determined by the client, while the counselor seeks to increase the client's insight and self-understanding through informal questions. Three attitudes on the part of the counselor are central to the productivity of person-centered therapy. They are congruence, unconditional positive regard, and what?
    A) complimentary
    B) positive reaction
    C) empathy
    D) coerciveness

78. While discussing the SCID-5 with a colleague, you say you are confident that you are evaluating for the major diagnoses in the *DSM-5*, also known as the "core coverage." How many core diagnoses are included in the SCID-5?
    A) six
    B) eight
    C) ten
    D) twelve

79. You are preparing for a support group designed for people who have experienced domestic violence and spend time reviewing material from John Gottman and his colleagues that discusses the two main types of batterers. "Pit bulls" are individuals whose heart rate increases when they are verbally aggressive. The second type of batterer experiences a decrease in heart rate when being verbally aggressive. These batterers tend to be antisocial and violent with most individuals in their lives. Which term is used to describe the second type of batterer?
    A) viper
    B) cobra
    C) adder
    D) python

80. A counselor working at an inpatient addiction rehab program plans to give a psychoeducational lecture to the program participants. What would be an appropriate topic for this lecture?
    A) vocational opportunities
    B) coping with trauma
    C) nutrition
    D) relapse prevention

81. You are meeting with Monica, a new client who notes on her intake paperwork that she has been struggling with anxiety for a couple of months. She reports that her partner struggles with anger management and lashes out when he is angry. During your assessment, what will be your primary focus?
    A) exploring her anxiety symptoms
    B) psychoeducation about healthy coping skills
    C) assessing the level of violence and abuse
    D) identifying her healthy supports

82. Erica was diagnosed with bipolar disorder four years ago. She wants to start individual therapy sessions to help manage her symptoms. After sharing with her psychiatrist that she was beginning to struggle with depressive symptoms, she was referred to a counseling practice. What is the MOST important information the counselor should request before working with Erica?
    A) records from her psychiatrist
    B) records from her graduate school
    C) records from her primary care physician
    D) records from her current employer

83. Your private practice office is in a building with an elevator, which has a pass code to deter people from using it excessively. You have an initial intake with an individual who is unable to walk long distances due to medical concerns. How would you proceed?
    A) refer the client to a different practice
    B) have the meeting on the first floor
    C) provide the code to the client before the session
    D) see if he can use the stairs before providing the code

84. A colleague prefers conducting unstructured clinical interviews, rather than structured interviews using the SCID-5. What are some of the typical topics covered in an unstructured clinical interview?
    A) enjoyable activities, exercise routine, and eating habits
    B) career goals, finances, and dating history
    C) social activities, physical and mental health history, and drug and alcohol use
    D) sources of guilt and shame, legal history, and leisure activities

85. You are working with a college student who has poor sleep hygiene. Ryan sleeps for only five hours and often struggles to pay attention in school. After deciding that he would benefit from receiving psychoeducation about sleep, you discuss sleep cycles. How many stages are there in a sleep cycle?
    A) three
    B) four
    C) five
    D) six

86. A client who has been receiving counseling services for a fee is overdue on the payments despite agreeing to the set rate stated in his contract. The counselor decides to terminate services. Is it ethical to close a case based on nonpayment?
    A) No. Clients should rectify payment issues with the counselor's supervisor.
    B) No. Clients have a legal right to receive counseling services even if they cannot pay.
    C) No. Counselors should redo payment contracts to accommodate the financial needs of clients.
    D) Yes. Counselors can terminate services if there is no imminent danger to the clients or others.

87. A teenager who is mixed race is seeing a social worker due to home issues. The client lives with his mother, who is White, and sees his father, who is Black, on weekends. The client reports feeling angry when at his mother's house due to his lack of opportunities to connect with his racial identity. What should the social worker do NEXT?
    A) assess for possible emotional abuse from the mother
    B) reflect and acknowledge the client's feelings of anger
    C) explore with the client the possibility of moving in with his father to better support his racial identity
    D) suggest that the client seek out more opportunities to explore his racial background

88. You receive a referral for a new client, a twenty-eight-year-old male who has been having difficulty at work. He has received a written warning for not completing his tasks as expected and is now experiencing anxiety symptoms and significant worry about losing his job. In the paperwork, he notes having difficulty sleeping, specifically, waking up several times at night and not feeling rested in the morning. The sleep difficulties started almost four months ago and occur four to five nights a week. Which diagnosis would you investigate?
    A) generalized anxiety disorder
    B) hypersomnolence disorder
    C) insomnia disorder
    D) central sleep apnea

89. You have been working with Anthony for twelve weeks to address his history of trauma. Anthony has been receptive to DBT, and you have been introducing him to emotion regulation skills. Which of the following acronyms can help him with emotion regulation?
    A) SAD
    B) HALT
    C) CAGE
    D) PLEASE

90. Jia started therapy when her youngest child began attending college. Jia has her master's degree in journalism and had a successful career as a journalist. When she and her husband wanted to settle down, she decided to stop working to become a stay-at-home mother. This quickly became her identity, and Jia began to disengage from her hobbies and interests. When Jia's youngest started college, Jia began struggling with the idea of an empty nest. She does not enjoy her hobbies and has not wanted to return to writing. She has also been sleeping more than usual and has noticed that her clothes are fitting more loosely. Which diagnosis would you investigate?
    A) adjustment disorder
    B) major depressive disorder
    C) disruptive mood dysregulation disorder
    D) dysthymia

91. A counselor is reviewing the limitations of confidentiality with new clients. What is a limit clients should be aware of?
    A) Their spouse can have limited access to their records.
    B) Their emergency contact can have limited access to their records.
    C) Their records may be viewed during a state or federal audit.
    D) Their records are not protected by confidentiality in death.

92. A client is seeking assistance from the local food bank; his family does not have enough money to purchase food for the week. Which level on Maslow's hierarchy does this client's need BEST fit?
    A) physiological needs
    B) safety needs
    C) love and belonging needs
    D) self-esteem

93. Which of the following is a benefit of an unstructured interview?
    A) It allows the counselor to cover a variety of mental health concerns.
    B) A standardized list of questions guides the counselor.
    C) Unstructured interviews reveal more context and details for relevant topics.
    D) The more a counselor uses an unstructured interview, the easier it is to administer.

94. Your client Samantha has had depressive symptoms for two months: a depressed mood, loss of interest in hobbies and friends, and sleeping more than normal. She is drinking six to eight beers after work four to five days a week. Samantha feels guilty about driving to work while impaired and working the full day not feeling well. She explained that in the past, she drank one to two drinks on occasion. Based on the information, which idea should you discuss with your supervisor?
    A) refer her to an inpatient addiction treatment program
    B) refer her to a counselor who is in recovery
    C) refer her to your supervisor for assessment
    D) continue working with her and monitoring her alcohol use

95. Which of the following behaviors could a group leader model to group members to encourage active listening?
    A) drinking his coffee
    B) chewing gum
    C) nodding his head
    D) playing with a pen

96. You are the director of a mental health practice. What is an example of advocacy you could participate in for client concerns?
    A) creating a social media account providing psychoeducation on coping skills
    B) lobbying for laws that protect the liability of client safety
    C) talking to your colleagues about your concerns
    D) encouraging your colleagues to make phone calls and emails regarding your concerns

97. Pedro is a forty-seven-year-old man who has reached out to you to gain perspective and guidance. He has been caring for his older mother and has noticed some concerning symptoms: his mother's energy level and appetite have decreased, and she has been complaining to her doctors about stomach pains, but there are no physical reasons for the complaints. Pedro has recently heard his mother weeping in her room in the evenings and is unsure how he can help her. You notice Pedro's pressured speech. He appears anxious and is in clear distress. How can you help Pedro?
    A) listen and validate his concerns
    B) provide him with referrals for his mother
    C) speak with his mother about her symptoms
    D) discuss common concerns for older adults

98. You are running an intensive outpatient program group. A group member shares that she received Narcan last night after relapsing and overdosing on heroin. She denied seeking medical attention. Your clinic has a medical staff member present when it is open. What is the BEST action to take?
    A) process her relapse and continue with the group
    B) consult with your supervisor after the group session concludes
    C) focus on relapse prevention skills
    D) escort her to meet with the medical staff for assessment

99. A fifty-seven-year-old man has been meeting with a counselor to address his alcohol dependence and has cut down on his drinking over the past few weeks. He arrives at his appointment sweating, says that he has been vomiting, and has a noticeable tremor in his hands. What should the counselor do?
    A) call 911, even if the client refuses to consent, as he is likely detoxing and may experience seizures or possibly death
    B) explain the possible dangers of alcohol withdrawal and collaborate with the client to decide whether to seek medical help
    C) encourage the client to withstand the uncomfortable symptoms for a few days, as they will likely pass after the painful detox process
    D) encourage the client to decrease his alcohol intake more slowly, as he will be less likely to experience such serious withdrawal symptoms

100. You have been working with Rachel, a nineteen-year-old female with trauma symptoms and a history of childhood abuse and neglect. Rachel said that you remind her of her childhood neighbor who would give her juice boxes and invite her for lunch. She shared that she was fond of this neighbor because she seemed to care when her parents did not. She said that she feels the same about you and that no one else in her life has taken the time to listen to her thoughts and feelings. Based on the information, what is Rachel exhibiting?
    A) codependency
    B) transference
    C) countertransference
    D) building rapport

101. Which of the following should a counselor do when working with any client?
    A) accept the client in a positive way while remaining objective
    B) understand that most clients will be negative and hard to deal with
    C) be optimistic and permissive
    D) disagree with clients until a long-standing foundation of trust is built

102. During an interview, a client relates his family situation, saying, "Two of my kids are in school, but my oldest, who is now nineteen . . ." He pauses and does not continue. What should the counselor do?
    A) ask if the oldest child works
    B) ask if the oldest child left school
    C) quickly ask about the last child
    D) patiently wait for the client to continue

103. During an interview, a curious client asks several questions about the counselor's private life. How should the counselor respond?
    A) refuse to answer such questions
    B) answer the questions fully
    C) explain that your primary concern is with her problems and that discussion of your personal affairs will not help meet her needs
    D) explain that it is the responsibility of the interviewer to ask questions and not to answer them

104. You began working with a single mother, Lucy, and her fourteen-year-old daughter Erin. Lucy reached out for counseling because she gets overwhelmed with the frequency of arguments that she and her daughter have. Lucy was honest and shared that they both get angry and hostile and say mean things. Lucy is looking for ways to decrease the amount of conflict she and Erin have. What would be MOST helpful for both mother and daughter?
    A) discussing body language
    B) emotion regulation skills
    C) walking away
    D) journaling

105. A counselor is working on value clarification with a client who has alcohol dependence. He is also assisting her in recognizing the consequences and the impact her behaviors have on others. The counselor uses a readiness ruler to help assess the client's readiness to change. These methods are most likely to be effective when the client is in which stage of the transtheoretical model?
    A) action
    B) maintenance
    C) preparation
    D) pre-contemplation

106. You have been working with Elizabeth for approximately two years for various mental health concerns including anxiety. She is four months pregnant and is concerned because her husband made a comment after observing her eating chalk. Elizabeth shares that she knows it sounds odd, but she has a craving for chalk. She thinks it is just a pregnancy craving, but her husband thinks it is something more. What is your next step?
- A) refer her to her ob-gyn
- B) refer her to her primary care physician
- C) refer for pica assessment
- D) refer for nutrition assessment

107. You are speaking with a colleague who thinks that the initial assessment he just completed could have gone poorly. He explains that he was feeling tired, hungry, and distracted, which got in the way of demonstrating positive regard. How can you show your colleague positive regard?
- A) offer to do his next assessment so he can take a needed break
- B) take him out to get food and allow him to voice his concerns
- C) explain that this does not negate his work as a skilled clinician
- D) encourage him to contact the client and apologize for his performance

108. You are working with Nina, a twenty-two-year-old female who has been struggling with suicidal ideation while coping with her recent diagnosis of bipolar disorder. Nina has shared that she has thoughts about death daily and finds that by evening, her thoughts turn to a desire to die. She has had passive thoughts about suicide recently, and this concerns her. You validate her concern and work to develop a safety plan. She has agreed that keeping a small card with her safety plan in her wallet would be ideal. What is something that could be written on her safety card?
- A) her employer's phone number
- B) list of mental health concerns
- C) phone number for a supportive person
- D) phone number for her ex-partner

109. Nina calls you and shares that she is currently struggling with suicidal ideation. She explains that she has had a tough day and feels like giving up. Nina lets you know that she is home alone and has access to prescription medications that she has been thinking about taking. She is tearful and says that she called because she does not want to die but does not know what else to do. How should you proceed?
- A) tell her you are concerned about her safety and will be calling for a wellness check
- B) tell her you are concerned and that you can meet with her individually tomorrow
- C) tell her you are concerned and encourage her to call her close friends for support
- D) tell her you are concerned and encourage her to use her emotion regulation skills

110. You are a counselor in an inpatient rehab setting and have just completed an intake assessment for a twenty-two-year-old female who has been struggling with heroin addiction for about a year and a half. During your assessment, you learned that she has a history of trauma and binge eating. Which treatment approach would you recommend?
- A) focusing on her opioid addiction
- B) focusing on her trauma history
- C) focusing on her disordered eating behaviors
- D) a holistic approach addressing all concerns

111. You have been working with Molly for several months regarding her anxiety symptoms. Molly has increased her coping skills and changed her lifestyle and now feels that she can better manage her symptoms. She has moved on to figuring out healthy changes she can make at home that would improve her familial relationships. Molly has shared that her partner and children have distanced themselves from her because they never know how she is feeling. Which of the following could help improve their relationships?
   A) scheduling family activities
   B) talking about Molly's progress
   C) letting her family come to her
   D) waiting until she feels more improvement

112. You have been working with Cruz, a fourteen-year-old who has been questioning his gender identity. He has shared that his parents try to be supportive, but he feels that they do not fully understand his struggle and how they can support him. You offer to meet with his parents to provide them with psychoeducation on gender identity, sexuality, and how they can support him in his journey. Cruz is agreeable. During your family session, Cruz's mother asks you to explain gender identity. What is the BEST response?
   A) Gender identity is the sex a person is born with.
   B) Gender identity is how others perceive a person.
   C) Gender identity is how someone expresses and identifies.
   D) Gender identity is the same as a person's sex.

113. You are working as a counselor in an inpatient addiction rehab program. When should you begin planning to discharge your clients?
   A) during their intake
   B) halfway through treatment
   C) one month before discharge
   D) two weeks before discharge

114. You are an intake counselor at an outpatient drug rehab program. After meeting with a young woman who has been struggling with opioids, you decide that she meets the criteria for opioid use disorder, severe. Part of your role is to determine if she is appropriate for the level of care you provide, and, if so, to develop a treatment plan. You are concerned that she has continued to use opioids and is unable to stop. As a result, you conclude that she needs a different level of care. Which level of care would be the MOST appropriate, given the diagnosis?
   A) detoxification program
   B) inpatient rehab program
   C) partial hospitalization program
   D) intensive outpatient program

115. You are reviewing the intake paperwork for a new client before an intake session. You notice that the client has written "bigender" for sexual identity. What does this indicate about the individual you are about to meet with?
    A) The client identifies as both feminine and masculine.
    B) The client identifies as the sex they were born with.
    C) The client's identity shifts between feminine and masculine.
    D) The client does not identify as feminine or masculine.

116. You have been working for a virtual mental health provider as an individual counselor for two months. Before you meet with a new client, which step will you take at the beginning of your session?
    A) confirm her physical location
    B) confirm her time zone
    C) discuss your theoretical background
    D) discuss your educational background

117. You have been working with Thomas for three weeks. He shared that his anxiety symptoms are interfering with his job performance. He would like to contribute more during staff meetings, but when others begin to talk over him, he stops speaking. Thomas would like to reach a point where he does not let others talk over him. Which of the following resources could help Thomas with this goal?
    A) mindfulness strategies
    B) emotion regulation skills
    C) assertiveness training
    D) safety planning

118. During a psychoeducation session for parents of LGBTQIA+ youth, you are asked to describe sexuality. Which of the following is the BEST description?
    A) Sexuality is the gender a person is assigned at birth.
    B) Sexuality is who a person is or is not attracted to.
    C) Sexuality is how people identify their gender.
    D) Sexuality is how others perceive one's gender.

119. You are meeting with a new client, James, for the second time. Your first session focused on your biopsychosocial interview. For this session, you want to further explore the concerns that came up when you were discussing his mental health history. James reported that every few months he has a four-day period when he sleeps less, is more productive, and feels good about himself. He is more talkative than usual, has racing thoughts, and is easily distracted. Despite these changes, his work and other responsibilities have not been impacted. This is typically followed by a period when he feels lethargic, sleeps more, loses interest in enjoyable activities, and has had passive suicidal ideation for a little under a week. He has never been hospitalized for these changes and has never engaged in any dangerous activities when he feels good. He denied all suicidal concerns at the time of intake. Based on the symptoms, what diagnosis would be the MOST appropriate?
    A) major depressive disorder
    B) bipolar I
    C) bipolar II
    D) cyclothymic disorder

120. You are seeing a father who learned that his child identifies as pansexual. He is trying to be supportive and encouraging, but he does not understand what this means. What is the MOST appropriate explanation?
    A) Pansexual is being attracted to the opposite gender.
    B) Pansexual is being attracted to a person's personality regardless of their gender.
    C) Pansexual means that someone does not need to engage in sexual behaviors.
    D) Pansexual means that someone needs to have a strong emotional connection to engage in sexual behaviors.

121. You are running a family therapy program for family members with a loved one attending an inpatient rehab program. Which of the following is an appropriate psychoeducation topic for this group?
    A) different methods of substance use
    B) financial cost of addiction
    C) the disease concept of addiction
    D) common mental health concerns

122. You are a career counselor working with high school students to explore career options they may be interested in. You use a personality assessment and then discuss which careers match well with the students' results. Your preferred assessment looks at four traits: their energy, how they process information, how they make decisions, and their style of organization. The combination of their answers will create a unique profile that can then be compared with career options. Which personality assessment are you using?
    A) thematic apperception test
    B) word association test
    C) Winslow Personality Profile
    D) Myers–Briggs Type Indicator

123. You have just completed an intake interview with Sarah, a fourteen-year-old girl whose mother brought her in for an assessment after her school counselor expressed concern about her behavior. Over the school year, Sarah has lost a significant amount of body weight and has a low weight compared to her peers. She discussed with the school counselor her anxiety about gaining weight and the negative impact these thoughts have on her functioning. Sarah shared that she only eats when she is hungry, usually has one piece of fruit for each meal, and drinks water throughout the day to stay hydrated. Sarah did not appear to recognize the significance of her behaviors and weight when she met with her counselor. Which diagnosis would you choose after learning her symptoms?
    A) avoidant/restrictive food intake disorder
    B) anorexia nervosa, restrictive type
    C) anorexia nervosa, binge eating/purging type
    D) bulimia nervosa

124. You are a high school counselor working with a junior who feels conflicted about college. Oscar shares that his parents expect him to go to college, but he has no interest in that. He explains that learning has been hard for him, and he feels like he would be taking out loans to continue struggling. He recently spoke to an Army recruiter and feels like the military could be a good fit. Oscar enjoys exercise, and he admired his grandfather, who was in the military. He asks you for suggestions about what he should do next. Which of his ideas would you support?
    A) enlisting before talking to his parents
    B) conforming to his parents' expectations
    C) taking a year off to consider both options
    D) talking to an army recruiter to learn more

125. You are about to conduct an initial assessment with a new client. Your supervisor encouraged you to summarize more during these appointments to make sure you fully understand the client. How often would you summarize during the appointment?
    A) twice; halfway and at the end
    B) at the end of each section
    C) at the end only
    D) dismiss your supervisor's suggestion

126. You have been working with Susan, a twenty-eight-year-old female who has been coping with the changes from her divorce. Over the past two sessions, you have asked how she is managing emotionally, but she keeps focusing on her job and family. Which skill would help you learn more about her emotions regarding her divorce?
    A) active listening
    B) summarizing
    C) redirecting
    D) unconditional positive regard

127. You have been working with Zane since he lost his job. He has been struggling with feelings of worthlessness, hopelessness, and sadness. He enjoyed his job as an art teacher, but his position was cut due to budgeting. He now feels concerned about paying his rent and student loans. Zane has taken this loss as a reflection of his performance, despite receiving several offers for personal references for future job applications. Which cognitive behavioral therapy technique could be helpful for Zane?
    A) cognitive restructuring
    B) guided discovery
    C) journaling and thought records
    D) successive approximation

128. You currently facilitate five groups at your outpatient treatment program. Which of the following groups would have the LEAST impact on new members?
    A) a closed group for widows and widowers
    B) a psychoeducational session on relapse prevention
    C) an open group for coping with anxiety
    D) a telehealth closed session for PTSD

129. You are working with an individual who has been having a hard time communicating with her partner. She shares that she always feels defensive, which you believe contributes to her inability to shift her perspective. During your session, you discuss emotion regulation skills that can help her manage her emotions better in the moment, which will allow her to better communicate her thoughts and emotions. Which of the following is an emotion regulation skill you could recommend?
   A) box breathing
   B) ignoring the conflict
   C) matching her partner's tone
   D) screaming

130. You are reviewing a client's referral paperwork before an intake interview. Sandra is a twenty-eight-year-old woman who has been struggling with a depressed mood for about two and a half years. During these moods, she has a hard time controlling her eating habits, sleeps more than normal, and feels hopeless. She was unable to recall any time longer than three weeks that she did not struggle with her depressed mood. No symptoms of a manic or hypomanic episode, psychotic disorders, or substance use disorders were noted in the paperwork. Based on the information, which diagnosis should you investigate during your intake interview?
   A) disruptive mood dysregulation disorder
   B) major depressive disorder
   C) persistent depressive disorder (dysthymia)
   D) premenstrual dysphoric disorder

131. You are working in an outpatient addiction treatment program. During your initial assessment with a new client, she appeared resistant to treatment, so you tried to validate her experiences and provide support. In return, the client asked what business you have helping someone with an addiction, because it is obvious you do not have one. You have been in recovery for five years and feel that self-disclosure may help the client be more open with you. What is an appropriate way to share your experience?
   A) be dishonest about your experience to avoid embarrassment
   B) provide all the details of how you hit rock bottom
   C) share that you are in recovery with minimal details
   D) encourage the client to come to an AA meeting with you

132. At the end of a one-hour interview with a client, she begins to discuss another issue that will take additional time to consider. You have another client scheduled shortly after this interview. What is the BEST way to proceed?
   A) finish the initial interview and schedule a second appointment with that client to discuss the new issue
   B) skip the next client's appointment and allow the current client to continue, using all the time she needs to explain the new issue
   C) ask the client to give a clear rationale for why she feels the need to talk about the new issue near the end of the interview
   D) let the client know that her scheduled hour has expired, and you have someone else to meet

133. You just finished a session with Declan, a forty-six-year-old man who has experienced significant changes in the past few weeks. Declan's wife had an affair, which led to their mutual decision to get a divorce. When Declan looked over his finances, he realized that he cannot afford to continue with his debt payment schedule on his salary alone. Declan has a history of major depressive disorder and shares that he reached out to you because his symptoms have started to return; specifically, his lack of appetite, insomnia, fatigue, feelings of hopelessness, and suicidal ideation. Declan denies having any intent or means for suicide at this time. What is your treatment recommendation?
    A) individual counseling
    B) medication-assisted therapy (MAT)
    C) counseling and MAT
    D) inpatient mental health program

134. The focus of interviews is always on clients and their situations. Accordingly, which statement is MOST correct regarding interview focus?
    A) Counselors should get clients to focus on factual information.
    B) Counselors are responsible for assisting clients to focus on anything related to their problems.
    C) Counselors must help clients focus on their feelings, which are often behind many of the problems they face.
    D) Counselors should not direct interviews; rather, they should allow clients to speak as they wish.

135. You have been working with Laura for three months. She became a stay-at-home mother about four years ago when her children were born. She has been missing her career but feels guilty because she loves her time with her kids and feels that she should be grateful she is able to stay home with them. Which skill would be appropriate to use with Laura?
    A) unconditional positive regard
    B) summarizing
    C) reflective statements
    D) self-disclosure

136. You just completed an intake session for Yasmin, a twenty-nine-year-old female who identifies as bisexual. Yasmin shares that she was raised in a religious home and that her family stopped talking to her when she told them she is bisexual. Since then, she has had difficulty building meaningful relationships and is worried that if she lets someone truly get to know her, that person will choose to end the relationship. Her goal is to learn to build healthy relationships with others. When discussing her treatment options, you talk about the benefits of having a corrective emotional experience and how she can try this approach in counseling. How would you describe a corrective emotional experience to Yasmin?
    A) similar to cognitive restructuring, modifying the way she perceives her family's response to her sexuality
    B) working to repair the relationship she has with her family and processing their reactions during her sessions
    C) developing an open therapeutic relationship in which she can be her true self and feel supported
    D) working through the emotions she has been holding on to regarding her family's reactions and moving on

137. You are facilitating a group therapy session for individuals who struggle with a variety of mental health concerns, such as anxiety, depression, and bipolar disorder. Wade shared that he was struggling to get out of bed this morning. You remember that Maria, another group member, had a similar concern last week. Once Wade has talked about his issue, you ask Maria to speak about what helped her last week when she was struggling. What is this process called?
- A) blocking
- B) linking
- C) facilitating
- D) processing

138. You are running a group therapy session in an outpatient setting for parents whose children have terminal diseases. One of your group members is a mental health provider who has, unintentionally, been providing feedback that is not typical of other members. You have not yet talked about this observation with the member. If it happens again, how would you proceed?
- A) continue as normal with no follow-up
- B) allow the group to proceed, and follow up individually
- C) discuss the feedback in the group setting when it happens
- D) talk to your supervisor about the situation

139. You are running a psychoeducational group on suicide rates among various races and ethnicities. Which ethnicity has the highest rate of completed suicides?
- A) Hispanic or Latino
- B) non-Hispanic White
- C) non-Hispanic Black or African American
- D) non-Hispanic American Indian or Alaska Native

140. Mary, a former client, is returning to therapy. She was receptive to talk therapy and needed a safe place to talk through her thoughts and worries. She did not have any diagnosable mental health concerns when you worked with her in the past, and she decided to stop meeting with you when she was doing well. At Mary's first session in a year, she shared that she has been having panic attacks since she lost her job when the COVID-19 pandemic began. She worries about paying for her children's education and other expenses. Mary stated that she has had three panic attacks and worries about the "what ifs" for another one. Since her panic attacks, Mary spends hours each day searching for side job opportunities, which has negatively impacted her sleep. She does not have any known medical concerns and denies the use of drugs and alcohol. What diagnosis is the BEST fit for Mary's symptoms?
- A) unspecified anxiety disorder
- B) generalized anxiety disorder
- C) obsessive-compulsive disorder
- D) panic disorder

141. You are working in a family therapy clinic and are meeting with Tim and Mary, the parents of a thirteen-year-old named Susie. Tim and Mary have been concerned about Susie's behaviors since her aunt died unexpectedly two months ago. Since then, Susie has stopped spending time with her friends, and her grades have dropped significantly. They also recently found a pack of cigarettes and empty beer bottles in the garage. Tim and Mary denied that any of these behaviors were present before the family's loss. They shared that when they tried talking to Susie about their concerns, she became angry and missed the points they were trying to make. Which of the following exercises would allow you to model ideal behaviors that Tim and Mary could use to share their concerns with Susie?
    A) journaling
    B) meditation
    C) role-playing
    D) empty chair technique

142. You are meeting with a client who you feel could benefit from attending Alcoholics Anonymous meetings. When you explore her reasons for not going, she explains that she is not religious and is not interested in going to meetings to hear about God. How could you explain spirituality?
    A) feeling connected to other aspects of organized religion
    B) identifying with other religious materials
    C) a deep connection to something that makes you feel whole
    D) a deep connection to others that makes you feel whole

143. You are conducting an intake interview with John, who was referred by his primary care physician due to his concerning mental health symptoms. When John met with his doctor, he presented with disorganized speech and diminished emotional expression. On the referral form, John describes hallucinations and seeing family members who have died. He told his doctor that he had been seeing family members for about five weeks, and his wife reported that the other symptoms the doctor observed started around the same time. Despite these symptoms, John has not experienced a major depressive episode, manic episode, or hypomanic episode. His wife said that he had not been using alcohol or other drugs. Based on the information, which diagnosis should you investigate during your session with John?
    A) brief psychotic disorder
    B) schizophreniform disorder
    C) schizophrenia
    D) schizoaffective disorder

144. You are working with the parents of a young girl who has begun acting out and not doing her schoolwork. They need suggestions for how to stop her negative behaviors from progressing. You tell them that research shows that children who have a particular belief system are less likely to use tobacco, alcohol, and drugs. What is this belief system?
    A) religion
    B) spirituality
    C) moral code
    D) philosophy

145. You have been working with Ally for six months regarding her depressive symptoms. She has been in a committed relationship for four months and is having a hard time relating to her partner's family relationships. Ally is an only child who has a strained relationship with her family, and her partner is close with her parents, siblings, and extended family. Ally's partner wants to spend more time with Ally at family events compared to earlier in their relationship when it was just the two of them. Ally and her partner have agreed to a couple's session. Which of the following would be the MOST helpful topic to explore?
    A) boundaries
    B) healthy communication
    C) values clarification
    D) long-term goals

146. You have just conducted an intake interview with Sandy, a twenty-four-year-old woman, who shared that she is having a hard time feeling comfortable at work. She feels uncomfortable in her own skin and is embarrassed by her hairline. Sandy explained that she has hair extensions that help her feel more comfortable, but there is still some distress. You noticed her receding hairline and areas with significantly less hair. Sandy explained that she has been pulling her hair out since she was a teenager. Over the years, this has occurred with other places on her body, and most recently it has been focused on her head. Which diagnosis would be appropriate for Sandy?
    A) obsessive-compulsive disorder
    B) body dysmorphic disorder
    C) generalized anxiety disorder
    D) trichotillomania

147. You are working as a high school counselor. Mark, a senior, was just caught in a physical altercation with another student. Mark presents as angry due to his harsh tone of voice, choice of words, and body language. Your goal is to understand what led up to the fight and how Mark can avoid conflict in the future. What would you do FIRST?
    A) breathing exercises with Mark to help him calm himself
    B) call his parents to take him home from school
    C) let Mark verbalize his thoughts
    D) keep him from class for the rest of the day

148. You are a group counselor at an inpatient drug and alcohol treatment program, where you run a specialized group for individuals with dual diagnosis. Anthony is a new participant who came to treatment after being arrested for possession of cocaine. During his initial interview, Anthony said that he had been using drugs to cope with his depressed mood and feelings of worthlessness. He explained that he has "dark periods" that last about two weeks, during which he struggles to get his work done and keep his home clean. He also mentioned changes in his appetite and sleeping behaviors and a loss of energy before he began using drugs regularly. Anthony explained that using drugs helps him be more productive and get work done. Based on the information, what do you suspect his diagnosis to be?
    A) disruptive mood dysregulation disorder
    B) bipolar II disorder
    C) major depressive disorder
    D) persistent depressive disorder

149. Your supervisor asked you to get some long-term follow-ups for clients you worked with in the past. Which group of clients would be ideal for this task?
    A) clients who completed treatment one month ago
    B) clients who completed treatment two months ago
    C) clients who completed treatment three months ago
    D) clients who completed treatment six months ago

150. Many individuals live with dual diagnosis. For those dealing with a substance use disorder and another mental health issue, what should their treatment focus on after detoxification?
    A) substance use
    B) mental health concern
    C) whichever occurred first
    D) both at the same time

Answer Explanations 1

1. B: When dealing with a new treatment like play therapy, it is important to grasp how techniques and awareness can improve. Meeting with her supervisor would help the counselor gain insight into child behavior indicators.

2. A: Anxiety becomes a severe problem when it interferes with problem-solving. Anxiety disorder is apparent when an individual feels that the problems or issues will continue without letup. Continued thoughts and emotional responses to these problems cause the person to forgo problem-solving.

3. C: Before making any recommendations or decisions, the social worker should first assess the client's support system for possible housing. Referring the client to a shelter may be appropriate, but that will not be known until the client has been assessed. Because the client is over 21 and is not incapacitated, reporting the boyfriend is not appropriate without the client's express permission as it violates confidentiality. Offering housing with the social worker is never appropriate as it crosses ethical boundaries.

4. B: While all options are appropriate, option B is the only response that acknowledges Marcus's current struggle with anger. This can also be a validating statement that allows him to further reflect on his experience. Option A demonstrates reflecting.

5. A: The categories listed would best be addressed during a biopsychosocial interview. *Biopsychosocial* is made up of the terms: *biology*, *psychological*, and *social*.

6. D: Continuing education (CE) courses are required for counselors to maintain an active license in most states. These courses offer new training certifications and provide an opportunity to learn about new practices while refreshing the counselor's knowledge on existing practices.

7. A: The counselor's primary responsibility is to provide a full range of assistance, including creating a treatment plan with a diagnosis and goals.

8. C: Eye movement desensitization and reprocessing (EMDR) is an evidence-based approach to treating trauma. With EMDR clients can experience a decrease in their symptoms, replace negative thought processes, and reduce their responses to triggers.

9. C: It is important to be open and friendly but remain professional. Remember that patience is an important attribute in a counselor.

10. B: The symptoms described are associated with bipolar disorder, which indicates the need for a diagnostic interview. A structured interview assessing the client's symptoms would allow you to identify a diagnosis.

11. D: Qualitative research aims to investigate how and why things happen. It focuses on a small number of participants, which allows topics to be further explored than other forms of studies. Results from these studies tend to produce additional topics for research.

12. C: Acculturation describes the degree to which a person is accustomed to and familiar with the dominant culture of the land that she lives in and best describes what the social worker should assess.

Assimilation is an outdated term that refers to the erasure of a people's traditional culture. Racial discrimination does not describe this situation. The outdated term *melting pot* refers to cultural mixing in the US to create one mega culture.

13. C: An anxiety disorder due to prostate cancer is the best choice because John's symptoms are directly caused by his medical diagnosis, and he has no history of mental health concerns. A medical exam, lab work, and a verbal history will determine an individual's history of mental health concerns. A key component of this diagnosis is that symptoms significantly impact a client's social life, work, and other important areas of functioning.

14. D: Option C is not the main focus for the counselor. Suicide rates are statistically lower among Black individuals, so Option B is incorrect; however, the client should still be monitored for his suicide risk. The most concerning part of the client's suicide risk is his inability to identify protective factors, which can include future goals and relationships.

15. B: Although problems among clients may be similar, every situation is unique and may require a different solution. Counselors must learn as much as possible about each client before working on a solution.

16. A: Having the client focus on helping her child is the main objective. This is best accomplished by helping her solve the problem while alleviating her fears concerning the diagnosis.

17. C: Counselors should not impose their personal opinions upon clients.

18. A: Since you may see the client in public settings, it is appropriate to establish boundaries so you both understand how to act toward each other.

19. C: The best option is to discuss the policy up front and answer any of the client's questions. Printing the policy is an additional option, but the client may not read it.

20. C: Cognitive behavioral therapy (CBT) is the best therapeutic approach for Toby. This therapy can help him change his emotions by changing his automatic thoughts. The counselor would work with Toby to challenge his automatic thoughts and replace them with newer, healthier thought patterns.

21. D: Individuals who experience depressive symptoms, especially those struggling with suicidal ideation, should be continuously monitored for risk. The *DSM-5* states that while having a history of suicide attempts is serious, most individuals who complete suicide do not have previous, failed attempts. Other factors that can increase a person's risk are being male, living alone, being single, feeling hopelessness, and living with borderline personality disorder.

22. D: A counselor must know when to seek the help of a professional in another discipline and refer the client to this source. The counselor must also coordinate activities with the other professional.

23. B: Exploring the client's stated fears is the most appropriate first step. Only after emotional exploration can the social worker begin building a case plan with the client. Reassuring the client that the father will not win is not an appropriate response because the social worker cannot be sure that this is true. Assessing the client's current safety is not necessary since the client is currently safely residing in the shelter.

24. C: The cultural formulation interview is a sixteen-question assessment that helps counselors better understand how people's cultural experiences have impacted them. Culture refers to information, rules, and practices that are passed down from generation to generation. As a result, individuals may have different interpretations of mental illness and its associated symptoms.

25. D: Options A, B, and C are all part of understanding the client's concerns and developing a treatment plan. If the client has a mental health concern, this would be incorporated. If the client is presenting with suicidal ideation (SI) concerns, you will assess for risk and determine if he should be seen at a hospital. If the client is not appropriate for the counselor's experience, a referral is the appropriate treatment recommendation.

26. D: The best way to obtain reliable information and lessen the chance of misunderstandings in an interview is to make sure the client understands both the reasons for the questions and how truthful, accurate answers will help solve problems. Option A may result in misunderstandings, option B in prevarication, and option C in resentment.

27. A: Body language can send significant messages to a client. If a counselor makes inconsistent eye contact or moves frequently in his chair, he might seem uninterested in what the client is sharing.

28. C: Showing an appropriate level of empathy will depend on what is being shared. Appearing inauthentic or over-empathetic can damage the therapeutic relationship. Failing to show empathy can make the counselor appear cold and uninterested.

29. B: Ann is likely living with disruptive mood dysregulation disorder. She is experiencing verbal rages in more than one setting, and these outbursts have been occurring for the past year. The minimum requirement for outbursts for this disorder is three per week, and Ann's mother reports that they are more frequent than that. This diagnosis can only be made for individuals between the ages of six and eighteen.

30. B: Such diagnoses are known as "provisional diagnoses."

31. C: Solution-focused brief therapy (SFBT) applies in this situation because it is effective in three to ten sessions. In a relapse prevention group, members can identify their goals and determine which solutions have helped them before. This approach can also help members identify plans to address any barriers they face in working toward their goals.

32. B: There are currently five versions of the SCID-5: Research Version (SCID-5-RV), Clinician Version (SCID-5-CV), Clinical Trials Version (SCID-5-CT), Personality Disorders Version (SCID-5-PD), and the Alternative Model for Personality Disorders Version (SCID-5-AMPD).

33. C: Congruence is a term used by psychologist Carl Rogers when he was developing person-centered therapy. Rogers defined congruence as genuineness that is needed for a counselor to provide unconditional positive regard and empathy.

34. A: Using therapies you are not trained in is not only unethical; insurance providers may not pay for the sessions.

35. A: Collaborative care occurs when a variety of professionals provide care to a client. This is a common approach in several hospital programs, including psychiatric programs and addiction treatment programs. Collaborative care allows professionals to work together to provide the best care to the client.

36. A: Social workers are mandated reporters and must report suspected abuse of people who are vulnerable, including older adults. The social worker should report the son for suspected elder abuse. Conducting a family session is not appropriate in the case of suspected abuse, while confronting the son is unsafe. Asking the client if she may have misplaced the cash avoids the social worker's duty to report.

37. C: Intermittent explosive disorder is the most likely option. This diagnosis requires the individual to have verbal outbursts OR a minimum of three behavioral outbursts that involve the destruction of property. The magnitude of the outburst needs to be extreme for the situation and not premeditated. Individuals with this diagnosis can experience distress from their reactions or impairment in their interpersonal and occupational functioning. The onset of behaviors associated with this diagnosis typically begins in late childhood or adolescence and rarely begins after age forty. The outbursts will continue to arise for several years and can be episodic.

38. C: Canceling appointments based on a client's demographics is unethical. The best option is to proceed with the scheduled appointment. If you have concerns about working with clients with different backgrounds than yourself, you should process this with a supervisor.

39. A: Treatment goals should include learning new skills that can be used to solve problems. This can also benefit other relationships they have.

40. A: The counselor should guide the couple to set treatment goals to improve communication. This will help them learn new skills they can use to address disagreements as well as other problems in their relationship.

41. D: Unless you are using a social media account as a psychoeducational platform, being friends with clients online can change your relationship's dynamics and harm your therapeutic alliance.

42. B: The overarching concern for Thomas and Derrick is the codependency patterns that have developed. By focusing on Derrick's needs, Thomas is negatively impacted. Derrick does not need to take care of his responsibilities because he knows that Thomas will do so. By addressing their codependency behaviors, you will help Thomas and Derrick establish new boundaries and improve their communication patterns. This will lead to Derrick learning to manage his own responsibilities without Thomas's help.

43. C: Clients should not share personal information in emails because confidentiality cannot be ensured. Most counselors are not available 24/7. Any emails sent or received should be documented in the client's chart as a form of communication.

44. D: A counselor should help clients by providing them with an objective perspective. This helps ensure that goals are realistic and attainable, and that they work toward the progress clients would like to see.

45. D: The expectations from Jerry's family are part of the family system, which is therefore the best system to evaluate. The academic system is putting Jerry under some pressure, but it is not creating conflict with his goals. The political system and church system do not play roles in this situation.

46. D: This client would benefit from being in an environment where he feels comfortable and safe to explore his sexuality and the concerns he has about his family's support. He may not have other people in his life who can give him a safe place to talk about his thoughts, feelings, and struggles. A counselor practicing positive regard projects an attitude of acceptance of the client as a person and understands that seeing every person is worthy of dignity and respect.

47. C: Partial hospitalization programs are appropriate for individuals who need more support after completing an inpatient rehab program. These programs have a similar structure to a typical day at inpatient rehab, the key difference being that the individual can return home at the end of the day. People at this level of treatment are in the early stages of their recovery and require a healthy and supportive home environment. Being active in Narcotics Anonymous, Terry is more likely to succeed in a partial hospitalization program, where he can work to build healthy relationships. Terry should not necessarily expect his family to forget about his past transgressions, but he should feel like he can be open about his struggles and successes at home. Family therapy can be used to help strengthen the support that can be found at home.

48. C: While you provide Lucia with emotional support, you can also offer a counseling session with her husband. This way, you could help both individuals express their thoughts and concerns in a healthy manner with the goal of improving their understanding of each other. With improved understanding, the couple can work to determine which option is right for them and their family.

49. D: There are four main reasons to use the SCID-5: To make sure the counselor is evaluating for all the major *DSM-5* diagnoses, to help select the population for a study, to help identify current and past mental health concerns within a study's population, and to help students and new mental health professionals improve their clinical interviewing skills.

50. A: Group rules can help members know what to expect and what is expected of them. They address concerns such as late arrivals, missing group, interacting outside of group, having food and drinks in the group, and managing cross talk.

51. C: Short-term goals can work toward a person's long-term goals and are typically associated with a one-month period. Short-term goals are achievable and stack up to help the client achieve long-term goals.

52. A: The hiring team is questioning the client's ability to do her job based on the fact that she has children. This is considered discrimination. Stereotyping is the act of making assumptions about someone based on gender, race, culture and so on. Ethnocentrism is when one considers his ethnicity or culture to be superior. In consciousness raising, a group coalesces and works to raise awareness on a specific issue or concern.

53. D: When a client presents a new problem, the first step to take is always to acknowledge the feelings of the client. It is not appropriate to bring the partner into the session without first gaining a better understanding of the dynamics and determining the goal behind bringing the partner in. It has not been established that the client will ever meet his partner's family, so teaching coping skills for the meeting is irrelevant. Every family has different norms and expectations, but that should not be the first topic when the client brings up his problem.

54. B: The self-directed search (SDS) was developed by John L. Holland and is a test that can help Mary find career opportunities that align with her interests and skills. Taking the SDS is a simple short-term goal that clearly works toward her long-term goal of finding a new career path. Knowing the desired salary can help narrow down a job search, but Mary would have to gauge the importance of salary versus other aspects of a job that could be more important to her.

55. C: The hero tends to be a high-achieving child. Individuals who take on the family role of hero can struggle with people-pleasing behaviors and boundary-setting and may find that they need external validation more than others.

56. A: Codependency is a common unhealthy relationship behavior found among individuals who are struggling with an addiction. The codependent person tends to focus on the individual who is struggling, which leads to the codependent person putting her needs on the back burner. This behavior can also enable the individual in active addiction.

57. B: Children who take on the role of the lost child can often feel forgotten. They can be detached from the family and find meaning in fantasy through books or games.

58. C: The behaviors Richard has been using are examples of conflict resolution skills. Other skills include being patient with the other person, remaining unbiased, keeping calm, avoiding lecturing, being mindful of one's body language, and observing other people.

59. C: Option C would allow your client to discuss how she has been impacted by the family's move and how this has influenced her identity. Focusing only on the present moment would fail to acknowledge the importance of the client's familial experiences with reform schools.

60. B: The Beck Anxiety Inventory (BAI) is a short assessment that measures the severity of anxiety symptoms. It is used during intake and later in treatment to assess for progress and other notable changes.

61. B: Treatment plans, progress, and setbacks should be reviewed every thirty days. Readministering the Beck anxiety inventory (BAI) after thirty days would help show the effectiveness of the interventions Dan is working on.

62. D: When a client has physical concerns, the social worker should always refer out to a physician or health care provider to screen for medical causes. Only once a physician rules out medical concerns, would it be appropriate to explore mind-body connections between stress and physical symptoms. Dizziness and bright lights do not indicate a need to assess for visual or auditory hallucinations, so is not appropriate. A client presenting with stress is not an appropriate reason to reschedule; instead, the stress should be addressed in session.

63. B: To provide informed consent, the client must understand the risks associated with participating, the potential benefits, the procedure, and the possible consequences. Most states require that an informed consent be signed and dated rather than offered verbally.

64. A: The correct format of an "I statement" is "I feel (emotion), when (event)." The overall goal of "I statements" is to take ownership of one's feelings and not blame them on the other person. It is important to avoid phrases like "Because you ____" and "You made me feel ____" because these can make the other person feel defensive.

65. B: Addiction treatment can take a holistic approach and address a person's mind, body, and spirit. Spirituality is a topic that can arise in self-help groups, such as Alcoholics Anonymous and Narcotics Anonymous. Spirituality does not necessarily have to tie into religion.

66. C: Evelyn Duvall proposed the first family life cycle version in 1956. Since then, her model has been replaced by other versions, including: the life cycle of the intact middle-class nuclear family, the life cycle of the single-parent family, and the life cycle of the blended family.

67. C: The counselor is providing Nader with psychoeducation about his intake assessment. It makes sense that he would be apprehensive if he has never been in therapy before and is unsure what to expect. All clients will come to sessions with an expectation of what they will experience; unfortunately, this expectation is not always accurate or helpful. Taking time to explain the process can also help build rapport with Nader.

68. B: The six stages for this cycle include: single adults leaving home, the new couple, families with young children, families with adolescents, families launching children and moving on, and families in later life.

69. A: Using open-ended questions can help Mark share more than "yes" or "no" answers. Even if his answers are short, he can still lead the discussion. While he may benefit from some psychoeducation, it does not need to be the focus of the sessions.

70. B: Role-playing would allow Samantha to run through situations that may arise during her workday. It can provide her with a safe place to try new communication skills and practice doing things differently.

71. D: Supporting the child and helping him learn that he will not go without food is important in assisting him to overcome the fear and anxiety he continues to experience because of the former neglect.

72. C: Support groups, such as Alcoholics Anonymous and Narcotics Anonymous, help individuals in recovery make connections with other people in recovery. Individuals who are active in these groups are encouraged to work closely with a sponsor who can provide guidance and support in their recovery. Group counselors often advise against building relationships with other group members because it can change the dynamic of the group. A support group in a clinical setting would be an exception to this.

73. C: A resolution refers to an outcome that Elaine and Joey both work toward. Their improved emotion regulation skills may have been an individual goal, and because of their individual goals, they were able to work toward improving their relationship by decreasing the amount of arguing.

74. B: Contemplation is the stage during which individuals begin to see that a behavior is a concern, but they are not ready to change that behavior.

75. B: The second of the three stages involve individuals accepting their new roles in the relationship. This requires patience, open communication, and working on boundaries within the family. Elijah and Mary both need to establish boundaries with previous partners and family regarding co-parenting.

76. B: Before making any decisions, the social worker must first assess what steps the client has taken and what she needs to do next. Creating an action plan is only appropriate after assessing where the client is in the process. Educating the client is not appropriate until the social worker knows what the client needs to be educated on. Calling the disability center is generally not appropriate because it is a best practice to empower the clients to call for themselves.

77. C: For person-centered therapy to be successful, the counselor must create a supportive environment and be as open, nonjudgmental, and empathetic as possible.

78. C: There are ten core diagnoses covered in the SCID-5:

> **1.** mood episodes, cyclothymic disorder, persistent depressive disorder, and premenstrual dysphoric disorder
>
> **2.** psychotic and associated symptoms

3. differential diagnosis of psychotic disorders

4. differential diagnosis of mood disorders

5. substance use disorders

6. anxiety disorder

7. obsessive-compulsive and related disorders

8. feeding and eating disorders

9. externalizing disorders

10. trauma- and stressor-related disorders

79. B: "Cobra" is the term John Gottman uses to describe individuals whose heart rate decreases when they become abusive. These perpetrators tend to struggle with anger and can be dangerous to others.

80. D: Relapse prevention is an appropriate psychoeducational topic for an addiction rehab program. While some of the participants could benefit from the other topics, all participants are engaging in treatment for an addiction concern.

81. C: When counselors work with a client who is in an abusive relationship, the primary focus should be on assessing and continuing to assess the level of violence and danger in the environment. This includes exploring emotional abuse, verbal abuse, physical abuse, and sexual abuse. The two levels of abuse are common couple violence and severe abuse violence.

82. A: Since Erica is being referred by her psychiatrist, it is important to request those records to better understand her symptoms, their severity, and any related hospitalizations.

83. C: If the client has a physical condition that hinders his ability to use stairs, he should receive reasonable accommodations to allow him access. Providing the code before the session will make it easier for the client to get to therapy.

84. C: The main topics covered in an unstructured clinical interview include the following:

- age and sex
- reason for seeking counseling
- client's work and education history
- client's current social activities
- any physical and mental health concerns, past and present
- current medications and any drug and/or alcohol use
- family history of mental health and physical health concerns
- the counselor's observations of a client's behavior during the session (for example, anxious, detached, euthymic)

While the topics listed in Options A, B, and C may come up in an interview, they typically occur within the counselor's investigation into the common areas.

85. B: Sleep cycles have four stages that can last from 90 to 120 minutes. Once one sleep cycle ends, the cycle begins again. People's bodies respond differently to each of the sleep stages.

86. D: As long as clients are not a danger to themselves or others, counselors can terminate services. It would be unethical to terminate services to a client who is, for example, suicidal or showing signs of violent schizophrenia.

87. B: The social worker should first reflect the client's feelings. Assessing for emotional abuse is not relevant in the given example without further information that might indicate abuse. Suggesting that the client move in with his father is not appropriate without adequate knowledge of custody and better understanding about the presenting issue. Suggesting more opportunities to explore his racial background is a good idea, but it is not the first step that the social worker should take.

88. C: Insomnia disorder is the correct option to explore. The giveaway is that this client is not getting adequate sleep and is reporting frequent waking at night. He has begun to experience negative consequences from the lack of proper sleep. To be diagnosed with an insomnia disorder, an individual must have a hard time falling asleep or staying asleep or wake up earlier than intended. This change will negatively impact one or more areas of functioning. The sleep disturbance must be present for a minimum of three months, at least three days a week.

89. D: The acronym *PLEASE* is used in dialectical behavior therapy (DBT) to reference self-care. Addressing these areas regularly can help people regulate their emotions appropriately. The acronym stands for the following: PL (physical illness), E (healthy eating), A (avoid mood-altering substances), S (sleep), and E (exercise).

90. B: Jia may be struggling with major depressive disorder. While some adults rejoice at the idea of an empty nest, many others struggle with the transition from raising their children to supporting them as they become independent. This can be a time to encourage Jia to learn more about herself, her interests, and her passions.

91. C: Limits to confidentiality include:

- being reviewed during a state or federal audit
- sharing records for record keeping and billing purposes
- sharing records with a supervisor or colleagues for consultation that would benefit the client
- sharing records if the counselor is concerned clients may harm themselves or others
- sharing records in a medical emergency
- sharing records if the client discloses abuse that falls into required mandated reporting
- sharing information if the client brings another person into the session
- a court requiring that a counselor disclose client information.

92. A: Access to food is a physiological need. Safety needs would include housing and shelter. Love and belonging needs include safe and loving relationships. Self-esteem is the ability to think highly of oneself or hold oneself in positive regard.

93. C: Unstructured interviews do not come with standardized questions, so the counselor can guide the interview in ways that he feels will lead to the most relevant information. This often allows for a more open discussion about the client's concerns, goals, and motivations. Unstructured interviews are heavily influenced by what the client shares as well as the counselor's theoretical approach. These interviews are different for each client due to their personalized nature.

94. A: Samantha's alcohol drinking has undergone a significant change, and she has driven and worked while impaired. She would likely benefit from an inpatient co-occurring treatment program and a medically supervised detox.

95. C: Body cues, such as nodding your head and making eye contact, show the speaker that you are listening. Counselors who are mindful of their body language can help show group members what is expected during a session.

96. B: Counselors can lobby for law changes when they find concerns to fight for, including laws and regulations regarding professional and client safety concerns.

97. A: Pedro is your client, and you should use your session with him to focus on his issues. Allowing him to lead the session can help you get better insight into the level of support he needs, as well as his need for psychoeducation. Normalizing his concerns and discussing coping skills for his anxiety would likely benefit Pedro.

98. D: All of the options are appropriate in this situation; however, the first priority should be the client's well-being and safety. Since there is a medical professional in the office, the client should be evaluated to see if further medical attention is necessary.

99. B: Vomiting and tremors do not necessarily indicate a medical emergency, but they do signal withdrawal. The counselor should explain the possible risks of alcohol withdrawal to the client and discuss whether he wants to seek medical treatment. The client should be encouraged to consult with a medical professional if these symptoms occur again.

100. B: This is a clear example of transference. Rachel has redirected the feelings she had toward her neighbor onto you. While these are positive feelings, addressing them during a session will benefit your therapeutic alliance in the long run.

101. A: A counselor must always provide an environment free from judgment and be aware that there is more to clients than what they present. It helps to be objective when developing an understanding of clients and their patterns.

102. D: Sometimes clients get lost in discussing a topic due to another thought. If they pause, avoiding leading or prompting their speech and allow them to work through their thought processes.

103. C: The best way to handle the situation is to remind the client that the two of you are focusing solely on her problems. A discussion of your personal affairs will not be useful in resolving any of her issues.

104. B: Healthy responses to conflict include remaining calm and clear in your communication. If both individuals are quick to anger, they would likely benefit from learning coping skills for their distress that they can use when they argue. This can help Lucy and Erin work toward healthier communication patterns.

105. D: All of these strategies are most likely to be effective with clients who are in the pre-contemplative stage, which means that they are not exhibiting an intention to take the actions needed to change their behaviors in the near future (typically defined as within the next six months).

106. C: It would be appropriate to share this information with Elizabeth's doctors, but if you are trained to assess for pica, you should do so. If you are not trained, you can provide her with a referral. Pica occurs when an individual eats nonnutritive and nonfood substances over a period of time for at least one month. To qualify as pica, the behavior cannot be culturally supported or considered a social norm.

107. C: Positive regard in this situation means showing your colleague kindness that he is not showing himself. He is aware of the factors that contributed to his performance, and this one assessment does not reflect his work as a whole.

108. C: A safety plan can include the phone numbers for supportive people in Nina's life as well as the 988 Suicide & Crisis Lifeline. Other common information on safety cards includes protective factors and coping skills.

109. A: Nina should be evaluated at the local hospital. She is distressed and has verbalized a plan as well as intent to follow through with the plan. The fact that she called you is a positive sign, and you can say so when you talk to her about calling for a wellness check. It is appropriate to keep her on the phone while contacting the authorities.

110. D: Research has shown that for co-occurring disorders, the best treatment outcomes are seen among individuals who are treated for all of their mental health concerns. In this case, the individual would likely receive specialized treatment for her trauma and disordered eating while engaging in the addiction treatment program. Her aftercare recommendations should continue to address all mental health concerns that she is struggling with.

111. A: Scheduling a family activity, such as an outing or a dinner, could help Molly's family reconnect with her. Scheduling the event ensures that all members are available and expecting it to occur.

112. C: Gender identity is how people choose to identify themselves. This may or may not be consistent with their sex. People can change their gender identity throughout their life. Gender identity can be expressed through clothing, makeup, and behaviors.

113. A: Discharge planning should begin at the time of intake. While a client may expect to be in treatment for a certain length of time, things change. Starting to plan at intake gives you ample opportunity to talk with your clients about their thoughts for discharge. Depending on the setting you work in, discharge planning can include continued mental health treatment at a different level of care.

114. A: Based on the client's diagnosis and presentation, she should be referred to a detox program. Being in a safe environment can allow her to fully detox so she can then engage in a treatment program. Withdrawal symptoms can interfere with a person's ability to fully participate in a treatment program, which is why detox programs contain more psychoeducational groups than process therapy groups do. While the symptoms of opioid withdrawal are not fatal, the combination of symptoms such as vomiting,

sweating, and diarrhea can lead to health concerns such as dehydration. Detox programs include 24/7 medical supervision to monitor for health crises.

115. A: Individuals who identify as bigender will show traits of both masculinity and femininity.

116. A: When providing telehealth services, it is important to confirm the client's physical location in case an emergency arises during the session, and you need to contact the authorities. The need for this can arise with a variety of mental health concerns, including suicidal ideation, depressive symptoms, and individuals in active addiction.

117. C: Assertiveness training can help Thomas manage his anxiety by developing the skills he needs to feel heard and acknowledged in his workplace.

118. B: Sexuality can also be referred to as "sexual orientation." Both terms are used to describe whom a person is or is not attracted to. Awareness and education about various sexual orientations can increase the general public's knowledge about sexuality.

119. C: The symptoms describe a hypomanic episode and a major depressive episode. James's symptoms do not align with a manic episode because they last four days, he does not engage in risky behaviors, and the symptoms have had little to no impact on his functioning. Since he has no history of manic episodes, he meets the criteria for bipolar II. Cyclothymic disorder requires that an individual has never fully met the criteria for a hypomanic episode. James's symptoms meet the criteria for a hypomanic episode and major depressive episode, meaning that he would not meet the criteria for cyclothymic disorder.

120. B: People who identify as pansexual are attracted to characteristics (personality, values, morals, and so forth) other than a person's gender. This means that the individuals they are attracted to can be of any gender.

121. C: Family programming in an addiction setting commonly provides education about the disease concept of addiction. This can help family members better understand how addiction changes the way the brain works and the challenges this can cause. Additionally, this would be an ideal time to discuss how the family could support their loved one's recovery efforts.

122. D: The Myers-Briggs Type Indicator assessment is used to highlight people's important values and traits that can then help them make informed decisions about their career options, which can narrow down the many options presented to students. Students should be encouraged to continue exploring their interests and understand that they may change their minds once they start exploring their options more.

123. B: The symptoms align with a diagnosis of anorexia nervosa, restrictive type. The specifier of "restrictive type" is appropriate because Sarah eats only one piece of fruit for each meal, which means she is restricting. Sarah is not engaging in behaviors related to binge eating/purging type.

124. D: It sounds like Oscar is still exploring his options. Rather than making a quick decision, he should consider all the possibilities, such as alternatives to college, such as trade school. Using a career assessment could help Oscar better understand how he can apply his values and interests to his career search.

125. B: Summarizing at the end of each section will likely make it easier for the client to understand the session and will avoid confusing different topics, like family and medical concerns. This will allow your client to add any forgotten details.

126. C: Redirecting allows you to change the topic to keep the session productive. This client may be using avoidance as a defense mechanism to avoid talking about a difficult topic.

127. A: Cognitive restructuring and reframing can help Zane adjust his negative thought patterns that automatically assume that he lost his job because of his performance. Colleagues offering personal references for future job opportunities is evidence that he did well at his job. If Zane can change his negative automatic thoughts into healthier thoughts, he will see a positive shift in his depressive symptoms.

128. C: Closed groups tend to experience a shift when members leave and join. Option B refers to a single session, so there would be no opportunity for a shift. Open groups tend to have a stronger focus on psychoeducation, whereas members of closed groups tend to develop rapport with each other.

129. A: Box breathing is an emotion regulation skill that your client can use in the moment to lessen her emotional reaction. Avoidance would not do her any good, nor would matching her partner's tone of voice. Screaming may be one way to cope but would not be appropriate in the moment since her partner could interpret this as an act of aggression.

130. C: Persistent depressive disorder is the appropriate diagnosis for individuals who have been struggling with major depressive disorder for over two years. It is important to rule out symptoms of manic and hypomanic episodes that would indicate the presence of bipolar I, bipolar II, or cyclothymic disorder.

131. C: Self-disclosure would likely make the client feel more comfortable by knowing that you also have struggled with an addiction. It is not necessary to share the details of your use, but you could talk about what has helped you in your recovery. It is important to make sure that whatever you do share is to the client's benefit—not yours.

132. A: Counselors must stick to their appointment schedules. Appointments should stay intact and only be interrupted if an emergency has arisen. When clients have additional issues to discuss, a new appointment should be scheduled to address those concerns.

133. C: Research has shown that the most effective approach for treating major depressive disorder is the combination of counseling and medication-assisted therapy. Declan would likely benefit from grief work for the loss of his marriage, as well as supportive counseling while he adjusts to the inevitable changes.

134. B: Helping clients focus on the actual situation is the best practice technique because it is the most conducive to resolution.

135. A: Laura is having an internal struggle between wanting to return to work and wanting to be a good parent. This is a common dilemma for women in similar situations, and she would benefit from having a safe, judgment-free environment where she can explore her thoughts and emotions.

136. C: Corrective emotional experiences require that the individual has a similar experience with the opposite outcome for a difficult situation. This applies to romantic relationships, friendships, or family relationships.

137. B: Linking occurs in a group session when one member helps another who is going through something that the first member can relate to. This is a helpful tool that members can use to relate to each other and focus on the positive outcome of their struggles.

138. D: There are many factors that might affect this situation, so consulting with your supervisor will help you determine the best course of action. Important details to consider are the nature of the feedback, how often it occurs, and if the group member is aware of the behavior.

139. D: A 2021 study finds that the highest rates of suicide are found among non-Hispanic American Indians or Alaska Natives followed by non-Hispanic Whites, Hispanics or Latinos, non-Hispanic Black, or African Americans, and non-Hispanic Asian or Pacific Islanders.

140. D: The symptoms described align with panic disorder. After Mary had several panic attacks, she became worried about having more panic attacks, and she changed her behavior as a result of her concerns (searching for side jobs to the extent that her sleep is interrupted). It is important to rule out any medical conditions, mental health conditions, or substance use that could be causing her panic attacks.

141. C: Role-playing during your session with Tim and Mary would show them how they can effectively communicate their concerns with their daughter. It would also allow you to give them feedback on the communication skills they have learned from you.

142. C: While the Big Book and other Alcoholics Anonymous (AA) literature do talk about God, one does not have to believe in God to benefit from the program. Spirituality is believing in something bigger than oneself. Research has shown that having a spiritual connection can benefit one's mental health. Other benefits include a sense of love, patience, faith, and hope.

143. B: A diagnosis of schizophreniform disorder can be made when a client has experienced at least two of the following symptoms for at least one month. One of the symptoms must be one of the first three options:

- delusions
- hallucinations
- disorganized speech
- grossly disorganized behaviors or catatonic behaviors
- negative symptoms (diminished emotional expression or avolition)

Additionally, several mental health diagnoses must be ruled out, including schizoaffective disorder, major depressive disorder, and bipolar disorder with psychotic features. This means that the symptoms associated with schizophreniform have not occurred at the same time as the disorders mentioned, or are present for only a short period. Medication and substance use must also be ruled out as a cause.

144. B: In addition to decreasing the risk of tobacco, alcohol, and drug use, spirituality can also lessen depressive symptoms in youth, according to a 2008 study by Abraham Verghese.

145. C: A values clarification exercise can help Ally and her partner gain a better understanding of what is important to them and the differences they may have. This can be used to facilitate a conversation about what they would like their relationship to look like.

146. D: Trichotillomania is also known as hairpulling disorder. Affected areas can include the head, eyelashes, eyebrows, pubic area, axillary region, and perirectal area, and these can change over time. The hairpulling can occur in brief episodes during the day or over longer periods (sometimes hours). Individuals may try to cover up the hair loss with makeup and wigs. The individual may have tried to stop the behavior but has been unable to do so. The hairpulling causes distress; however, *distress* is a vague term. People who experience trichotillomania usually feel embarrassed. These feelings can occur in social situations, at work, or in any other life areas. It is necessary to rule out dermatological conditions and body dysmorphia.

147. A: The point of this session is to gather information about an altercation Mark had with a classmate. Given his presentation, you are unlikely to get a clear picture of the events. Guiding Mark through some deep breathing exercises could help him relax and attain a calmer state, which would help him explain his thoughts in a more productive manner.

148. C: The symptoms meet the criteria for major depressive disorder. They include the following:

- depressed mood
- feeling worthless
- diminished ability to perform work duties
- appetite changes
- sleep disturbances
- loss of energy

Based on the information, Anthony seemed to be experiencing major depressive disorder before he began struggling with addiction. He reported using cocaine to increase his energy level, which aligns with his difficulty in getting work done.

149. D: Long-term follow-ups are completed with individuals who finished treatment six or more months ago. Short-term follow-ups typically occur one to three months after discharge.

150. D: Individuals who come to treatment for addiction and another mental health concern should be treated for both at the same time. Detoxification is the first step, regardless of the diagnosis. Detoxing usually causes uncomfortable symptoms such as nausea, vomiting, and diarrhea, which can impact an individual's ability to engage in therapy. Symptoms of addiction and a mental health concern are likely intertwined, which speaks to the importance of treating both. For example, if only the addiction is treated, a person will continue to struggle with mental health issues, which can bring on a relapse. Addiction changes the way the brain functions, so treating only the mental health concern does not address the whole issue.

Practice Test 2

1. After identifying the roles that the Smith family members fall into, you have decided to provide them with psychoeducation about these roles and use this as a tool to discuss goals they could work toward. Which of the following would be an appropriate goal for the Smith family?
    A) improve family communication
    B) improve family boundaries
    C) clarify family and individual values
    D) prioritize family time

2. Which term describes an opinion, typically negative, that a counselor can have based on an individual's race, religion, ethnicity, gender, age, sexual orientation, heritage, or ancestry?
    A) ignorance
    B) bias
    C) naivete
    D) indifference

3. Of the following individuals, who would be more likely to develop a specific phobia?
    A) Alex, a fourteen-year-old student
    B) Ahmed, a seven-year-old boy
    C) Robert, a fifty-two-year-old businessman
    D) Bernice, an active seventy-eight-year-old woman

4. During a mental status exam, your client begins talking about the role the sun plays in her behavior. She explains that when the sun is in the sky, it controls her behavior, which contributes to her inability to focus on work during the day. When the sun goes down in the evenings, her control returns, so she is able to focus on her work. How would you describe her thought content?
    A) delusion
    B) hallucination
    C) obsessions/compulsions
    D) other

5. Luis is a twenty-eight-year-old male who has been struggling with anxiety for about a year. Recently, he cannot think of a day when he has not felt anxious. Luis identifies feeling restless, fatigued, and irritable, and he struggles to concentrate at work. You diagnosis him with generalized anxiety disorder. What is the minimum number of symptoms Luis must have for criterion C to meet diagnostic criteria?
    A) one
    B) two
    C) three
    D) four

6. You are working in an addiction treatment program with Martha, who has been diagnosed with alcohol use disorder and binge eating disorder. You have training and experience as an addiction counselor but no exposure to eating disorder treatment since earning your degree three years ago. Which of the following should you do?
    A) talk to your supervisor about your competency with this client
    B) work with the client individually and focus on her addiction
    C) work with the client and research eating disorder treatment
    D) refer her to a colleague with more experience in eating disorder counseling

7. An outpatient counselor at a mental health private practice has been working with Amanda, a twenty-eight-year-old female with bipolar disorder. Amanda was diagnosed three years earlier at the hospital when she was in a manic episode. Since then, Amanda has continued working with the hospital on an outpatient basis for medication management. What would collaborative care look like with Amanda's prescribing doctor?
    A) having a joint treatment plan
    B) discussing her interpersonal concerns
    C) having a signed consent of release
    D) discussing the assessment measures you will use

8. Which of the following disorders is known to exist comorbid with major depressive disorder?
    A) obsessive-compulsive disorder
    B) oppositional defiant disorder
    C) paranoid personality disorder
    D) schizophrenia

9. A social worker has an older adult client who has been having trouble maintaining her finances. She recently moved in with her son, who is unemployed, to get some help keeping track of her expenses and doctor appointments. On her most recent visit, she stated that the son is wearing expensive new clothing and reported that several hundred dollars in cash she stashed in her drawer had recently gone missing. What is the BEST course of action for the social worker?
    A) report the son for suspected elder abuse
    B) conduct a family session to establish better boundaries between mother and son
    C) confront the son about where he purchased the clothes
    D) ask the client if she may have misplaced the cash

10. You are working with a nineteen-year-old Christian client who was raised in a religious home and has always had a strong relationship with God. Recently, your client unexpectedly lost a close friend. This has led him to question his spirituality, which he feels has contributed to his current struggle with depressive symptoms. Which therapeutic approach would be MOST helpful?
    A) giving advice
    B) referring him to his priest
    C) showing empathy
    D) focusing on depressive symptoms

11. You have been working with Samantha, a thirty-two-year-old female who has been struggling with anxiety. She recently started a new job and is hoping to improve her confidence during interactions with her colleagues. Which of the following exercises would help Samantha work toward her goal?
    A) the empty chair technique
    B) role-playing
    C) the miracle question
    D) journaling

12. Regarding the criteria for a major depressive disorder diagnosis, how many symptoms are listed that can be present during the same two-week period?
    A) six
    B) seven
    C) eight
    D) nine

13. Which behavior might make a client feel that her counselor is NOT being genuine?
    A) being defensive
    B) active listening
    C) encouragement
    D) empathy

14. When developing a treatment plan, it is important to discuss the diagnosis, challenges, and goals with the client. Which statement BEST includes the client in the treatment plan development?
    A) "How will you know when you are better?"
    B) "Decreased feelings of hopelessness can show progress."
    C) "Being active in taking your medication can reduce symptoms."
    D) "These are the changes my supervisor made."

15. An adult client comes to session in distress because he just came out as gay to his family and they were not accepting. What should the social worker do NEXT?
    A) refer the client to an LGBTQ friendly therapist
    B) encourage the client to stand up for himself with his family
    C) recommend a family session to begin helping the family understand the client's perspective
    D) assess the client's level of distress, including any indication of thoughts of self-harm or suicide

16. Marla is a forty-two-year-old woman who began working with you individually after struggling to support her daughter who is living with opioid addiction. After a few weeks, you recognize that Marla struggles with codependent behaviors. She has been so focused on her daughter's needs that she has been neglecting her own. This has led Marla to feel overwhelmed, irritable, and exhausted. How would you proceed with Marla regarding her codependency behaviors?
    A) introduce DBT skills
    B) introduce goal setting
    C) improve boundaries
    D) introduce mindfulness

17. Robby is a three-year-old boy whose parents have enrolled him in a half-day preschool program. Robby has a speech delay and was actively engaging in speech therapy for eight months. When school began, he stopped going to speech therapy because the counselor was pleased with his progress and language use. Robby's parents informed the preschool of this, and the teachers there have been patient with him. After four months of school for three days a week, Robby still has not talked in the classroom. He communicates with his teacher by using hand signs and other body movements. At home, Robby uses words when communicating with his parents. He does not speak to individuals he is unfamiliar with, even with his parents present. Which diagnosis would BEST fit Robby?
   A) pragmatic communication disorder
   B) autism spectrum disorder
   C) social anxiety disorder
   D) selective mutism

18. You are reviewing a session with a female client who you believe has been struggling with premenstrual dysphoric disorder. Before you can be confident in your diagnosis, which differential diagnosis should you evaluate?
   A) major depressive disorder
   B) borderline personality disorder
   C) generalized anxiety disorder
   D) intermittent explosive disorder

19. After eight weeks of working with you on his alcohol use, Nathan realizes that his drinking behaviors are hurting his work performance. This includes decreased focus, concentration, and feeling sick at work. Nathan has recently been open to talking about changes he can make to his behavior that would promote sobriety. Which of the five stages of change is Nathan in?
   A) contemplation
   B) preparation
   C) action
   D) maintenance

20. Which of the following accurately describes quantitative research?
   A) It relies on data that can be measured.
   B) It is not intended to be applied to practice.
   C) It uses a small number of participants.
   D) It investigates how and why things happen.

21. You are running a group counseling session for professionals who are struggling with mental health concerns. Two group members have been contributing open-ended questions, which you feel is inappropriate. How can you appropriately encourage group participation?
   A) ask members to use their own experiences when sharing
   B) ignore the behaviors because the members are participating
   C) wait until another group member shares an observation
   D) ask the two members to not attend the next session

22. You have been working with Michael for three weeks. He was encouraged to seek professional help by his wife when she noticed that he had been withdrawing from his family and friendships. Michael was in a billiards tournament league and has stopped attending the matches. Additionally, he missed his son's last three soccer games. Michael shares that he has been struggling with feelings of hopelessness, fatigue, and passing thoughts of death. Based on the information, which mental health diagnosis should you assess for?
   A) bipolar disorder
   B) cyclothymic disorder
   C) major depressive disorder
   D) hypomanic episode

23. You have been working with Amanda and Leslie for about four weeks on how they can improve their relationship. During your session, you asked them to read the **1997** book *A Couple's Guide to Communication*. What is this therapeutic approach called?
   A) homework
   B) bibliotherapy
   C) marriage enrichment
   D) marriage encounter program

24. Before meeting with two new clients, you are reviewing the initial paperwork and see that their concerns stem from infidelity. When you work with clients on infidelity, you use an integrated approach developed by Snyder, Baucom, and Gordon. The model is based on which three stages?
   A) dealing with the impact of the infidelity, exploring the context and finding meaning, moving on
   B) dealing with the impact of the infidelity, exploring the context and finding meaning, forgiveness
   C) exploring the reason for the infidelity, exploring the context for the infidelity, forgiveness
   D) full disclosure of the infidelity, dealing with the impact of the infidelity, finding meaning again

25. You are reviewing the mental status exam so that you can use it in your upcoming intake assessment. Which area of assessment covers the following options?
   - poverty of thought
   - blocking
   - racing thoughts, flight of ideas
   - loose associations
   - circumstantiality
   - tangentiality

   A) thought content
   B) affect
   C) perceptions
   D) thought process or form

26. You are working at a college campus student counseling center. When your clients arrive late, it disturbs your schedule for the rest of the day because you have been giving them the full session length. How might you address this concern?
    A) do nothing and continue having full sessions when clients arrive late
    B) develop a zero-tolerance policy for tardiness
    C) talk to your supervisor about having shorter sessions when clients arrive late
    D) add "buffer" time to your schedule to allow for clients' lateness

27. You work at an addiction treatment center providing group and individual counseling sessions and encourage your clients to consider attending a support group for people in recovery, by people in recovery. What group would you recommend to Jane, a twenty-nine-year-old female recovering from alcohol addiction?
    A) Narcotics Anonymous
    B) Alcoholics Anonymous
    C) your aftercare group
    D) a colleague's group session

28. You have been working as an initial assessment counselor in an outpatient addiction treatment program. Your new client arrives for her session, and you notice the smell of alcohol in the room. She reports driving herself to the appointment. She consents to taking a breathalyzer; her BAC comes up as 0.10. You inform her that you cannot complete the intake with her under the influence, and the client is agreeable to rescheduling. What is the appropriate next step?
    A) refer her to AA
    B) arrange for her to be picked up
    C) call the police
    D) reschedule the assessment

29. You are supervising a master's student working toward her degree in counseling. After reviewing one of her recent sessions, you notice that she appears rigid and stiff and uses psychology jargon that the client is unable to fully understand. Which of the following characteristics would you talk to her about?
    A) empathy
    B) consistency
    C) congruence
    D) professionalism

30. You are meeting with a new client. Which topic should you be familiar with?
    A) payment, fee, and insurance benefit issues
    B) the client's availability
    C) your upcoming overtime schedules
    D) alternative office locations

31. A counselor is discussing the damage social media use can cause clients, including body dysmorphia, anxiety, and depressive symptoms. When it comes to mental health, what is a positive use of social media?
    A) creating a mental health educational account
    B) limiting exposure to germs and viral infections
    C) creating new employment opportunities
    D) helping avoid boredom

32. You are working with a young man who has been struggling with social anxiety. He would like to build his support network and feels that once he makes a few close friends, his quality of life may improve. You are developing a treatment plan and need to include your therapeutic approach in your notes. Which approach would be the BEST option for this individual?
    A) person-centered therapy
    B) motivational interviewing
    C) cognitive behavioral therapy
    D) gestalt therapy

33. How many types of hallucinations are listed in the mental status exam?
    A) four
    B) five
    C) six
    D) seven

34. A client comes into an LGBTQ clinic with bruises and a bloody lip. He reports that he was holding hands while walking down the street with his boyfriend when three men jumped them and beat them up. Which of the following terms BEST describes the experience of the client?
    A) hate crime
    B) patriarchy
    C) transphobia
    D) homophobia

35. Johnathan sought counseling after learning that his wife of thirteen years had been having an affair for the past four months. He owns a construction business that causes him to work long hours and take trips out of town a few times a month. Johnathan still loves his wife and wants to try to move past this. After providing support and validation, you discuss the pattern of stages that spouses typically experience after learning of their partner's infidelity. What are these three stages?
    A) shock, moratorium, forgiveness
    B) emotional roller coaster, moratorium, trust-building
    C) emotional roller coaster, trust-building, forgiveness
    D) shock, emotional roller coaster, trust-building

36. You have been working with Sally, an eleven-year-old female with a history of physical abuse. Her mother reported that Sally witnessed her stepfather being abusive to her mother. Since you have been meeting with Sally, she has not been able to talk about the event and shared that she cannot remember the details. What defense mechanism is this?
    A) denial
    B) repression
    C) displacement
    D) rationalization

37. Your supervisor wants you to include a disclaimer at the end of your email signature. Which information is MOST appropriate to include?
    A) a reminder that email is not a secure form of communication
    B) your phone number
    C) your office's location
    D) your hours of work

38. Laura is a thirty-five-year-old woman who has been in counseling for six months. She is unhappy in her marriage but does not feel brave or strong enough to leave her husband. She denies experiencing any abuse and violence and notes that she is just unsatisfied. After discussing and exploring her options with you, she decides to file for a divorce. While working on goal setting with her, you focus on the strengths that could help her at this time. What are the four types of strengths you can pull from to help develop her goals?
    A) educational, relational, social, environmental
    B) social, environmental, financial, educational
    C) relational, educational, social, financial
    D) individual, relational, social, environmental

39. You are meeting with a new couple for couples counseling. After taking time to get to know them, you validate their concerns and emotions and commend them on seeking help. You explain that only a small number of couples who get divorced try counseling first. What percentage of couples who divorce try counseling before separating?
    A) **15** percent
    B) **20** percent
    C) **25** percent
    D) **30** percent

40. You are running a group therapy session in an outpatient treatment program and notice that group members are hesitant to be vulnerable in their sessions. Which exercise would help create trust within the group?
    A) develop group rules together
    B) use icebreaker exercises
    C) call on group members to share
    D) avoid processing group exercises

41. How many characteristics of speech are included in the mental status exam?
    A) two
    B) three
    C) four
    D) five

42. You are working as a school counselor at a local university and your client wants to talk about the different nonverbal communication categories that she learned about in one of her classes. What is an example of a nonverbal communication category?
    A) one's clothing
    B) body odor
    C) body gestures
    D) coughing

43. You are working as a school counselor and have been meeting regularly with a high school junior named Aleida, who has recently increased her self-awareness regarding her academic abilities, social skills, and emotions. This has allowed her to set realistic goals for her future and work with you on improving her emotion regulation skills. What has Aleida successfully developed?
    A) idealization
    B) realization
    C) intrinsic understanding
    D) planful competence

44. As an intake counselor, you usually use the MMSE during your intake sessions. What are the five sections that make up the MMSE?
    A) appearance, behavior, mood, affect, and language
    B) registration, attention and calculation, affect, thought process, and mood
    C) mood, orientation, thought content, perception, and attitude
    D) orientation, registration, attention and calculation, recall, and language

45. A **16**-year-old male client has been seeing a school social worker for a while for attendance and homework issues in school. At his most recent session, he expressed feelings of gender dysphoria and that he would like to transition to being a woman. What should the social worker do NEXT?
    A) check in with the client to see if he has told his parents or other adults about these new feelings
    B) acknowledge the feelings of gender dysphoria that the client has disclosed
    C) refer the client to a well-respected gender clinic in the area
    D) assess the client to determine the best diagnosis given his disclosure

46. Anthony, a nineteen-year-old male, struggles with procrastination. Even talking about setting goals is overwhelming. The counselor discusses the components that go into making healthy goals and describes the acronym *SMART* for goal setting. What does this acronym stand for?
    A) sensitive, measurable, attainable, realistic, tailor-made
    B) specific, measurable, attainable, realistic, time-restricted
    C) sensitive, meaningful, attainable, realistic, time-restricted
    D) specific, meaningful, attainable, realistic, tailor-made

47. You are facilitating an LGBTQIA+ group for adolescents in your area. Which of the following would be the MOST appropriate topic for your session?
    A) identifying safe, enjoyable hobbies and interests
    B) psychoeducation about medication-assisted therapy
    C) psychoeducation about family dynamics
    D) identifying triggers for self-harm

48. You have been meeting with Marilyn for several months regarding her grief over her husband's death. Marilyn has also been navigating her boomerang son. Which situation accurately describes a boomerang child?
    A) a child returning to his childhood home after living in a supported living setting
    B) a child returning to his childhood home after becoming unemployed
    C) a child living at home due to being physically dependent on his mother
    D) a child living at home throughout his adult life due to a developmental condition

49. You have been working as a school counselor and have been meeting individually with a student named Bianca, whose family immigrated to the United States from Mexico. During her session, Bianca shared that she yelled at a peer on the school bus because her peer was making jokes about her parents' inability to speak English. Bianca was disciplined for the argument; the peer was not. She reported feeling intimidated by the principal and was unable to explain what her peer had said. Which skill would be important for Bianca to work on?
    A) emotion-regulation skills
    B) walking away
    C) tolerating ignorance
    D) advocating for herself

50. You are in an individual session with Jay, who tells you about an argument he had with his wife. He explained that his wife said he does not spend time with her, which made him angry. He said that he has been working overtime to buy a new car because the family vehicle keeps breaking down and is unreliable. When you ask him how he felt when she made that comment, he said "frustrated, unappreciated, and overwhelmed." He shared that he feels like he cannot please her. Which strategy could you recommend to Jay?
    A) walking away
    B) improving his communication skills
    C) stop working overtime
    D) delaying the vehicle purchase

51. A parent comes to the school social worker and wants her child assessed for a learning or intellectual disability. Which of the following would be the BEST assessment to use to determine if the child has any intellectual deficiencies?
    A) WAIS-R
    B) WISC-R
    C) MMPI
    D) PHQ-9

52. Sara is a young adult who was admitted to an inpatient mental health program because her parents were concerned about her erratic behavior. She experienced a manic episode that led to her hospitalization for assessment and treatment. During her manic episode, Sara quit her job as a retail store manager. What would be an effective long-term goal for Sara?
    A) find a new prescribing doctor within two weeks of discharge
    B) begin individual counseling within one month of discharge
    C) be consistent in taking her medications for twelve weeks
    D) find a new job within eight weeks of discharge

53. You are meeting with a client who has been arguing with his parents daily about his behaviors. Adam is a sixteen-year-old male who does not feel that he needs to tell his parents every detail about his life. His parents have asked him to go to counseling because they are unhappy that he will not talk to them about his friends and romantic interests. When you meet with Adam, he appears resistant to counseling and says that you are "on his parents' side." He expresses frustration with his parents, raising his voice and making harsh comments about them. His parents joined the session for about ten minutes, which resulted in an argument between them and Adam. You maintain a calm demeanor and give Adam the space he needs to verbalize his frustration once his parents leave. Which skill BEST describes your behavior in this situation?
    A) conflict tolerance
    B) mindfulness
    C) confrontation
    D) patience

54. During your second session with Adam, you ask him what he feels he might get out of counseling. He is unsure, but he would appreciate his parents backing off. Adam explained that he talks to his parents about his classes, sports teams, interests, and hobbies; however, he does not want to "gossip," as he sees it, about his friends or any romantic interests. What is an appropriate resolution skill to work on with Adam?
    A) mindfulness
    B) deep breathing
    C) communication
    D) distress tolerance

55. You have been working with a single mother, Sarah, for about four months regarding her depressive symptoms. You recently referred her to a single-parent support group to increase her social support and allow her to practice her social skills. You mentioned to her the distinct types of single-parent families she might encounter in the group. How many distinct types of single-parent families are there?
    A) three
    B) four
    C) five
    D) six

56. You are working with Nina, a twenty-two-year-old female who has been struggling with suicidal ideation while coping with her recent diagnosis of bipolar disorder. Nina has shared that she has thoughts about death daily and finds that by evening, her thoughts turn to a desire to die. She has had passive thoughts about suicide recently, and this concerns her. You validate her concern and work to develop a safety plan. She has agreed that keeping a small card with her safety plan in her wallet would be ideal. What is something that could be written on her safety card?
    A) her employer's phone number
    B) list of mental health concerns
    C) phone number for a supportive person
    D) phone number for her ex-partner

57. Nina calls you and shares that she is currently struggling with suicidal ideation. She explains that she has had a tough day and feels like giving up. Nina lets you know that she is home alone and has access to prescription medications that she has been thinking about taking. She is tearful and says that she called because she does not want to die but does not know what else to do. How should you proceed?
   A) tell her you are concerned about her safety and will be calling for a wellness check
   B) tell her you are concerned and that you can meet with her individually tomorrow
   C) tell her you are concerned and encourage her to call her close friends for support
   D) tell her you are concerned and encourage her to use her emotion regulation skills

58. You are a high school counselor meeting with juniors to discuss their thoughts about what comes after graduation. You just finished talking with Amar, a student who can be described as a parentified child. Which statement BEST describes a child in this situation?
   A) Amar will be attending a four-year university in the fall to get distance from his family.
   B) Amar will be attending a trade school so he can open his own business one day.
   C) Amar will be working full time to help his single mother with his siblings.
   D) Amar does not have plans for after graduation and is planning to take a year to travel.

59. You have been getting routine supervision while providing counseling services on a telehealth platform. During your supervision today, you discussed barriers to effective treatment while providing telehealth. What is a barrier you may experience with this catalyst for counseling services?
   A) clients forgetting appointments
   B) not having access to quality internet
   C) differences in time zones
   D) not having the privacy of an office

60. A 42-year-old male client who is Hispanic is seeing a social worker for help getting a job in the US He reports having difficulty with the job applications as they are all in English and his English proficiency is not high yet. What is the BEST response for the social worker to make?
   A) find a translator for the client to help him fill out the applications
   B) help the client research jobs that do not require English proficiency
   C) refer the client to an ESL program at the rec center
   D) fill out the applications for the client

61. A counselor is discussing goal setting with a client—specifically, the difference between intrinsic and extrinsic motivation. Which of the following is an example of intrinsic motivation that the counselor could share?
   A) receiving a bonus after a year of work at a new clinic
   B) working out because it is fun and feels good afterward
   C) making the honors list after working hard at school
   D) buying a nice house in a desirable neighborhood

62. You are an intake counselor at an inpatient substance use rehab. Which assessment tool are you using when you ask the following questions:
    - Have you ever tried to cut down on how much you drink?
    - Do you find yourself getting annoyed when others criticize your drinking behaviors?
    - Do you feel guilty about drinking?
    - Are you having eye-openers when you wake up?

    A) Alcohol Use Disorders Identification Test (AUDIT)
    B) CAGE questionnaire
    C) Drug Abuse Screening Test (DAST-10)
    D) Michigan Alcohol Screening Test (MAST)

63. You are a school counselor who has been meeting with an eight-year-old boy, Max. Max was referred to you by his teacher after she noticed that he was having a hard time in class. Max has been in the foster care system and was recently adopted by his foster parents. Max has shared that he is happy with his adoptive parents and is trying to find his place in the family. Max's teacher told you that he appears to make "silly" mistakes in his work when he knows the correct answers. He has a hard time staying focused during lessons and is sometimes unaware when the teacher calls on him. The teacher has noticed that his folders are messy, which makes it hard for him to find his work. Which diagnosis would you investigate?
    A) adjustment disorder
    B) attention-deficit/hyperactivity disorder, inattention presentation
    C) autism spectrum disorder
    D) attention-deficit/hyperactivity, combined presentation

64. Katy is a single mother who has been working two jobs to provide for her two toddlers. She shared with you that she feels burned out and constantly feels like she is being pulled in different directions and knows that it is unhealthy. You have begun introducing her to stress management skills. Which of the following is a skill you could recommend to Katy?
    A) meditation
    B) having snacks
    C) time management
    D) finding a higher-paying job

65. You are conducting a research project and find a personality assessment that investigates six categories of characteristics and rates each one on a high-to-low scale. You believe this assessment will help you gauge the differences among your participants. Which assessment are you using?
    A) personality assessment system
    B) HEXACO personality inventory
    C) Myers–Briggs Type Indicator (MBTI)
    D) DiSC assessment

66. You are meeting with Laylah, a twelve-year-old female who was referred by her school counselor. Laylah has shown some concerning behaviors both at school and at home, including moodiness and difficulty regulating her anger. This leads to her arguing with anyone who disagrees with her, which can lead to resentment. Laylah has a difficult time taking responsibility for her actions and often feels like others are to blame for her poor behavior. She has sought "revenge" when she felt that others treated her poorly, twice with peers at school and once with her adoptive brother. Laylah's teacher and her adoptive mother both state that the behavior disturbance began around the holiday season, which was about seven months ago. Because of her behavior at school, Laylah has been suspended twice and kicked off the volleyball team. Which diagnosis would you investigate?

- A) adjustment disorder
- B) oppositional defiant disorder
- C) intermittent explosive disorder
- D) conduct disorder

67. You have been working with Jonah, who has been in a domestic partnership for nine years. Jonah has discussed several times that his partner has been physically abusive, leaving him with bruises. After this occurs, his partner buys an expensive gift as an apology and promises to get help. Everything seems fine for a week or two, but then his partner becomes aggressive and eventually abusive again. To the best of Jonah's knowledge, his partner has not gotten help for his anger issues. Which of the following would be an appropriate psychoeducation topic?

- A) emotion regulation skills
- B) the cycle of violence
- C) antisocial personality education
- D) self-defense skills

68. You have been working with a twenty-eight-year-old woman who has experienced domestic violence. You are encouraging her to identify the aspects of her previous relationship that were abusive, using the power and control wheel from E. Pence and M. Paymar as a learning tool. In order to discuss qualities of a healthy relationship, you use another tool developed by E. Pence and M. Paymar that discusses honesty and accountability, trust and support, responsible parenting, shared responsibility, economic partnership, negotiation and fairness, nonthreatening behavior, and respect. What tool are you using?

- A) equality wheel
- B) relational wheel
- C) health and wellness wheel
- D) intimate wheel

69. You are a school counselor working with a sixteen-year-old female named Marla, who was removed from her parents' care after being physically and verbally abused by them. She has begun to struggle with suicidal ideation and self-harm behaviors—specifically, cutting herself. What would you do first in your session with Marla?

- A) explore how she is doing in her classes
- B) discuss her child protective service case
- C) assess for suicidal risk and harm
- D) sign a no-harm contract

70. You are meeting with a client who presents as anxious with rapid speech and are having a hard time following what he is sharing with you because he jumps between topics. What would be an appropriate skill to use?
    A) summarizing
    B) redirecting
    C) taking notes in session
    D) breathing exercises

71. You were asked by your supervisor to conduct a personality assessment for a new client. You choose one that has thirty items and several uses. This assessment can be used to make a diagnosis of PTSD within the last month, lead to a diagnosis of PTSD at a different point in a person's life, and assess for PTSD symptoms over the past week. This tool aligns with the *DSM-5* criteria for post-traumatic stress disorder. Which assessment will you use?
    A) Global Psychotrauma Screen
    B) PTSD Checklist for *DSM-5* (PCL-5)
    C) Posttrauma Risky Behaviors Questionnaire
    D) Clinician-Administered PTSD Scale for *DSM-5* (CAPS-5)

72. Who helped develop the concept of empathy into what it is known as today?
    A) Alfred Adler
    B) Sigmund Freud
    C) Carl Rogers
    D) Aaron Beck

73. You are meeting with Ethan, a thirty-one-year-old male who was referred to you by his health care physician for his anxiety symptoms. He began a new corporate job four months ago and is concerned about making a good impression. He was happy at his last job; however, the company had to downsize during the COVID-19 pandemic. Ethan feels that he now needs to prove himself to be a valued member of the team. He reports doing well so far and says that he has been trying to cope with sensations in his legs that typically occur during longer meetings. Ethan explains that when this happens, he has to shift his position in his chair, and he worries that he appears disengaged from the meeting. Additionally, he has a hard time "settling" when he tries to fall asleep. You learn that Ethan has been experiencing these sensations for three and a half months, at least three days a week. Which diagnosis would be the MOST appropriate for Ethan?
    A) generalized anxiety disorder
    B) restless legs syndrome
    C) attention-deficit/hyperactivity disorder
    D) panic disorder

74. You have been working with Sally for a month and are focusing your treatment on her struggle with anxiety symptoms. After deciding that it would be helpful to use an assessment to gauge the severity of her symptoms, you choose a twenty-one-item tool that has Sally rate the severity of her symptoms. Examples of symptoms assessed include feeling hot, unsteady legs, and feeling shaky or unstable. After Sally has rated her symptoms, you can add the numbers to see if they fall into a low, moderate, or potentially concerning category. Which assessment have you selected?
   A) generalized anxiety disorder seven-item (GAD-7)
   B) Beck Anxiety Inventory (BAI)
   C) State-Trait Anxiety Inventory
   D) Hamilton Anxiety Rating Scale (HARS)

75. Florian was referred to you for an assessment by his wife who is a registered nurse. When she returned home from work early one morning, Florian walked into their bedroom. When she tried talking to him, he was unresponsive and not fully awake. She watched him for about five minutes, then he got into bed and went back to sleep. The next morning, he did not remember getting up and had no idea why he was out of bed at that time. Florian does not drink or use drugs, so he and his wife found this to be a concerning event. Which disorder would you investigate?
   A) non-rapid eye movement sleep arousal disorder, sleepwalking
   B) rapid eye movement sleep behavior disorder
   C) unspecified sleep-wake disorder
   D) insomnia disorder

76. James is a 15-year-old male client who is gay and seeking assistance from a social worker to help him come out to his family. His family is deeply religious and attends a church that has spoken critically about people who are gay. From a systems perspective, which of the following BEST describes the role the church has in James's life?
   A) The church is peripheral to James' life.
   B) The church has a significant impact on James' parents, but not on James.
   C) The church is part of James' exosystem and therefore not important to James' family.
   D) The church is part of James' exosystem and therefore has an indirect emphasis on James' life.

77. Deliah was referred to you by her nursing home staff, who noticed that since her arrival a year ago, her memory has declined and she seems to have a harder time understanding others when they talk to her. The staff started noticing the concerns with her memory when she was forgetting to come for her afternoon medications. Which diagnosis should be investigated?
   A) delirium
   B) major and mild neurocognitive disorder
   C) major or mild neurocognitive disorder due to Alzheimer's disease
   D) major or mild neurocognitive disorder with Lewy bodies

78. You have been working with Joanna in the aftermath of her divorce. She was originally reluctant to talk about her divorce but has recently begun to open up. Joanna reported feeling frustrated and "stupid" for missing the signs of her partner's affair. She had been working opposite schedules as him and did not think anything of his frequent "work dinners." Which statement is an example of how she could reframe her thoughts?
    A) I trusted my partner, which is why I didn't question him.
    B) I was naive in my marriage, which is why I missed the signs of an affair.
    C) I was too distracted with work to notice his behavior changes.
    D) I was busy with work and didn't spend time with him.

79. You have just completed an intake assessment with a sixty-eight-year-old female at an inpatient addiction treatment program. Laura has been binge drinking on and off since she was in her twenties. She says that she has been able to stop drinking when she wanted to, so she has never thought her drinking was a concern. She has been drinking about five days a week for the past few months and confirms feeling "shaky" in the mornings after she drinks. She denies that her job, family, or other responsibilities are impacted by her drinking. Laura was referred to treatment by her doctor following a fatty liver diagnosis. What would you recommend to Laura?
    A) partial hospitalization program
    B) detoxification
    C) intensive outpatient program
    D) inpatient rehab program

80. Chloe, an 8-year-old girl, has recently been experiencing bullying at school from a classmate. The school is aware and is working on creating a solution that will keep Chloe safe and build conflict resolution between the two girls. Which of the following BEST describes Chloe's situation?
    A) Chloe's microsystem is having a positive impact on the situation, and the mesosystem is creating the stressor.
    B) Chloe's mesosystem is having a positive impact on the situation, and the microsystem is creating the stressor.
    C) The stressor and resolution are both part of the microsystem.
    D) The stressor and resolution are both part of the mesosystem.

81. Your client John recently shared that his sister stated that she does not feel comfortable talking to him about her problems. John's sister feels that John minimizes her struggles and tends to offer suggestions to fix them rather than listening and providing support. John is wondering what he could do differently to make his sister feel more comfortable talking to him. What would be an appropriate suggestion?
    A) avoid offering suggestions
    B) be more reserved in conversations
    C) communicate through email for a short time
    D) practice reflective listening

82. You are meeting with a new client for an intake interview at an outpatient addiction treatment program. While conducting the assessment, it becomes clear that the client is struggling with alcohol use and depressive symptoms. What is the BEST therapeutic strategy for this client?
- A) treat the client's addiction concerns and then address the depressive symptoms
- B) treat the client's depressive symptoms first, followed by addiction treatment
- C) treat the presenting addiction, then reassess for depressive symptoms
- D) treat the addiction concerns and the mental health concerns at the same time

83. While walking in a common area of your office you overheard a colleague share with his client that he was tired because his baby was up all night and he was struggling before their session began. What is an appropriate action for you to take?
- A) confront your colleague before his session
- B) confront your colleague after his session
- C) reach out to his client personally
- D) voice your concern to your supervisor

84. You have been working with Adrien at an inpatient addiction treatment program for two and a half months. He has successfully met his treatment goals and is expected to complete this program in two weeks. After speaking with Adrien about his goals after treatment, you have both agreed that he would benefit from continuing in treatment. Adrien states that his days have little structure since he is unemployed, and he is worried about being bored at home. He reports having a healthy home environment that is sober and supportive of his recovery. Which treatment option would provide him with a structured environment that will allow him to focus on his recovery?
- A) outpatient treatment program
- B) intensive outpatient treatment program
- C) aftercare programming
- D) partial hospitalization programming

85. A social worker is organizing a community coalition in her city. The residents have reported dissatisfaction with the local streets and sidewalks, saying that they are not safe for their children to use. The residents want improved road safety and fixed sidewalks. What should the social worker do NEXT?
- A) educate the residents on the process of contacting their local politicians
- B) educate the residents on the difficulty of getting laws and funding changed
- C) lead the residents in a discussion of their concerns and practice speaking to local leaders
- D) contact the local aldermen and invite them to the meeting

86. You have been working individually with Scott in an outpatient addiction treatment program. He has been in treatment for ten months and has twelve months of sobriety. Scott was in an inpatient treatment program for eight weeks before outpatient treatment. Which of the following factors BEST supports the decision to complete his treatment?
- A) He has maintained sobriety in his toxic home environment.
- B) He has made changes to his routine and friendships and uses healthy coping skills.
- C) He has not missed an individual session since he started treatment.
- D) He has paid off the remaining balance of his copays.

87. You are working with a new client, a child, in your mental health practice. The parents meet with you to discuss their concerns about their child. The mother explains that compared to her other children, this child does not seem to be learning as quickly. For example, he started speaking right before his third birthday, has a difficult time with his fine and gross motor skills, and has a BMI in the fifteenth percentile. You give the parents an at-home assessment to complete and bring to the next session. Which assessment have you chosen?
    A) Ages & Stages Questionnaires (ASQ)
    B) Battelle Developmental Inventory Screening Tool, 2nd ed (BDI-ST)
    C) Child Development Inventory (CDI)
    D) BRIGANCE Screens-II

88. Your client Sheila is a single mother of three children. She shared that she has not been able to feed her children well lately because she has no money. She has been asking her children to play at their friends' houses so they can eat full meals. You are concerned about her children's safety despite their mother's efforts. What should you do next?
    A) give her some money and ask her to buy her children more food
    B) empathize and try to change the topic of conversation
    C) explain your legal responsibilities and call CPS
    D) empathize, change the topic, then call CPS

89. You are working in an inpatient mental health treatment program that specializes in treating individuals with eating disorders. You are meeting with a new client who was diagnosed with bulimia nervosa and are discussing what he can expect from the treatment program. You let him know that his days will be structured and will include supervised mealtime, group therapy, individual therapy, alternative therapies, and specialized therapies as appropriate. When he asks which therapeutic approach is used in the program, what is the BEST answer?
    A) solution-focused therapy
    B) EDMR
    C) interpersonal psychotherapy
    D) cognitive behavioral therapy

90. You are meeting with a client who you suspect has a substance use disorder, and you want to use an assessment that is more thorough than the CAGE questionnaire. You decide on an assessment with ten questions rated on a zero-to-four scale. Once all the questions are answered, you add them to get a risk level regarding the presence of a substance use disorder. Which assessment are you using?
    A) Drug Abuse Screening Test (DAST-10)
    B) Alcohol Use Disorders Identification Test (AUDIT)
    C) Michigan Alcohol Screening Test (MAST)
    D) Alcohol, Smoking, and Substance Involvement Screening Test (ASSIST)

91. Rudy began working with you a year ago when he was experiencing depression. He met the criteria for major depressive disorder and has recently begun struggling with his symptoms again. You decide to use a depression screener at your next session to investigate the severity of his depressed mood, guilt, suicidal ideation, insomnia, work and interests, retardation, agitation, and anxiety. Which assessment are you planning to use?
    A) Burns Depression Test
    B) Hamilton Depression Scale
    C) Montgomery–Asberg Depression Rating Scale
    D) Zung Self-Rating Depression Scale

92. You are about to engage in a group session that provides psychoeducation on eating disorders for parents who are concerned about their children. In this group, what would you say is the most common eating disorder in the United States?
    A) anorexia nervosa
    B) bulimia nervosa
    C) binge eating disorder
    D) avoidant/restrictive food intake disorder

93. Martha has generalized anxiety. In the session, the counselor notices that Martha appears anxious and her speech is rapid and pressured. She talks about something that happened a week ago, then abruptly changes the subject to a future event. The counselor communicates his observation to Martha and suggests using a coping skill during the session to see if it relieves any of her anxiety symptoms. Which of the following should the counselor try?
    A) jumping jacks for exercise
    B) a three-minute guided meditation
    C) a twenty-minute guided meditation
    D) eating a snack

94. After completing the emotion regulation exercise, Martha reports feeling calm and ready to continue. Which skill might the counselor use to get the session back on track?
    A) summarizing
    B) redirecting
    C) soft confrontation
    D) paraphrasing

95. Your client has been struggling with depressive symptoms since her husband passed away suddenly. Since the loss, she has been sleeping more than normal, has a depressed mood, and has lost a significant amount of weight. Based on these symptoms, you use the SAFE-T assessment. What is the correct order of events for this assessment?
    A) document, identify risk factors, conduct suicide inquiry, identify protective factors, and determine risk level/intervention
    B) identify risk factors, identify protective factors, conduct suicide inquiry, determine risk level/intervention, and document
    C) conduct suicide inquiry, identify protective factors, identify risk factors, determine risk level/intervention, and document
    D) conduct suicide inquiry, identify risk factors, identify protective factors, determine risk level/intervention, and document

96. You are providing a psychoeducational session for parents who want to learn how to support their LGBTQIA+ child. One of the parents asks you to provide an example of cisgender. What is the MOST appropriate response?
    A) an individual who was born a female and identifies as male
    B) an individual who was born a male and identifies as female
    C) an individual who was born a female and identifies as neither male nor female
    D) an individual who was born a male and identifies as male

97. You are running a relapse prevention group in an outpatient addiction treatment program. One of the group rules is that members do not come to group impaired. When the group begins, you observe that a member appears impaired. You ask her to step outside, then have another staff member take her to the doctor on staff for assessment. Which behavior are you demonstrating?
    A) blocking
    B) linking
    C) facilitating
    D) creating safety

98. Alana is a client in an outpatient addiction treatment program. She began treatment three weeks ago to get sober from opiates and has been attending individual and group counseling and twelve-step meetings. In an individual session, Alana shared that she is only attending treatment because she wants to avoid criminal court for a possession charge. She lives with her partner, who actively uses opioids, and she works in a pub where her coworkers use drugs during their shifts. Which type of challenge has she been experiencing?
    A) consequences of addiction
    B) barriers to sobriety
    C) failure to comply with treatment
    D) lack of motivation

99. Which term describes a study whose results can be repeated when other studies are conducted with the same conditions?
   A) qualitative
   B) valid
   C) reliable
   D) generalizable

100. Which of the following is an example of a counselor-imposed barrier to treatment?
   A) using EMDR for a client with generalized anxiety disorder
   B) maintaining a consistent treatment schedule for clients
   C) closing the office on a recognized federal holiday
   D) having more than one office available for appointments

101. You are working in a private practice setting and have recently begun meeting with Lennon, a sixteen-year-old who identifies as transgender. Lennon's parents suggested that he engage in therapy for support since his peers have not been kind during his transition. Lennon has experienced verbal and physical abuse at school and at public places like the local mall. Lennon's parents are supportive of his transition and are helping him the best they can. When you meet with Lennon, you observe that he often talks about struggling in situations like lunchtime, class projects, and gym class. He shares that he gets sweaty, mumbles his words, and feels like everyone is watching him. When he knows one of these times is approaching, he tries to find a way out of it. Lennon is worried because his grades are beginning to slip, and he has a strong desire to attend college. Which disorder should you investigate?
   A) generalized anxiety disorder
   B) major depression episode
   C) social anxiety disorder
   D) panic disorder

102. You are halfway through your group session when Karen shares about her struggle with depressive symptoms. Another group member, Kim, starts talking about emotion regulation skills and begins to discuss some of them. You feel that Kim is providing more education than support for Karen. Which of the following is an appropriate response?
   A) let Kim continue, and follow up after the group session
   B) let Kim continue, and ignore it; she did nothing wrong
   C) politely interject and provide more information about helpful skills
   D) redirect and ask Kim to share what skills have worked best for her

103. You are working as a counselor in a high school. Christopher is meeting with you after receiving a referral from his Spanish teacher. He has been defiant in classes and disrespectful to the faculty and staff. Christopher spent the first ten minutes of your session loudly venting about his interpretation of the events and said he believes that all the staff and faculty—including you—are trying to prevent him from graduating on time. You want to show him unconditional positive regard and empathize with him while staying calm. Which emotion regulation skills can you use to manage your reaction?
   A) seek supervision
   B) box breathing
   C) visualization
   D) physical exercise

104. You have been working with Matthew for about six months regarding his depressive symptoms. He is unhappy in his marriage and struggles to find happiness. He began dating his wife at a young age and feels like he "missed out" on experiencing other relationships because of this. He is now in his mid-thirties and questioning his sexuality. What is the BEST approach to take?
    A) encourage couples counseling for him and his wife
    B) provide a safe and supportive environment for him to explore his feelings
    C) provide information about various sexual orientations that he may identify with
    D) encourage him to look for an LGBTQIA+ support group

105. Franco is a twenty-four-year-old male in counseling for support. He recently decided to tell his family that he is gay, and he did not get the positive and supportive reactions he was hoping for. Franco explained that he comes from a large, loud, extended family where everyone is active in each other's lives. This includes weekly Sunday dinners, which he has been asked not to attend for the past two weeks. This has led to him feeling sad, let down, and angry. How can you best support him?
    A) encourage him to distance himself from his family
    B) invite him to your family dinners
    C) provide him with unconditional positive regard
    D) encourage him to go to dinner this weekend

106. Which term describes a study that measures what it is supposed to measure?
    A) reliable
    B) generalizable
    C) valid
    D) qualitative

107. You have been working with Robert for five months regarding his struggles with depression and anxiety. You review his treatment plan with him, as it has been four weeks since you last did so. He asks why you do this every month. What is the BEST response?
    A) You are mandated to do so monthly.
    B) It decreases your professional liability.
    C) It lets you track his progress from last month.
    D) It helps guide a conversation about changes he needs to make.

108. You and your group coleader are running the first process group of the day in an addiction treatment rehab. A client named Jeanine began complaining about the care she has received. Agitated, she made negative comments and judgments about other group members. What is the BEST course of action?
    A) redirect the group to change topics
    B) ask her to step out with your coleader while you process the experience with the group
    C) have the group engage in a box breathing exercise followed by processing the experience
    D) wait to see what other group members' reactions and responses are before acting

109. You have been working individually with a transgender woman throughout her transition. She originally came to you with anxiety and depressive symptoms, and throughout your time together she has been responsive to CBT techniques and new coping skills. She currently reports feeling "much better" regarding her mental health. She wants to continue treatment for support, as she is still adjusting to the many changes in her life. She has limited social support and has been working hard to make healthy connections with individuals in the LGBTQIA+ community. What treatment recommendations could you suggest to her?
   A) biweekly individual sessions with you
   B) medication-assisted therapy
   C) an LGBTQIA+ support group
   D) volunteering at a local youth center

110. Jill, thirty-two, is a successful businesswoman. She comes from a traditional family that expects women to stop working and raise their families when they get married. Jill got married about three years ago and has no interest in having children. She says she does feel guilty for putting her career before her family and noted that her family has made their thoughts about the matter quite clear. How can you support Jill?
   A) recommend more exercise
   B) refer her to women's group therapy
   C) refer her to a psychiatrist for medication
   D) refer her to her ob-gyn to discuss fertility

111. When researchers repeat a study with different participants than the original study, what are they testing?
   A) generalizability
   B) reliability
   C) validity
   D) whether it is qualitative

112. When working with a client who is under the age of consent in your state, what should you get from her in addition to her legal guardian's signed informed consent?
   A) the client's assent
   B) verbal participation
   C) written participation
   D) approval of study content

113. You are meeting with a new client who has been admitted to your inpatient mental health program. This client has shared that she is uncomfortable with group therapy and does not believe that attending group sessions will be helpful. She later explained that her ambivalence came from how group therapy has been portrayed in movies and television, not her own experience. How could you provide education about group therapy to her?
   A) The group facilitator will provide feedback when needed but otherwise is relatively quiet.
   B) The group is led by peers, which can help her learn to speak up for herself.
   C) One group member will talk for most of the session; she would likely have little opportunity to do so.
   D) Group therapy allows her to feel validation in terms of emotions and experiences.

114. You have been working with Adell for five months after the unexpected loss of her husband. Adell shares that she is able to find some happy moments in her day, but most days she stays in her home. Which of the following could be a helpful referral for Adell?
    A) grief support group
    B) psychiatrist
    C) volunteer centers
    D) family time

115. A social worker is employed by a state lobbying agency. The organization is working to pass a law focused on expanding maternity leave for people who are pregnant in their state. Most of the state legislature remains opposed to the bill. The state's residents are largely in favor of the bill. Which of the following BEST describes the social worker's situation?
    A) The political environment is majority opposed, but the public environment is largely in favor of the bill.
    B) The political environment is majority in favor, but the public environment is largely opposed to the bill.
    C) Both the public and political environment oppose the bill.
    D) Both the public and political environment are in favor of the bill.

116. Helena has worked as a customer service representative for a local grocery store chain for one month. She began seeing you about three months ago when she was unemployed. Since she began working, her reported anxiety symptoms have decreased. Helena shared that she felt uncomfortable after a conversation with a coworker who said that she is unqualified for her job and that he thought she was given the job for other reasons. She explained that when he said this, he pointed to her body. She immediately felt uncomfortable and found an excuse to walk away. Which term BEST describes Helena's experience?
    A) jealousy
    B) workplace harassment
    C) condescending behavior
    D) sexual assault

117. You are facilitating a support group for first-year university students. Group members have recently reported feeling uncomfortable with group class assignments. They are unable to advocate for themselves, which results in them doing more work than they feel is fair. Which group activity would be appropriate?
    A) role-playing
    B) psychoeducation
    C) icebreaker game
    D) the miracle question

118. Martha has been working for her employer for sixteen years. She has been actively searching for new employment opportunities for about six months because she feels like she has no growth opportunities with her current employer. She recently received a job offer and has been feeling anxious about starting over with a new company. She reports having racing thoughts, feeling warm, and having difficulty concentrating. Which coping skills would you recommend to help her manage her anxiety?
   A) box breathing
   B) reading
   C) coloring a mandala
   D) taking prescription medication

119. During your group session, you notice that Eddie has been quiet and shared very little. He does appear engaged while others are talking by making eye contact and nodding. You do not know Eddie and his case well, but you would like to encourage group participation. Which of the following would you consider?
   A) put him on the spot in group
   B) talk to him individually after group
   C) facilitate a group activity
   D) give him a week to get comfortable

120. You are involved in a new medication trial for alcohol use disorder. Your results show that this medication is effective for opioid use disorder. It is then determined that a new study should be conducted to investigate the medications used for opioid use disorder to ensure that your study has what?
   A) reliability
   B) validity
   C) generalizability
   D) effective treatment

121. You have been working with Louisa, a college senior who is about to graduate with her BA degree in psychology. Louisa is not planning to pursue higher education after graduation and has recently started looking for full-time employment. She is beginning to feel discouraged with her options, explaining that she has a significant amount of student debt, and the starting salaries for positions she is considering will barely cover her monthly expenses. Louisa reports feeling depressed most of the day, accompanied by feelings of worthlessness and a decreased interest in her hobbies. She has been feeling fatigued, has lost about five pounds, and has little to no appetite. Louisa shares that her partner expressed concern, which led to Louisa talking to you. It has been about three weeks since Louisa felt like "herself." What do you believe Louisa is struggling with?
   A) persistent depressive disorder
   B) major depressive disorder
   C) major depressive episode
   D) adjustment disorder

122. Which of the following behaviors is MOST likely to encourage your group members to talk to you?
   A) be available before or after the group session
   B) provide them with your email and phone number
   C) consistently arrive on time for group
   D) have a snack during the group

123. You have recently begun facilitating a group for individuals struggling with depressive disorders. Their previous group leader unexpectedly fell ill and was unable to provide closure and ease the transition to you. You have noticed that group members have limited participation and are not as active as they were before. Which of the following could help encourage members to participate?
   A) play an icebreaker game
   B) conduct a meditation exercise
   C) lead guided imagery
   D) request a new counselor

124. A high school counselor has received several referrals from teachers who are concerned about students. These students were working with a counselor who retired last year. How can the current counselor establish therapeutic rapport with the students?
   A) ask what was helpful about their previous counselor
   B) ask for their class schedules
   C) ask for their emergency contact information
   D) ask for restaurant recommendations

125. Several group members have been showing their reactions while others are sharing. This has led to a shift within your group and a decrease in group participation. You have decided to discuss the benefits of being nonjudgmental in group sessions. Which of the following reasons would be the MOST important to discuss?
   A) It makes everyone feel safe.
   B) It keeps the group going.
   C) It keeps the group on track.
   D) It allows group to end early.

126. Theresa was married to her husband for thirty-four years before he was killed by a drunk driver eight months ago. She had been a stay-at-home mom in her younger years, and there had been no need for her to work as her children grew. Theresa's children are concerned about her since their father's passing because she has not accepted that her life is going to change now that he is gone. After looking through Theresa's finances, her oldest child saw that there was not enough money for her to maintain her current lifestyle. He encouraged her to consider returning to work or changing her lifestyle. Theresa has not made any changes to her routine and refuses to talk to her children about returning to work. The children are also concerned because she tends to focus on their father throughout the day, which contributes to extreme sadness and feelings of helplessness. She blames herself for her husband's death because he was on his way to pick up her medication from the pharmacy when his vehicle was struck. What do you suspect Theresa is struggling with?
   A) major depressive episode
   B) denial
   C) adjustment disorder
   D) complicated grief

127. You are running a support group for parents of teens who struggle with various mental health concerns, including bipolar disorder, ADHD, and major depressive disorder. Which of the following would be the MOST appropriate topic for psychoeducation for this group?
    A) the twelve-step model
    B) codependency concerns
    C) medication-assisted therapy
    D) treatment levels of care

128. You are working with Grace, a thirty-eight-year-old single mother who has been trying to improve her relationship with her nine-year-old son. Grace shared that when her son told her that he failed a test, she shamed him for his grade. She feels that she could have responded better because her son was visibly upset. Which of the following statements would have shown her son positive regard?
    A) I know you're smarter than this.
    B) You could have tried harder.
    C) Your grade is not reflective of your intelligence.
    D) You should study more for future tests.

129. You discussed with Grace the benefits that she may observe in her relationship with her son. Which of the following is a benefit of positive regard she may experience?
    A) Her son will come to her when he is struggling.
    B) Her son will do better on his next test.
    C) Her son will be more attentive at school.
    D) Her son will be less resistant to chores.

130. Gillette has been in your aftercare group since completing an inpatient rehab program for alcohol use disorder. She is active in the sessions and has made progress in her recovery. Lately her sharing has been focused on how she can apply the skills she has learned to her recovery and processing her challenges and successes. Which of the group stages would BEST describe Gillette's experience?
    A) orientation
    B) transition
    C) work
    D) consolidation

131. You recently began working with a new client, Paulo, a twenty-six-year-old gay man. He struggles with worrying, becomes fixated on issues, and has difficulty moving past them. Paulo shared that his partner did not respond to his text message quickly like he usually does, and Paulo began to worry that he had done something wrong and that his partner was going to leave him. Paulo also struggles with concentration, fatigue, and feeling on edge. His partner has pointed out that he is irritable when he gets "worked up." After exploring Paulo's history with these symptoms, you learn that they started when he was around sixteen. Paulo came out to his parents when he was fifteen, and they sent him to a conversion camp to "get well." When Paulo returned, he pretended that the camp was successful to appease his parents. He began to notice the same symptoms when he would worry that his parents would catch him in a lie. What do you suspect Paulo is struggling with?
    A) childhood trauma
    B) post-traumatic stress disorder
    C) generalized anxiety disorder
    D) major depressive disorder

132. Three members appear to be struggling with engagement during your group session. They have been closing their eyes, slouching, and making noises that communicate their discomfort. How would you describe this type of behavior?
    A) intellectualizing
    B) withdrawing
    C) reframing
    D) aggressive

133. Michael is a twenty-five-year-old Black male who was just admitted to the inpatient mental health program where you work. During his initial assessment, Michael shared that he has been feeling down for about a month. He has not been able to sleep, has no interest in eating, feels worthless, cannot concentrate, and does not want to spend time with his friends. About a month ago, he was pulled over by police on his way home from work. He followed directions and was still asked to exit the car and watch as the police searched his car without telling him why. When he asked why he was pulled over, he was told that he ran a stop sign, which he knew was not true. You asked Michael if he thinks this experience is related to his current symptoms, and he said that he had not thought about it that way. Michaels's partner called **911** two days ago when he began talking about wanting to die to end his pain. What do you suspect Michael is struggling with?
    A) major depressive episode
    B) trauma
    C) major depressive disorder
    D) post-traumatic stress disorder

134. Lucas chose to attend addiction treatment rather than serve a jail sentence for a recent drug-related arrest. As a condition of his deal, he must provide an update from the treatment provider to the court once every eight weeks. Lucas does not like these updates and believes his treatment should be kept private. How can the counselor comply with his deal while maintaining a therapeutic rapport?
    A) omit from the report the challenges Lucas has faced in the past eight weeks
    B) exaggerate the details of his progress in the past eight weeks
    C) be truthful, and review the report with Lucas before sending it
    D) allow Lucas to fill out his own progress forms for the court

135. A social worker is organizing a community coalition focused on addressing racism in the community. Several hate crime attacks against Asian community members occurred in recent weeks. The social worker is working with the community to organize neighborhood watch patrols and to collaborate with local law enforcement on providing better supervision in the neighborhood. Which of the following BEST describes the social worker's activities?
    A) social justice advocacy
    B) mediation
    C) community researcher
    D) case management

136. Shawn began therapy four months ago when he and his wife separated. Since then, he has consistently attended weekly individual sessions and has worked on managing his depressive symptoms while adjusting to his life changes. Shawn has an eye condition that makes it difficult for him to see at night, and he is concerned about being able to drive to his sessions when the days get shorter. Which of the following is an appropriate action to take?
    A) terminate his counseling relationship
    B) refer him to a new counselor
    C) move his appointments to earlier in the day
    D) end his sessions until the spring

137. A group for professionals with mental health concerns has been meeting weekly for five months. The counselor and group members have developed a good rapport and a safe environment. Members are making strides toward the goals identified during their first session. Which group activity would be appropriate for the performing stage?
    A) checking in
    B) two truths and a lie
    C) members sharing self-care routines
    D) members writing their own eulogies

138. You work in an outpatient addiction treatment center and are meeting with a new colleague to discuss the use of session fading in your treatment program. How can you explain session fading to this professional?
    A) As clients progress in their recovery and satisfy their treatment plan goals, their treatment schedules include fewer sessions.
    B) As clients progress in their recovery, the group counselors allow them to have more active roles in the group.
    C) During clients' last three months of counseling, they are required to attend fewer group therapy sessions.
    D) During clients' last month of treatment, they only need to attend individual counseling sessions.

139. The federal law HIPAA was enacted in 1996 to create national standards to protect client health information, such as mental health care records. What does HIPAA stand for?
    A) Health Information Privacy and Advocacy Act
    B) Health Insurance Portability and Accountability Act
    C) Health Institution Privacy and Advocacy Act
    D) Health Insurance Privacy and Accountability Act

140. You are in an individual session with a fifty-five-year-old male who has been questioning his spirituality since his adult son was diagnosed with stage 3 pancreatic cancer. Before the diagnosis, Eliot had a sense of hope and connection and a belief that there was something greater than him. He was able to feel connected and relaxed during meditation and yoga. In Eliot's mind, his son is healthy, a good man, and accomplished, so this illness should not have happened to him. What is the BEST approach to use during this session?
    A) active listening
    B) close-ended questions
    C) offer your opinion
    D) focus on the illness

141. A counselor is discussing how group members should act when they see each other in public. What is the BEST way to approach this?
    A) The group should decide together what to do.
    B) Group members can never acknowledge each other.
    C) It does not matter what they do.
    D) Members must act friendly toward each other in public.

142. Your supervisor tasked you with developing and sending a newsletter to clients who have completed your treatment program. He asks that you include information about staff changes, changes within the treatment center (such as new groups), and information about the annual alumni event. Which type of outreach is this?
    A) long-term follow-up
    B) planned discharge follow-up
    C) preventive outreach
    D) community outreach

143. How can counselors stay active and up to date on professional concerns?
    A) watching the news
    B) taking continuing education courses
    C) joining professional organizations
    D) talking to colleagues

144. You have been facilitating a process group for individuals in recovery from a variety of substances. You have learned that several members have been socializing outside of the group session, but they have not included all members. How can you explain this as a concern to your group?
    A) that it breaks group confidentiality
    B) that socializing can isolate group members
    C) that there is no counselor present
    D) that it takes away from the group contributions

145. A social worker is collaborating with local leaders on creating a fair housing policy to address rising rents and economic instability in her community. Which of the following terms BEST describes the social worker's activities?
    A) urban planning
    B) victim advocacy
    C) economic justice
    D) educator

146. A client is referred by a mental health court for wraparound services, and the counselor is required to report weekly to the care team. Which of the following is NOT appropriate to share with the care team?
    A) client's appointment attendance
    B) client's diagnosis and treatment plan
    C) details of the client's trauma history
    D) reported side effects of prescribed medication

147. You are working in an outpatient addiction treatment program and facilitating a closed group for individuals who completed an inpatient treatment program. Over the past two weeks, one group member has struggled with her mental health and sobriety. Since then, she has returned to the inpatient treatment program. What is the BEST way to begin processing the change in the group?
    A) ask for the group's opinion of the member who left the group
    B) ask how having this member leave makes them feel
    C) ask if they saw any signs that the member was struggling
    D) inform them that the member is no longer in the group, and proceed as normal

148. Which of the following can be done during supervision to help you understand your limits regarding cases you take?
    A) self-assessment
    B) self-reflection
    C) trainings
    D) self-care practices

149. Active listening is a skill that counselors can use to show that they are engaged in the session with the client. What is an example of an active listening skill?
    A) maintaining eye contact
    B) asking yes or no questions
    C) projecting onto the client
    D) congruence

150. When you are conducting a virtual intake assessment, which piece of evidence is challenging to gather?
    A) description of a client's environment
    B) body language
    C) context for a client's struggles
    D) mental health history

Answer Explanations 2

1. B: By changing the boundaries among the family, the Smiths can work to get out of the roles they have been put in or taken on. These roles are associated with a dysfunctional family, which can make psychoeducation vital for improving their relationships. They cannot change what they do not know is unhealthy.

2. B: Counselor bias can negatively impact the therapeutic alliance and should be explored and addressed in supervision. If a counselor has a bias toward a client that she cannot work past, it is not appropriate for her to continue working with that client.

3. B: Specific phobias typically develop before an individual's tenth birthday. Research has identified seven through eleven as the median ages for onset. These phobias can change as children get older and are more likely to last among those whose phobias continue into adolescence and adulthood. While specific phobias are not uncommon among older adults, they are associated with a decreased quality of life. This could be a red flag for neurocognitive disorders.

4. A: The scenario describes delusional thought. According to the *DSM-5*, there are four types of delusions: bizarre delusions, non-bizarre delusions, mood-congruent delusions, and mood-incongruent delusions. This client is exhibiting mood-incongruent delusions, which are not impacted by her mood. Her theme tends to include control and nihilism.

5. C: The *DSM-5* requires that an adult have a minimum of three of the following symptoms to satisfy the requirements. Children must have one symptom.

- restlessness or feeling keyed up or on edge
- being easily fatigued
- irritability
- muscle tension
- sleep disturbances (difficulty falling or staying asleep, or restless, unsatisfying sleep)

6. A: You should discuss with your supervisor your ability to ethically provide treatment. Individuals with co-occurring disorders have more success if they receive treatment for both concerns at the same time. If you cannot provide a particular treatment, you should refer the client to the appropriate professional.

7. C: Consent of release is required for the counselor to discuss any components of Amanda's care with anyone other than Amanda, including other mental health professionals she is working with. Without consent of release, the counselor is directly violating her confidentiality. Exceptions to confidentiality include concerns for her physical safety, concerns she would harm others, and abuse and neglect of children and other vulnerable populations.

8. A: According to the *DSM-5*, disorders known to occur at the same time as major depressive disorder include the following:

- substance use disorders
- panic disorder
- obsessive-compulsive disorder
- anorexia nervosa
- bulimia nervosa
- borderline personality disorder

9. A: Social workers are mandated reporters and must report suspected abuse of people who are vulnerable, including older adults. The social worker should report the son for suspected elder abuse. Conducting a family session is not appropriate in the case of suspected abuse, while confronting the son is unsafe. Asking the client if she may have misplaced the cash avoids the social worker's duty to report.

10. C: Empathy can give your client the space needed to work through his struggle with spirituality as well as his current experience with grief. While referring the client to his priest may be helpful, using empathy as a therapeutic approach will allow you to support him during your sessions.

11. B: Role-playing would allow Samantha to run through situations that may arise during her workday. It can provide her with a safe place to try new communication skills and practice doing things differently.

12. D: There are nine symptoms listed for this disorder. To meet the criteria, one of the symptoms present must be either a depressed mood or a loss of interest in pleasure. Additionally, there must be significant impairment in the individual's daily functioning. The symptoms listed include the following:

- depressed mood most of the day, nearly every day
- diminished interest or pleasure in all, or almost all, activities
- unintended weight loss or gain
- insomnia or hypersomnia
- psychomotor agitation or retardation
- fatigue or loss of energy
- feeling worthless, or having inappropriate guilt
- inability to concentrate or being indecisive
- recurrent thoughts of death, suicidal ideation without a plan, a suicide attempt, or a plan to commit suicide

13. A: If a counselor becomes defensive in a session, he should debrief and consult with his supervisor to understand what brought on this reaction.

14. A: Asking clients to observe changes in how they feel can help counselors better understand their goals and how to incorporate them into the treatment plan. If a treatment plan does not align with what is important to clients, it will be hard for them to meet goals set by the counselor.

15. D: When a client is presenting in distress, assessing his distress level is a vital first step in therapeutic practice. LGBTQ issues are within a social worker's scope of practice, so referring out is not appropriate. Encouraging the client to stand up for himself with his family may be emotionally beneficial but is not the first step that should be taken. Similarly, a family session may be helpful but is not the first step the social worker should take.

16. C: Codependency occurs in relationships with poor or no boundaries. Providing Marla with an understanding of codependency can help lead to a discussion about how she can shift her boundaries in her relationship with her daughter.

17. D: Children with selective mutism are able to comprehend what others are saying and are capable of using the language themselves. This difference is not related to a communication disorder or autism spectrum disorder. Children with selective mutism often do not speak at school, with peers, and sometimes even with family members. They tend to use other forms of communication, such as pointing and grunting to get their needs met.

18. A: Potential differential diagnoses for premenstrual dysphoric disorder include premenstrual syndrome, dysmenorrhea, bipolar disorder, major depressive disorder, and persistent depressive disorder. The onset of premenstrual dysphoric disorder can occur at any point once menarche begins. For many, symptoms worsen when menopause begins.

19. B: Nathan has recognized that his behavior is a concern and is beginning to see the benefits of changing his behaviors, which has added internal motivation. At this point, he is talking about changes rather than acting to make changes. When he begins making the changes, then he will be in the action stage.

20. A: Quantitative research uses standardized assessments and measurable data to investigate behaviors. Important components of this research include the methods that are used, limitations of the study, and whether other research supports its findings.

21. A: You can encourage members to talk about their experiences, what they have learned, and what helped them when they were struggling. Focusing on this can help them stay out of the counselor role while in the group session.

22. C: Individuals struggling with major depressive disorder often withdraw from their relationships or lose interest in activities they previously enjoyed.

23. B: Bibliotherapy occurs when a counselor asks clients to read books and/or other forms of literature to learn more about how to make healthy changes to their relationship. Book recommendation topics can include communication, conflict resolution, and increasing intimacy.

24. A: The 2008 model for working with infidelity from Snyder, Baucom, and Gordon lists three stages that do not have to be progressive. The order of the steps will depend on the clients and their experiences with infidelity. This approach will help both individuals learn skills for emotion regulation and decision-making.

As with other couples' intervention strategies, the overall goal is to help them strengthen their relationship and see the other side of their negative experience.

25. D: Poverty of thought, blocking, racing thoughts, flight of ideas, loose associations, circumstantiality, and tangentiality appear on the MSE under thought process and form.

26. C: Talking to your supervisor before making any changes will provide feedback on the logistics of the concern and the feasibility of your proposed solution.

27. B: Bill Wilson (Bill W.) founded Alcoholics Anonymous (AA) in 1935. Since then, the fellowship has expanded and meetings can be found across the world. These meetings are run by alcoholics in recovery, so they differ from a therapeutic support group. There are two types of meetings: those that are open to the public, and those that are open only to those in recovery. Alcoholics Anonymous encourages participants to work through a twelve-step model to strengthen their recovery.

28. B: While it may be appropriate to discuss Alcoholics Anonymous (AA) and reschedule the appointment, your focus should be on the client's safety. Since her blood alcohol concentration (BAC) is 0.10, she should not drive herself home. You can work with her to find a safe alternative, like a ride share, bus, friend, or family member.

29. C: When your supervisee appears uncomfortable and uses language that is not natural to her, she is at risk of appearing ungenuine to her client. This works against creating the safe and welcoming environment needed for impactful sessions.

30. A: Counselors should be aware of payment, fee, and insurance benefit concerns. For example, if a client's insurance requires prior authorization, you may need to provide the relevant clinical information. Counselors with an administrative staff may not need to know all the details about these concerns, but they should have a working understanding so they can inform potential clients.

31. A: Social media can be used to provide psychoeducation about mental health concerns and healthy coping skills, thereby increasing awareness and decreasing the stigma associated with mental health concerns.

32. C: Research has proven the effectiveness of cognitive behavioral therapy (CBT) in conjunction with medication for the treatment of social anxiety disorder. Techniques including exposure therapy are particularly effective.

33. C: Under the thought content section, there are six options for hallucinations: visual, auditory, olfactory, gustatory, tactile, haptic, hypnagogic.

34. A: Hate crime is the best description for the event. While the men beat up the client due to homophobia, that term does not fully encompass the criminal nature of assault. Patriarchy is a social system where men are the leaders in society. Transphobia is when a person is afraid of or expresses hate for people who are transgender.

35. B: The three stages are emotional roller coaster, moratorium, and trust-building. These do not necessarily occur in this order, and some people may regress at times, which is fine. Everyone's experience is different, so their healing processes will be different as well. Emotions experienced can include anger, sadness, and isolation. Individual therapy can provide Johnathan with a safe place to feel, sit with, and begin to process his emotions regarding his wife's infidelity.

36. B: Repression is a common defense mechanism in individuals who have experienced trauma. Memories associated with the traumatic event are blocked from their conscious minds.

37. A: Your signature should always include your phone and fax numbers and office location. Option A is an appropriate disclaimer: content of emails is confidential and intended only for the person addressed in the email.

38. D: Examples of individual strengths can be positive self-esteem, hard work, drive, and resilience. Relational strengths can describe the individuals in her life who she feels would support her in her decision to file a divorce. Social strengths can refer to social organizations she belongs to, such as a book club or religious organization. Environmental strengths include location, healthy coping skills, and leisure activities that she can use when she is distressed.

39. C: Approximately one out of every four couples, or 25 percent, who get divorced try couples counseling first. Those who do try counseling tend to wait years after problems begin to get help. While some couples may be able to pinpoint a specific reason for wanting a divorce, not all couples have that experience.

40. A: Having the group work together to develop rules or norms can help create an environment where members feel safe. They can address their concerns, such as keeping what is said in group sessions private, which can help members feel that they are all on the same page.

41. C: In the mental status exam (MSE), the counselor documents four characteristics: the client's speech volume (appropriate, soft, loud), speech rate (controlled/appropriate, rapid/pressured/slowed, deliberate/monotonous), speech quantity (appropriate/concise, minimal/monosyllables, detailed/elaborate), and speech quality (appropriate/clear, stutters/slurred/mumbled, impediments/ESL).

42. C: Nonverbal communication categories include facial expressions, gestures, eye contact, touch, space, and body movement. These behaviors send messages to the people you communicate with. For example, if a counselor is avoiding eye contact, she may appear uninterested in what the client is telling her.

43. D: Planful competence occurs among families with adolescents and is strongly influenced by the child's environment and caregivers. Research has shown that healthier children have both parents equally involved in their upbringing.

44. D: The five sections of the mini-mental state exam (MMSE) listed in Option D make up the possible thirty points that a client can score. The sections described in Options A, B, and C are from the full version of the mental status exam and the brief mental status exam.

45. B: The first step when clients disclose emotions is to acknowledge and reflect their feelings. Assessing the client is an appropriate step but should only be done after processing and acknowledging feelings. Checking in about to whom the client has disclosed this information should only be done after reflection of feelings. Clients who are LGBTQ are within a social worker's scope of practice, so referring out is not appropriate.

46. B: The SMART strategy breaks down a large goal into smaller goals that can feel more attainable. Each small goal provides the client with the steps needed to meet the large goal, which can help set the client up for success. After a successful experience, the client can feel the positive emotions that come from accomplishing a goal. This approach also helps the client track progress moving forward.

47. A: A helpful group exercise would be to identify hobbies and interests to promote mental health. This can also help group members learn more about each other while enhancing your group cohesiveness. Not all clients will be affected by addiction or self-harm, so options B and D are not the best choices. Psychoeducation about family dynamics could be helpful, but it will not help group members to connect as well as option A.

48. B: Boomerang children typically experience financial hardship that causes them to move back in with their parent or parents. This can be the result of unemployment or the accumulation of debt. They may be reluctant to regain their independence, which may indicate some codependent behaviors.

49. D: Focusing on advocating for herself can help prepare Bianca for a variety of future situations when it will be important to clearly communicate her experience and explain her actions.

50. B: Jay would likely benefit from improving his communication patterns. This can include learning to cope with the negative emotions that arise, as well as communicating his thoughts in a way that avoids placing blame on his wife.

51. B: The Wechsler Intelligence Scale for Children–Revised (WISC-R) is the best assessment for childhood intellectual functioning. The Wechsler Adult Intelligence Scale–Revised (WAIS-R) is best used for adults. The Minnesota Multiphasic Personality Inventory (MMPI) assesses personality and psychopathology. The Patient Health Questionnaire (PHQ-9) is a depression scale used for assessment and monitoring.

52. C: Long-term goals take place three months or more in the future. If Sara can be consistent with taking her medications, she will likely have a better quality of life and be able to manage her manic symptoms. While individual therapy would be beneficial, a one-month goal is considered a short-term goal.

53. A: Maintaining composure while Adam expresses his frustration and argues with his parents can help strengthen your rapport with him since he will see that you do not automatically side with his parents, as he may have been expecting.

54. C: By improving his communication skills, Adam can learn to more effectively explain to his parents the boundaries he wishes to have in their relationship and the reasons why. It appears that Adam has been open with his parents about his interests and schooling, but he wants privacy when it comes to his social supports.

55. B: The four types of single-parent families are: Single parenthood due to divorce, single parenthood due to death, single parenthood by choice, and single parenthood due to temporary factors.

56. C: A safety plan can include the phone numbers for supportive people in Nina's life as well as the 988 Suicide & Crisis Lifeline. Other common information on safety cards includes protective factors and coping skills.

57. A: Nina should be evaluated at the local hospital. She is distressed and has verbalized a plan as well as intent to follow through with the plan. The fact that she called you is a positive sign, and you can say so when you talk to her about calling for a wellness check. It is appropriate to keep her on the phone while contacting the authorities.

58. C: Parentified children are common in single-parent families. This phenomenon occurs when a child is unable to engage in typical age-appropriate childhood or young adult behaviors and needs to take on adult

responsibilities within the family. Family therapy aims to address this concern and establish clear and healthy boundaries within the family.

59. B: A potential barrier to telehealth is a poor internet connection for you or your client. You should develop a plan with your clients about how to proceed if your call is interrupted because of a poor connection. Even with telehealth services, you should be in a private location to ensure that Health Insurance Portability and Accountability Act (HIPAA) regulations are being met.

60. B: Helping the client find jobs that do not require English proficiency is the best response. A translator may be helpful in the short term, but if the job requires English, relying on a translator will ultimately set the client back. Referring the client to an English as a Second Language (ESL) program will likely help his long-term job prospects but will not help him find a job immediately. It is not appropriate for the social worker to fill out the application for the client as that undermines client autonomy.

61. B: Extrinsic motivation comes from sources outside of the self, such as material rewards, validation or acclaim from others, and recognition. Intrinsic motivation is internally powered, making outside recognition irrelevant.

62. B: The acronym *CAGE* stands for "cut down, annoyed, guilt, and eye-opener." This is a simple questionnaire that can be used in an intake assessment or an individual session. The AUDIT is a ten-item tool that can help counselors recognize when clients' drinking behaviors have become dangerous to their health. The DAST is a twenty- and twenty-eight-item test that helps identify consequences that clients have experienced from their drug use without being specific to the substance being used. The MAST is a twenty-five-item test that helps counselors better understand the lifetime severity of a client's alcohol use; it is often used to help guide treatment plans.

63. B: It would be appropriate to assess for attention-deficit/hyperactivity disorder (ADHD), inattention presentation. While Max has four symptoms reported by his teacher, six are needed to make an accurate diagnosis. Margaret Keyes published a study in the *Archives of Pediatrics & Adolescent Medicine* that discusses the higher rates of ADHD among adopted children compared to their non-adopted peers.

64. A: Meditation is a stress management skill that she can try adding to her routine. There are a variety of approaches to meditation, and the exercises can vary in length, which means she could do a short meditation if she is feeling overwhelmed throughout the day.

65. B: The HEXACO personality inventory looks at six characteristics: humility, emotionality, extraversion, agreeableness, conscientiousness, and openness to experience. This assessment uses a scale to score, so you can gauge the significance of the characteristics. The main criticism of this tool is that there is no reflection of cultural influences.

66. B: The information meets the criteria for a diagnosis of oppositional defiant disorder (ODD); however, other conditions such as conduct disorder, attention-deficit/hyperactivity disorder (ADHD), disruptive mood dysregulation disorder, and intermittent explosive disorder should be ruled out. A 2008 study by Margaret Keyes and colleagues investigated the prevalence of conduct disorders among adopted children. Oppositional defiant disorder was more common among individuals who were adopted domestically compared to their non-adopted peers and those who were adopted internationally. Other common concerns among adopted individuals are externalizing symptoms and ADHD.

67. B: The cycle of violence would address the several stages that can help Jonah identify the pattern within his partner's behaviors, including being abusive, buying a gift as an apology, a honeymoon phase, and a repeated tension buildup.

68. A: The equality wheel and the power and control wheel can be used in therapy sessions to help clients understand healthy and unhealthy qualities of a relationship. These tools provide examples for each aspect, which can lead to discussion points and help guide a therapy session for an ambivalent client.

69. C: The priority is making sure Marla is safe by assessing for suicidal ideation, intent, and plan, as well as discussing her recent self-injurious behaviors. Children who have been abused commonly struggle with aggression, acting out, academics, and other mental health concerns. There is no "cookie-cutter" approach for children who have been abused, so it will be important to tailor your approach to the individual child.

70. A: Summarizing would be appropriate and would give you the clarifying details you need. Additionally, you can check in with your client about how he is feeling and note any changes you observe in his speech.

71. D: The Clinician-Administered PTSD Scale for *DSM-5* (CAPS-5) can take from forty-five to sixty minutes to complete and can be used for clinical purposes as well as research. The assessment aligns with criteria B, C, D, and E for post-traumatic stress disorder. Additionally, this assessment looks at the duration of symptoms, the symptoms' level of distress on the client, and the impact the symptoms have on the client's social and occupational functioning.

72. C: Carl Rogers viewed empathy as a "state of being" for counselors that facilitates being nonjudgmental and accepting.

73. B: The primary concern is Ethan's sleep-wake disorder: restless legs syndrome. While he does seem to be struggling with anxiety symptoms, it is apparent that the restless legs syndrome is contributing to a significant amount of those symptoms. To accurately assess for an anxiety disorder, Ethan should first be referred to a physician to treat his restless legs syndrome.

74. B: The Beck Anxiety Inventory (BAI) is an anxiety screening tool that can be completed fairly quickly. It can be done orally during a session or self-reported before a session. The symptoms included in the BAI are effective predictors of anxiety disorders, which make this a helpful tool when trying to formulate a diagnosis. The BAI can gauge progress after the client completes it a second time, and the results are compared once the client has begun therapy and/or medications. The BAI has been found to produce valid results.

75. A: It would be appropriate to assess for a sleepwalking disorder. The information meets some of the criteria; however, more details are needed to make an accurate diagnosis. For example, it would be necessary to investigate how many episodes Florian has had; the length of each episode; and if any other behaviors, such as eating, occur during the episodes. Additionally, it would have to be determined if the episodes cause distress in his daily functioning.

76. D: Church communities typically make up an individual's exosystem, having an indirect impact on his life. There is no way for the social worker to be sure of options B or C. The church may be peripheral to James' life, but it still has an impact on him.

77. B: There is not enough specific information to consider Alzheimer's disease or Lewy bodies. There is sufficient evidence of a major or mild neurocognitive disorder, but further testing is required to narrow down the etiological cause of the disorder.

78. A: Option A is the only statement that does not place blame on Joanna for her partner's affair. Joanna can use reframing as a tool to relieve herself of the blame for her partner's behaviors, over which she has no control.

79. B: Knowing that Laura has a history of binge drinking, a fatty liver, and has been drinking recently, she should go to a medical detox center. While Laura has not yet experienced some of the negative consequences typically associated with problematic drinking, long-term misuse of alcohol can have significant impacts on health, including cancer and heart and liver concerns. For many, it can take years to develop health consequences from binge drinking. Laura would likely benefit from psychoeducation about the potential dangers of sudden, unsupervised alcohol withdrawal, such as seizures and death.

80. B: The bully is the stressor and is part of the microsystem. The school, which is part of Chloe's mesosystem, is creating resolution. All other options do not accurately describe the situation.

81. D: Reflective listening would help John focus completely on his sister and what she is sharing. He will be more likely to pick up on the emotions for which his sister is trying to receive support. While being reserved may work in some situations, such a change to his normal behavior may make his sister even more uncomfortable.

82. D: Research has shown that the best approach is to treat both addiction and mental health concerns at the same time. Individuals struggling with dual diagnosis often have intertwined symptoms. For example, the client's depressive symptoms could lead to cravings and triggers, which would challenge her sobriety. By providing mental health treatment in conjunction with addiction treatment, the client will learn to manage her mental health symptoms in a healthier manner.

83. D: It would be best for your supervisor to handle the situation. You heard only a brief part of the conversation, so there may be more to it than you realize.

84. D: At a partial hospitalization program (PHP), Adrien would attend treatment for six to eight hours a day. For many, this form of treatment can be a bridge from inpatient treatment to returning home. Adrien is a candidate for a PHP program since he has a healthy and supportive home environment. While the other three options are possible, they will not provide Adrien with the structure that he is seeking for his routine at home.

85. C: Leading a discussion on the residents' concerns will help them hone their arguments and be better prepared to speak with local leaders. Educating the residents on the process of contacting local leaders will be an important step after goals are fleshed out and established. Educating the residents on the difficulty of changing laws is unnecessarily discouraging. Coalition work is best done when the social worker is supporting the residents in their actions instead of doing the work for them.

86. B: Treatment is completed when the client has shown growth and achieved identified treatment goals. Since Scott is in treatment for an addiction, he should be able to effectively manage stressors and triggers, have healthy sober support, and not struggle with other mental health concerns.

87. C: The Child Development Inventory (CDI) is a three-hundred-item screener that parents can complete at home and give to the counselor. This tool looks at the child's development in eight areas, including social, self-help, gross motor, fine motor, expressive language, language comprehension, letters, and numbers. The CDI also includes the General Development Scale, which investigates the child's health and growth, vision and hearing, and development behavior.

88. C: To maintain your therapeutic relationship, you can discuss with Sheila your concern about her children and the need to contact the proper authorities. Having this conversation is a way to be honest with her while fulfilling your legal and ethical responsibilities.

89. C: Interpersonal psychotherapy (IPT) is an evidence-based practice commonly used in the treatment of eating disorders, including bulimia nervosa and binge eating disorder. Research has shown that IPT is an effective alternative to cognitive behavioral therapy (CBT); however, this approach takes longer than CBT to reach the same results. This therapy can help individuals change the way they view themselves, which can help decrease the urge to control the way they look to others.

90. B: The Alcohol Use Disorders Identification Test (AUDIT) was developed by the World Health Organization (WHO) and is used to identify individuals whose drinking behaviors have become concerning for their health. Scoring for this assessment includes lower risk, increasing risk, higher risk, and possible dependence.

91. B: The Hamilton Depression Scale is a commonly used tool for individuals with a depressive disorder diagnosis. It is also referred to as the Hamilton Rating Scale for Depression and the Hamilton Depression Rating Scale. This tool can be used with both children and adults and currently comes in two versions: one with seventeen items, the other with twenty-one. The Montgomery–Asberg Depression Rating Scale is a ten-item tool that can be used to gain a better understanding of depressive symptoms in those who have a mood disorder. The Zung Self-Rating Depression Scale is a twenty-item assessment that rates four common symptoms of depression: pervasive effect, psychological equivalents, psychomotor activities, and other disturbances.

92. C: According to the National Eating Disorders Association, binge eating disorder is the most common eating disorder. This disorder is characterized by a loss of control when eating or by eating an amount of food larger than what most would eat in that period. These binges occur at least once a week for three months.

93. B: A short, guided meditation could give Martha the time needed to refocus her thoughts and relieve some of her anxiety symptoms. A longer meditation would be appropriate for her to try on her own since it would take up a large portion of her session with the counselor.

94. B: This is an appropriate time to redirect and get the session moving in a positive direction. Summarizing and paraphrasing could cause Martha to fall back into her previous pattern.

95. B: The counselor begins the SAFE-T assessment by identifying risk factors that can be changed to reduce the client's risk. Next, he determines what protective factors can be increased to reduce risk. This is followed by a suicide assessment that looks at the client's thoughts, plans, behaviors, and suicidal intent. Once the counselor has all the information, he can determine the client's risk level and formulate an appropriate response to ensure the client's safety. After discussing recommendations with the client and

developing a plan, the counselor should document his assessment of the client's risk level with supporting evidence discussed, the interventions used, and follow-up steps.

96. D: Cisgender is used to describe individuals who identify as the sex they were assigned at birth.

97. A: Blocking occurs when a counselor stops a behavior that could harm the group. An impaired group member violates the rules and expectations. Having the member assessed by a medical professional is an added measure to ensure her safety.

98. B: Everything Alana has listed is a barrier to sobriety. She does have extrinsic motivation to stay sober (pending legal charges). Even though her motivation is extrinsic, she is still attending sessions and meetings, so she is compliant with treatment. The term *consequences of addiction* usually refers to negative consequences that might push a person to addiction treatment (for example, loss of relationships, financial insecurity, or career and/or health problems).

99. C: *Reliable* is the term used in research to describe when an outcome can be repeated with subsequent research studies that have the same conditions.

100. A: Using a therapeutic approach or intervention that is not effective for the client's diagnosis is a counselor-imposed barrier. The use of eye movement desensitization and reprocessing (EMDR) is effective for clients with trauma or post-traumatic stress disorder (PTSD)—not anxiety disorders. Counselors should always work within their scope of practice and only use interventions for which they have proper training.

101. C: The information indicates a social anxiety disorder rather than the other anxiety disorders listed. A 2012 study estimates that approximately 25 percent of LGBTQIA+ youth struggle with an anxiety disorder. Other common mental health concerns include mood disorders and substance use disorders.

102. D: Kim likely has good intentions and is unaware that she has crossed into an area of providing psychoeducation rather than support for Karen. Redirecting Kim can be done in a subtle and kind manner that keeps the group productive.

103. B: Box breathing can be done discreetly during the session in response to distress you may experience. The other options do not apply; they would distract from the session. Debriefing with your supervisor can be helpful if you have a reaction to Christopher's outburst during the session.

104. B: The best approach is to let Matthew begin exploring his thoughts and feelings in a safe, nonjudgmental environment. He has likely never talked about his sexuality with anyone, so giving him the space to speak his truth is important. Once he has had time to process his thoughts and feelings, you can work together to determine what would be helpful for him.

105. C: You can best support Franco by providing him with unconditional positive regard while he navigates the changes within his family relationships. You can give him a safe area to process his thoughts and emotions that he may not be getting from others in his life.

106. C: *Valid* refers to the extent to which a study is measuring what it set out to measure.

107. C: Reviewing a treatment plan monthly allows the client to reflect on progress made over the past month and better understand what can be expected in future sessions. It also allows the client to verbalize any changes he would like to be reflected in his treatment plan.

108. B: Since you have a coleader, you can ask him to step out with Jeanine while you stay and process what happened with the group. Other members may have various reactions, including anger, empathy, and confusion. It would be unhealthy for the group if Jeanine continued talking negatively about other members during the session. The colleague who steps out with Jeanine can provide her with one-on-one support and try to understand what contributed to her behavior.

109. C: With her mental health symptoms being manageable, she would likely benefit from engaging in an LGBTQIA+ support group, where she would be with individuals who can relate to her and validate her thoughts and experiences. Individual counseling could occur biweekly; however, this would not change her support system as a support group would.

110. B: While you can provide support to Jill in your individual sessions, she would likely benefit from participating in a women's support group. Such a group can allow her to hear from women with a variety of backgrounds, which can help normalize her thoughts and feelings.

111. B: These researchers are testing for reliability of the study. Tests should be repeated at different times and with a variety of participants to test the reliability of the original research.

112. A: Obtaining assent from a client who is under the age of consent in your state can help build rapport before the study or procedure, which in turn could reduce potential limitations on your study.

113. D: Group therapy can provide clients with an opportunity to work on social skills that they may be lacking. They will also have the opportunity to feel validated by their peers when they notice similarities in their experiences. Group therapy sessions are led by a professional who will keep the session focused, productive, and healthy.

114. A: Adell may find that attending a grief support group is helpful. In such a group, she would be able to connect with other individuals who can relate to her grief and normalize her experience. This is different from meeting up with her friends, because a support group is guided by a counselor and focuses on members' experiences with grief and loss.

115. A: The political environment is majority opposed, yet the public remains in favor of the bill. The other options do not accurately describe the scenario.

116. B: This is an example of workplace harassment. Different companies have different ways to report these incidents, but a counselor can work with Helena to process her experience and help her feel validated about her reaction. The following behaviors are considered workplace harassment: Offensive jokes and comments, physical abuse and threats of abuse, insults, humiliation, derogatory slurs, name-calling, and abusing authority.

117. A: Role-playing can be used as a group activity to address a variety of topics, including communication, establishing boundaries, and increasing confidence. This can be a learning tool for members to receive feedback from you and their peers on their role-playing presentations.

118. A: Breathing is an effective self-regulation skill and can be used more readily than reading or coloring. It appears that Martha's anxiety symptoms are specific to her situation, so alternative skills should be used before recommending medication. Other effective coping skills include yoga, meditation, journaling, and exercise.

119. B: Since you do not have a rapport with Eddie, you should talk to him outside of group and explore barriers impacting his participation. Once you have learned more, you can work together to develop a plan to increase his participation.

120. B: The original study was designed to study the effects the medication had on those living with alcohol use disorder. For the study to be valid, it must be designed to investigate those struggling with opioid use disorder.

121. C: Louisa is currently struggling with a major depressive episode. She has had the minimum of five symptoms for at least two weeks needed to accurately make this diagnosis. Her depressive episode is likely influenced by her concern about her postgraduation finances, as well as the major life change that will come when she completes her degree.

122. A: All options can help you build rapport with group members, but being available to them before and after sessions gives them a consistent opportunity to speak with you individually. This is more effective than communicating via phone and email because you will not miss important body language cues. Being on time for the group can help members feel that you are dependable, but you will not have time to speak with them individually if you arrive right when the group starts. Snacking during group can be a distraction and serve as a barrier to participation.

123. A: Icebreaker games can facilitate discussion that feels safe. Once safety is established within the group, members are likely to participate more.

124. A: Asking clients about what they gained from a previous therapeutic relationship can give the counselor insight and help connect clients' current needs to their previous needs.

125. A: While maintaining a nonjudgmental environment can help keep the group on a productive path, the most important thing is that everyone in the group feels safe.

126. D: Theresa is likely struggling with complicated grief regarding the sudden loss of her husband. She has been dealing with guilt, sadness, and feelings of helplessness for a significant period. Another sign of complicated grief is that she has made little change to her routine and has not accepted that she needs to change her lifestyle to accommodate her financial situation.

127. B: This group would likely benefit the most from learning about issues and behaviors that can arise within codependency, such as enabling. You can build upon this topic by talking about healthy boundaries and communication patterns.

128. C: Positive regard is a skill anyone can use, not just counselors. Practicing this skill can enhance a personal relationship, such as one with children. Option C accepts the failing grade without equating it to a flaw within the child.

129. A: If Grace is able to show her son that he can talk to her about difficult things, such as failing a test, he will feel more comfortable coming to her with other challenges. This can help strengthen their relationship and allow Grace to model healthy coping skills for challenging emotions and situations.

130. D: Gillette is in the final stage of group therapy, where she applies what she has learned in group to her everyday life. For some outpatient aftercare groups, this may mean that she is almost finished with the group.

131. C: While Paulo's experience at the conversion camp could have been traumatic, the symptoms describe generalized anxiety disorder. The symptoms are not applicable for a post-traumatic stress disorder (PTSD) diagnosis or major depressive disorder. According to the Trevor Project, 13 percent of LGBTQIA+ youth report being exposed to conversion therapy, over 75 percent of which occurred under the age of eighteen.

132. B: These group members appear to be withdrawing from the group session, evidenced by their body language and nonverbal communication. As a leader, you could use skills such as redirecting to try to shift these behaviors to encourage group participation.

133. C: Michael has six identified negative symptoms that are needed to meet the criteria for major depressive disorder. His symptoms have been present longer than the two-week minimum and have had a significant impact on his function, considering that he was hospitalized for suicidal ideation. His experience with the police likely deepened his depressive symptoms.

134. C: Embellishing or neglecting relevant information is unethical. Reviewing the report with Lucas before sending it can open a dialogue about his concerns. For example, he may feel that he made progress in an area that is not mentioned in the report.

135. A: The social worker is engaged in social justice advocacy. Mediation is a form of conflict resolution between individuals. Community researchers lead community research projects. Case management is focused on addressing problems and goals with individual clients.

136. C: It would be appropriate to move his sessions to an earlier time that would make his commute easier. There is no need to terminate the counseling relationship as long as he continues to benefit from it.

137. D: Checking in is an exercise that should be done during each group session. Option B is more appropriate for the forming phase of group development. Writing their own eulogies requires members to put thought into the exercise. Since they are in the performing stage of development, they have created a safe environment where they can be vulnerable with each other. This can also give you more insight into their values.

138. A: Session fading is a strategy whereby the number of sessions decreases as clients accomplish goals on their treatment plans. This could be reflected in the number of individual, group, and psychoeducational sessions they are asked to attend.

139. B: The acronym *HIPAA* stands for Health Insurance Portability and Accountability Act.

140. A: Active listening is the best approach. Open-ended questions could allow Eliot to further discuss his thoughts and feelings. It is possible that he has not talked freely with his family about his concerns, so providing a safe place for him to do so could be of great benefit. He may choose to focus on the illness, or he may concentrate on another aspect of the situation. Understandably, his son's diagnosis has led Eliot to question his spirituality, so encouraging him to be patient and kind with himself could help him move forward.

141. A: Each group will be different; some groups may not want to acknowledge each other, while others may not mind. Regarding addiction treatment process groups, members may encounter each other at outside support groups like Alcoholics Anonymous or Narcotics Anonymous. Therefore, it can be helpful to have an agreed-upon response to seeing each other.

142. A: Long-term follow-up can include treatment evaluations, psychoeducation, and community events. This type of outreach can be sent via newsletter, text, phone call, or email.

143. C: Participation in professional organizations keeps counselors apprised of important advocacy concerns and opportunities to take action. The other options are good ways to stay informed but may not offer opportunities for activism.

144. B: When socializing members exclude other members, this can affect the group's sense of safety by making members feel like they are outsiders. Because of this, processing groups tend to discourage socialization.

145. C: The social worker is pushing for economic justice. Urban planning is specific to city infrastructure and design. Victim advocacy is not relevant in this example because there are no specific victims. Education is not the primary role of the social worker here.

146. C: The goal of the care team is to help the client through the process. Disclosures should only include the information focused on the client's progress. Disclosing the details of the client's trauma history is not relevant to care coordination and would be a breach of the client's confidentiality.

147. B: When a group member leaves a closed group, other members will inevitably be impacted. They can feel a variety of emotions ranging from worry and sadness to relief. While processing this transition, it is important to focus on the individuals who are still in the group and what this change means for them.

148. A: Self-assessments can help counselors understand their limitations when it comes to which mental health concerns they are competent to work with.

149. A: Eye contact is the only option that is related to active listening. Congruence is an important skill for a counselor, but it is not a listening skill.

150. B: When conducting virtual intake interviews and therapy sessions, you may miss valuable information that you can gather from the client's body language and other nonverbal cues. Other aspects of the sessions can proceed as normal. You will want to verify the client's location at the beginning of the session and be knowledgeable of the emergency services available in the area in case a need arises.

Online Resources

Trivium includes online resources with the purchase of this study guide to help you fully prepare for the exam.

Practice Tests

In addition to the practice tests included in this book, we also offer an online exam. Since many exams today are computer based, practicing your test-taking skills on the computer is a great way to prepare.

From Stress to Success

Watch "From Stress to Success," a brief but insightful YouTube video that offers the tips, tricks, and secrets experts use to score higher on the exam.

Reviews

Leave a review, send us helpful feedback, or sign up for Cirrus promotions—including free books!

Access these materials at: https://triviumtestprep.com/aswb-bachelors-online-resources

www.ingramcontent.com/pod-product-compliance
Lightning Source LLC
Chambersburg PA
CBHW081150290426
44108CB00018B/2495